Mastering the Art of Suspense
How to Write Legal Thrillers, Medical Mysteries, & Crime Fiction
by Andrea J. Johnson

Guidebooks for Success

WRITER PRODUCTIVITY SERIES – BOOK 2

Mastering the Art of Suspense. Copyright © 2022 by Andrea J. Johnson. Manufactured in the United States of America. All rights reserved. No part of this work may be sampled, copied, reproduced, distributed, stored in a database or information repository for later use, nor transmitted in any form or by any means — electronic, mechanical, or otherwise invented —without prior written consent by the author. Any replication of the text without the author's permission, except brief quotations in the context of a book review, is a violation of the copyright. First edition.

This book is for personal use only. Readers are responsible for undertaking any due diligence regarding the validity of the techniques and advice contained herein, and the author is not liable for any loss or damage caused by this book's use.

ISBN: 978-1-7376880-2-0

1. Detective and mystery stories—Technique. 2. Fiction Technique. 3. Authorship

To receive a monthly email newsletter full of free writing advice and updates about future Writer Productivity Series books, register at https://ajthenovelist.com/sign-up/

ANDREA JOHNSON

About the Author

Andrea J. Johnson is a writer and editor whose expertise lies in traditional mysteries and romance. She holds a B.A. in English from Swarthmore College, an M.F.A. in Writing Popular Fiction from Seton Hill University, and a copyediting certification from UC San Diego. Her craft essays have appeared on several websites such as *CrimeReads*, *Litreactor*, *DIY MFA*, *Submittable*, and *Funds for Writers*. She has also written for the women's lifestyle websites *Popsugar* and *The List Daily*. Andrea's novels include the cozy courtroom whodunit series the Victoria Justice Mysteries, whose stories focus on a trial stenographer turned amateur sleuth (think *Murder, She Wrote* meets *The Pelican Brief*). When she isn't researching or writing mysteries, you can find her helping novice writers develop their steamy contemporary romances.

Books by Andrea J. Johnson

Victoria Justice Mystery Series:
Poetic Justice
Deceptive Justice
Writer Productivity Series:
How to Craft a Killer Cozy Mystery
How to Craft Killer Dialogue

MASTERING THE ART OF SUSPENSE

Dedication

To my three favorite Williams, thank you for believing in me.

ANDREA JOHNSON

Introduction 9
Mastering the Art of Suspense 15

- › What's a Thriller? 15
- › Difference Between Thriller and Suspense 17
- › Thriller Subgenres 19
- › Legal Thrillers 22
- › Medical Thrillers 31
- › Noir 35
- › Thriller Plot Map 37
- › Building Suspense 46
- › Suspense Tips 50
- › Checklist: Building Suspense 55
- › Are Suspense and Tension the Same? 54
- › Checklist: Mastering the Art of Suspense 56
- › How to Write Contained Suspense 60
- › Checklist: Contained Suspense 64

Opening Hook 65

- › Suspenseful Opening Hooks 73
- › Inciting Incidents 75
- › Exercise: Opening Hooks 76
- › Checklist: Opening Hooks 76

Prologues 78

- › Prologue Pitfalls 82

Point of View 86

- › First-Person Viewpoint 87
- › Second-Person Viewpoint 90
- › Third-Person Objective Viewpoint 92

MASTERING THE ART OF SUSPENSE

- Third-Person Limited Viewpoint 93
- Third-Person Omniscient Viewpoint 95

Unreliable Narrators 98

- Types of Unreliable Narrators 102
- History of Unreliable Narrators 107
- Benefits of Unreliable Narration 109
- Tips for Creating an Unreliable Narrator 110
- Unreliable Narrators in Other Viewpoints 113
- FAQ: Unreliable Narrators 116

Characters 118

- Villains 119
- Bad Guy Behavior 123
- Checklist: Villains 124
- FAQ: Villains 125
- Heroes 126
- FAQ: Heroes 128
- Exercise: Villains and Heroes 128
- Checklist: Heroes 129
- Antiheros 130
- Secondary Characters 133

Conflict 136

- Types of Conflict in Fiction 139

Dialogue 141

- Eight D.I.A.L.O.G.U.E Tips 142
- Exposition in Dialogue 143
- Checklist: Dialogue 148

Setting 150

> Description 151
> Concrete Language 153
> Checklist: Setting and Description 155

Stakes 156

> How to Add Stakes 157
> A Word on Suffering 163

Pacing 165
Violence and Action 170

> Checklist: Violence and Action 177
> Chase Scenes 179
> Checklist: Chase Scenes 185

Exposition 187

> Flashbacks 189
> Frame Story 193
> Checklist: Exposition 194

Cliffhangers 196
Plot Twists 199

> Defining Plot Twists 203
> Checklist: Plot Twists 205
> FAQ: Plot Twists 207
> Types of Plot Twists 208
> Plot Reveals 211

Foreshadowing 213

MASTERING THE ART OF SUSPENSE

> Checklist: Foreshadowing 216
> Chekhov's Gun 217

Misdirection 219

> Red Herrings 220
> MacGuffin 224
> Checklist: Misdirection 226

Analyzing Evidence 230

> Checklist: Analyzing Evidence 229

The Climax 233

> Deus Ex Machina 234
> Denouement 235
> Checklist: Denouement 236
> Epilogue 236

Research 240

> FAQ: Research 242

Generating Ideas 245

> How to Write a Premise 247
> Checklist: Premise 250
> Subplots 251

Series or Standalone? 254

> Standalones 256
> Series 257

ANDREA JOHNSON

Revision 260

> Revision Questions 262
> Tracking Problems 265
> Critique Partner Feedback 267
> Editing Software 271
> Can a Writer Revise Too Much? 273

Conclusion 275
Author's Note 276
Glossary 277

Introduction

You can add suspense to any story...and in this book you'll find the tools.

First of all, what people actually mean when they use "suspense" as a genre is really "thriller" because the truth is **that every story can (and should!) contain suspense** — or at the very least tension, which is the anticipation of conflict or an emotionally strenuous situation. For example, in a sweet romance, the suspense lies in this question: *Will they or won't they overcome their differences to find love*? In contrast, a thriller finds its suspense in the action-packed battle of good versus evil, the detailed push and pull between the protagonist and the antagonist. But really, how is that so different?

When it comes to applying suspense to any genre, it simply boils down to degree and intensity — or should I say, the author's story goals and the audience's expectations. And what we can already take away from this for all of our novels, regardless of genre, is that good suspense ignites both the reader's intellectual and emotional curiosity. Writers want to do everything they can to encourage their audiences to worry for the characters and wonder how they will ever escape their dilemma.

In the opening chapters, we'll talk more about building suspense, but let's first outline exactly what this book has to offer and what I hope you'll learn.

This guide assumes you know the basics of narrative storytelling and how to infuse emotion into your fiction, so we will only touch on those concepts briefly. If you want additional help in the aforementioned areas, purchase *Scene & Structure* by Jack M. Bickham and *The Emotional Craft of Fiction: How to Write the Story Beneath the Surface* by Donald Maass.

Keep in mind, the thesis of this book is that suspense is something needed in all commercial fiction genres. Even though I have a section outlining the different thriller subgenres, **this book is for everyone**. Each section contains information that can apply to any fiction writer's work, and the tips are relayed in a manner that works for all writing levels. Every chapter ends in a checklist, grow tip, or a frequently asked question you can refer to when you need answers in a hurry.

Although we will eventually work to establish a clear definition for suspense and determine how it differs from the term "thriller," you will find that I use the word "suspense" throughout this book as a catchall for "your novel." Again, the idea is that regardless of what you're writing, you will need these tools to help you build the proper level of tension and suspense in your fiction.

Please review the table of contents for a more granular list of the topics covered. But generally speaking, this work will shine a light on the eleven elements needed to craft nail-biting suspense.

Suspense: On the most basic level, suspense is the anxiousness or uncertainty about how things will unfold. We also often hear about suspense raising a question, *will she succeed*, but drawing out the solution. However, this isn't about omitting things from the audience. It is about ensuring that the protagonist must struggle for the answer she seeks. Plans backfire. Fears manifest. Crisis erupt. Yet, your heroine's time and attention are pulled in another direction, making resolution seem impossible and putting the audience on the edge of their seat. We empathize with the protagonist — or at least her situation — so our connection further amplifies that suspense, or rather, amplifies our worry that she'll get the job done.

Tension: If suspense is about raising a question, then tension is the dread one feels when it is clear that the plan has gone to hell in a handbasket and the consequences are afoot, whether that be as minor as a knife to the gut or as major as a bomb demolishing a city. Tension can also be the excitement of escaping a conflict by the skin of one's teeth, but how it majorly differs from suspense is that its effects are more immediate. Tension is the reader's anticipation of conflict rising, so it can (and should!) appear to some degree in every scene.

Strong Opener: We refer to this as the story's hook because the first scene should draw the audience into your story. So start in the middle of things. Drop the audience into the center of a problem. Pose a difficult question. Create an unusual circumstance. These approaches activate the reader's brain as she struggles to understand the situation and the stakes. Of course, you as the writer need to be clever about relaying that information as quickly and seamlessly as possible, so spend a decent amount of time brainstorming exactly where your story should start.

Vicious Villain: Give your hero a worthy opponent whose intellect, talents, and strength matches — if not, surpasses — the attributes given to your hero. This will make the challenge behind your story, better known as the conflict or narrative question, more significant and lead to the uncertainty that is the backbone of suspense.

Passionate Protagonist: Give the audience someone to root for, someone they can empathize with. This person doesn't need to be perfect or even completely morally. They just need to be relatable and face universal obstacles that the audience can understand. Memorable leads are the key to any good fiction and are often why readers return to a series.

Compelling Conflict: Conflict drives the narrative and provides story tension by introducing the elements over which the two opposing forces (antagonist and protagonist) will struggle. A novel should have an overarching conflict that acts as the story question as well as mini-conflicts that arise during each scene. The smaller conflicts should help reveal each characters' motivations, values, and weakness.

High stakes: Story stakes are what will be won if the protagonist succeeds and lost if they fail. According to James Scott Bell's *Su-*

perstructure: The Key to Unleashing the Power of Story* (2015), this should always involve death whether that's an actual physical death, a professional one such as the jeopardizing of one's career, or a psychological one where the hero is battling some inner turmoil.

Upbeat Pace: The story should advance with every scene because even though we are prolonging the outcome, we don't want the audience to get ahead of us. Therefore, it is important that your story's forward progression moves at a decent pace.

Ample Action: Even suspense stories of a psychological nature should have some physical action. Remember, action — whether chases or fights — should do more than just thrill, they should also reveal character, amplify conflict, build tension, elicit emotion, and sustain suspense.

Plot Twists: A plot twist is an unexpected development that shatters what the characters thought they knew. Think of it as a story turn designed to drastically disrupt things the audience believes they already know and view the story in a whole new light. This can be a discovery, a revelation, a secret, et cetera. To get there, you can incorporate misdirection in the form of red herrings, unreliable narrators, reversals, MacGuffins, et cetera. But regardless of the tactic used, your twist must be properly foreshadowed or the audience will feel cheated.

Blurred Lines: When pushed to the brink, there often comes a point when the protagonist is faced with a dark choice. This can be breaking one's moral code or breaking the law, but this is always a tense moment because the heroine has nothing left in the tank and this choice has the potential to change things moving forward. This usually happens in the scene prior to the climax where the hero will need to dig deep or learn lessons that will aid them in the battle to come.

We will talk more about *how* to achieve those elements later in this book. Also, please note this text will focus on what it takes to write a full-length novel. Even though you will able to use most of this advice for novellas or short fiction, that is not our focus. With that in mind, here is a complete list of what this guide <u>will not</u> offer:

- ❖ Advice on drafting marketing or submission plan
- ❖ Advice on querying an agent or securing a book deal
- ❖ Advice on writing a series
- ❖ Advice on self-publishing
- ❖ A rigid way of doing things

The last point is important. While I want to give you a solid foundation for mastering suspense, the manner in which you go about this task should mesh with your skill and sensibilities. I am not here to dissuade anyone from doing something that has brought them positive results. I am, however, interested in making sure your manuscripts contain the necessary ingredients to get fans addicted to your work.

Therefore, this book is for anyone who needs a push getting started. You will receive a detailed roadmap that will help turn an idea into a work of art. You can read this guide in sections or from beginning to end, but I encourage you to take notes in your own hand so that the concepts get into your bones. You should also bookmark the glossary in the back in case there are terms that are unfamiliar. But most importantly, follow up on any supplemental material mentioned, particularly if it covers one of your weak spots.

As alluded to earlier, there are a number of elements that go into crafting good suspense. These tools are possible to learn on one's own, but the path is treacherous. So if you have chosen fiction for your career, I encourage you to embrace the concept of life-long learning because fiction, like any other art, has tricky nuances that are always changing.

During my writer's journey, I took this advice to the extreme by attending graduate school for an MFA in Writing Popular Fiction.

Of course, you don't have to go to such lengths (unless you want to!), especially when I've already done the work for you.

So with career growth as our mindset, consider this book my way of sharing what I've learned while getting you excited about your own projects and saving you a little time and money along the way. Whether you're a plotter or a pantser, my goal is for you to become passionate about taking your writing to the next level while giving you the tools to master the art of suspense.

Mastering the Art of Suspense

"Hitchcock knew that the closed door is much more frightening than the open one. Think of when you were a kid at night, staring at the closet door, wondering what was really in there. We filled the void with our imaginations. And we almost never thought that it was a kind fairy holding a puppy and some pudding....
The true nature of terror is the unknown. The truly terrible thrives in silence."
~*State of Terror* (2021) by Hillary Clinton and Louise Penny

What's a Thriller?

At the simplest level, a thriller is a fiction narrative that's so captivating the reader can't put it down. Thrillers are also considered one of mystery's prime subgenres because thriller plots often include some form of crime or wrongdoing. However, unlike many of its mystery counterparts, thrillers are defined less by what their stories encompass and more by the way they make the audience feel and the exciting manner in which they unfold:

- High-concept premise
- Vibrant settings
- Volatile conflicts
- Visceral action
- Escalating stakes
- Intense pacing
- Dark threats
- Pulse-pounding suspense
- Mind-bending plot twists

Thrillers draw us in through emotion, preying on our curiosity and fears — often thrusting a relatable but ordinary person like ourselves into an extraordinary situation that seemingly has no solution. So we bite our nails and keep turning pages until we reach the adrenaline-soaked climax where the protagonist narrowly escapes, worse for the wear but ultimately wiser.

Thrillers also demand the most from their setting, characters, and plot — to the extent that the reader walks away knowing more than he ever wanted to know about killer sharks, viral outbreaks, obsessed mistresses, or secret fight clubs. And yet, that's why thrillers are so addictive. They take the audience to the extreme, showing them something they never would have imagined.

And while some thriller authors like Dean Koontz, James Patterson, David Baldacci, and Lee Child rely on gunplay and international locales, others like Tess Gerritsen, Gillian Flynn, and Pamela Samuels Young delve into the psychological peril their characters face — which only goes to show how much variety there is within the genre, especially when it comes to exploring our society's various social and moral dilemmas.

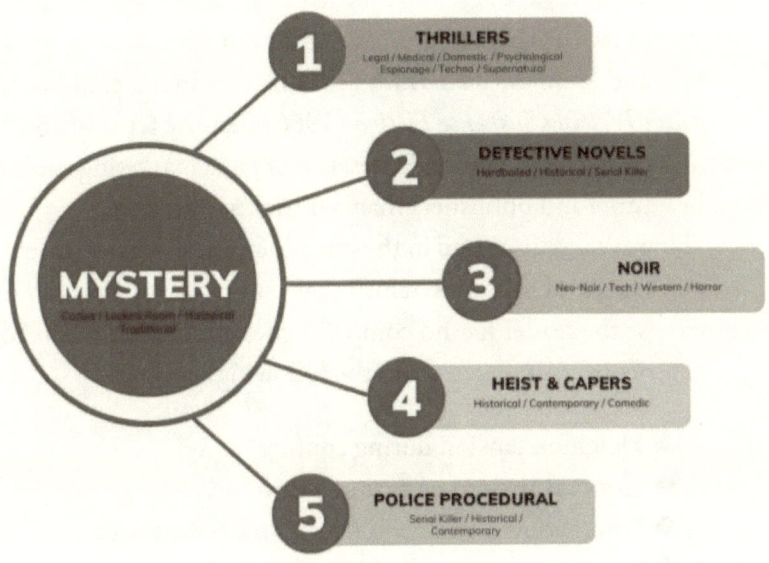

Please note this is not a comprehensive list, but simply a visual interpretation of this chapter's general argument. Obviously, each genre has audience expectations that help define their content, but this meant as a reflection of how things are often shelved at the bookstore or sorted on Amazon. As with anything, arguments can be made for overlap. We've also seen many of these subgenres mixed to great success and that is very much allowed — e.g. the detective/thriller *Mr. Mercedes* (2014) by Stephen King. But in general, this list speaks to the most popular subgenres as typically aligned by subject.

Difference Between Thriller and Suspense

If we are simply talking about separating fiction into genres, thrillers and suspense can be considered the same thing. That is to say, when the word "suspense" is used as a literary *category*, it refers to any story whose dominate efforts are to create apprehension and anxiety in the reader — whether the plot is small and sedentary in scope with character-specific stakes or larger in scope with world-specific ones. Basically, suspense is a much more loosely organized category than most genres. In fact, Patricia Highsmith, author of *The Talented Mr. Ripley* (1955) and *Strangers on a Train* (1950), notes in her craft book *Plotting and Writing Suspense Fiction* (1966) that the term "suspense fiction," as used in the United States, is more of a marketing tool adopted by editors and publishers than a distinctive grouping.

However, as discussed in the introduction, all stories should have some element of the uncertainty that comes with being *suspenseful* otherwise the reader has no compelling reason to continue reading.

Suspense can be used to do the following:

- Heighten tension during conflict
- Conceal answers as part of a slow reveal
- Foreshadow a twist and make it more powerful
- Engage your reader...and much more!

In fiction writing, suspense occurs on two levels: the suspense characters feel as they anticipate an outcome and the suspense the story arouses in the reader. There are different approaches to each, which we will cover in later sections, but the foundation is that suspense comes not just from an uncertainty about what's going to happen but also an uncertainty about what everyone thinks they know about what is really happening.

Narratively, this means that every story should have a long-term suspense problem that is posed at the start. That question is then slowly answered as the plot progresses. Typically, these are the suspense elements that your characters are most anxious about. However, since suspense requires both uncertainty and anticipation, the truth behind this narrative question shouldn't be revealed until the climax or conclusion. For example, in the Matrix trilogy, the main suspense questions are clear: *Is Neo really The One? Can he defeat Agent Smith and succeed in saving Zion from extinction?*

But to create a story that is truly addictive, you also need short-term suspense questions on a scene-by-scene level that elicit a similarly strong reaction from the reader. These may connect to the overall narrative question, create a point of contention in the subplot, or act as misdirection, but the answers come much more quickly. You can also use these moments as cliffhangers at the end of chapters, urging the reader to turn pages to find out what's next.

We will discuss this more in a later session, but just keep in mind that this is how we think of suspense when the term is aligned with the literary *techniques* authors use to arouse interest from the reader — and this will also act as the main focus of this guidebook moving forward.

Thriller Subgenres

The assumption is that if you have purchased this book, you have a general idea of what type of story you'd like to write. However, for your reference, I have included a short list of genres that commonly fall under suspense. This is not a comprehensive list, but I have included enough information to inspire further research if desired.

Domestic Thrillers: In a domestic thriller, the main focus is the struggle to defy the odds — a scenario where an ordinary person must overcome their underdog status to vanquish a larger-than-life problem. The transformative journey of survival and self-worth is the audience draw, and the suspense the reader feels is derived from the question of whether or not the protagonist will endure and succeed. Domestic thrillers essentially draw from the old Gothic tales by taking an implied threat and making it real. In those early stories, the protagonist is a woman in jeopardy without anyone to help her, except for a man with a hard heart that she can't always trust, and the setting is a spooky home with a dark past. While the contemporary approach to this subgenre can have either a male or female lead and often replaces the supernatural element with a more realistic threat like abuse or harassment, we can still look at this genre as an offshoot of novels such as Charlotte Brontë's *Jane Eyre* (1847) and *Rebecca* by Daphne du Maurier (1938).

Romantic Suspense: These are stories about the love connections that form amidst the investigation of a murder or potential crime. British author Mary Stewart is often regarded as one of the first to blend romance with thrills in novels such as *Wildfire at Midnight* (1956), *The Ivy Tree* (1961), and *Touch Not the Cat* (1976). Danger propels these stories forward, so the suspense derives from the uncertainty that a relationship can be cultivated under such circumstances — not to mention, the race against the clock to solve the crime. Modern stars in the field include J.D. Robb (aka Nora Roberts), Catherine Coulter, and Lisa Jackson.

Psychological Thrillers: These stories rely on fear, paranoia, and conspiracies to create plots where the characters question such things as their perceptions of reality, their personal identity, or the agenda and identity of the people around them. The protagonist can be impaired in some way — naivete, mental disease, addiction, et cetera — or be the victim of someone with these issues. The suspense, for both the reader and the protagonist, is derived from the uncertainty of the unknown and one's inability to trust the things their mind tells them. Psychological thrillers often take many forms, touching upon such tropes as stalkers, stolen identity, person in peril, mistaken identity, identity swap, and amnesia.

Espionage Thrillers: Some of the earliest recognized espionage thrillers are *The Spy* (1821) and *The Bravo* (1831), both by American author James Fenimore Cooper as well as *The Riddle of the Sands: A Record of Secret Service* (1903) by Erskine Childers. The latter is an adventure story that rose to popularity in the years before the first World War, and its success allowed for a different kind of storytelling that focused more on action and setting and less on the deductive reasoning and evidence gathering that had become synonymous with the detective stories and traditional mysteries of the time. The novel is reminiscent of the work of adventure romance writers like H. Rider Haggard, pioneer of the lost world adventure subgenre that had become popular during the late 1800s of the United Kingdom's Victorian Era.

Childers approach of using authentic details, such as yachting through the various Frisian Islands, inspired the work of Ian Fleming, John le Carré, and John Buchan. In fact, Buchan would produce a moniker for this style of writing in the subtitle for his work *The Thirty-Nine Steps: A "Shocker"* (1915) — first appearing, July through September, as a serial in *Blackwood's Magazine* with the byline "H de V" before the novel's publication in October of that same year. Today's readers may substitute "shocker" for "thriller"; but either way, the concept of a story designed to evoke excitement and suspense can be derived from this line of works.

Real-life espionage is akin to what the average person would call monotonous work: engaging in reconnaissance, researching biographical information on targets, cycling through historical records and financials, monitoring calls. Thus, it is your job as a writer to find ways to make those real-world aspects fascinating while maximizing those moments when the action reaches the thrilling high we're used to seeing with heroes like James Bond or Jason Bourne. A great way to achieve this is to take a cue from the old FOX television show *24* and have your tale start at the height of its problem where a ticking clock forces the hero to act in an immediate fashion. By condensing the action, you ensure that the most interesting aspects of the profession and the most crucial decisions take the forefront without diluting realism or wholly eliminating the aspects of the job that are more academic or cerebral.

Political Thrillers: These stories show the protagonist discovering a conspiracy that he either deliberately or accidentally becomes involved in while trying to expose or end the threat. The theme is often some variation on the corruption of power and that grab for dominance can take the form of a coverup, assassination, terrorist attack, or hostage situation. The history of the political thriller finds its roots in *The Three Musketeers* (1844) by Alexandre Dumas and *The Scarlet Pimpernel* (1905) by Baroness Orczy.

Techno-Thrillers: This subgenre covers a number of potential sources for innovation: militaristic, medical, genetics, robotics, nanotechnology, et cetera. These elements act as not only the setting for these stories but also tend to influence the controlling theme. In the same way that the underlying theme for most romances is "love conquers all," the subtextual message for all techno-thrillers is "technology run amok" — worse-case scenarios surrounding scientific, systematic, and mechanical discoveries — think *Jurassic Park* (1990) by Michael Crichton. Alternatives to this main theme are technology as savior or tech used as a weapon or source of power. The pitfall of this genre as an author is to overdo the technology to the point that you fail to excite. Plus, it is difficult to both explain new concepts and build memorable characters. If ever in doubt, splurge on the side of characterization as that's what connects the reader to your novel. Refer to Tom Clancy's *The Hunt for Red October* (1984) as one of the innovators for this genre even though Clancy himself looks to Jules Verne's *Twenty Thousand Leagues Under the Sea* (1870) and Frank Herbert's 1956 submarine novel *Under Pressure* as some of the inspirations for his early work.

Legal Thrillers

While the average reader may consider Erle Stanley Gardner's *The Case of the Velvet Claws* (1933) or Robert Traver's *Anatomy of a Murder* (1958) as the pioneering examples of the modern legal thriller, real-life criminal misdeeds and salacious trials were being repackaged and presented as entertainment as early as 399 B.C. when Plato wrote about Socrates' trial for impiety and corruption; see also Geoffrey Chaucer's *The Canterbury Tales* (1387) and William Shakespeare's *The Merchant of Venice* (1600).

But according to Marlyn Robinson, author of "Collins to Grisham: A Brief History of the Legal Thriller," the real boon was in the late seventeenth century. Most notably, German lawyer Georg Harsdorffer wrote *A Gallery of Horrible Tales of Murder* (1650), which highlighted the use of science to provide evidence and deduce guilt during a time when defendants' pleas were still gained through torture.

In the 1730s, a French lawyer, Francois Richer, edited a version of the *Causes Célèbres*, a collection of trial stories, where he included the preface, "I have taken care to arrange the material in such a way that the reader cannot spot at once how a case will end and what verdict will be pronounced. He remains in a state of uncertainty during the development of the action, and in that way, I believe each case will become more gripping.... The reader will remain curious up to the final page." Whereupon, the element of suspense was added to the world of mystery and crime in a manner that moved the focus from morality tales to thrilling ones.

Marlyn Robinson also notes that English playwright and novelist Wilkie Collins further contributed to this new genre when "The Lawyer's Story of a Stolen Letter" (1854) became one of the first to combine suspense, detection, conspiracies, and the legal system into the plight of the innocent turned accused. Wilkie also later wrote *The Woman in White* (1859), which helped solidify the genre and his place in the literary landscape.

Whether you're writing a full-blown legal thriller or a traditional mystery with a minor trial element, you must be familiar with courtroom etiquette, judicial rhetoric, and the laws for your chosen state. Like medical thrillers, this is a subgenre where audiences expect to be immersed in a realistic view, so do your research. Even if the plan is to approach the material from a unique angle, you need to know the procedures before you can bend them in the name of a suspenseful criminal verdict or ethical dilemma.

Invest in a copy of Black's Law Dictionary[1] or become familiar with the online version, and purchase *Principles of Legal Research: How to Find the Law* (2009) by Kent Olson. Also, because forensics and DNA technology have become such a vital part of criminal investigations, you may need to do additional research in the areas of ballistics, serology, dactyloscopy, and toxicology — which cover firearms, blood serums, fingerprints, and chemical substances, respectively. *Forensics: A Guide for Writers* (2008) by D.P. Lyle, M.D., is an excellent starting source for such information. Lastly, you'll need to know how and why the cops do what they do, so look for *Police Procedure & Investigation: A Guide for Writers* (2007) by Lee Lofland.

The great thing about legal thrillers is that there is a wide interpretation within the subgenre. You can choose to focus on a trial with a heavy moral dilemma that leads to an inwardly reflecting story like John Grisham's *A Time to Kill* (1989) or merely include the professional involvement of lawyers without using the courtroom as with Grisham's *The Firm* (1991). You can implement a frame story to focus on the legal woes of a family as done in *Defending Jacob* (2012) by William Landay or explore the real-time hardships of an attorney seeking justice for her bullied daughter as depicted in *Failure to Protect* (2019) by Pamela Samuels Young. Regardless of which structure you choose, tension and pacing must be carefully planned and plotted because they're still suspense stories.

What may help is to think of legal thrillers as having three basic story structures: mysteries, man on the run, and court based. The legal thriller steeped in mystery usually places the lawyer or other legal professional in the role of detective. The "man on the run" story is where the lead character finds himself entangled in some sort of le-

---

1. https://thelawdictionary.org/

gal conspiracy that they must expose. And of course, the court-based story places either the criminal attorney and their trial work, the jury and their deliberations, or the defendant and their quest for innocence at the forefront of the narrative. In each scenario, the stakes must be high with things like careers, freedoms, fortunes, families, and lives on the line. But again, how you tackle the story is up to you. Just remember that regardless of the approach, legal thrillers must answer two things by the story's climax: Does the justice system deliver on its promises, and what does it mean if it can't? The big audience response and the groundwork for your suspense will come when the audience senses an injustice. They will become engrossed in the plot and identify with your protagonist as the story vacillates between *will she or won't she* set things right.

So of course, your legal thriller should include a protagonist with a strong sense of truth and morality. Avid readers of the genre will find that this is often a young, idealistic underdog who acts as the antithesis of the corrupted corporations or firms that they face. The rest of the story is often populated with secondary characters who are more seasoned, but the advantage of this is that technical aspects of the law and other jargon can be explained to the naive protagonist (and hence, the reader) without seeming like an information dump. In addition, a newbie protagonist opens the door for the inclusion of a mystery genre staple: the mentor. Mentors are excellent fictional devices because they are designed to help the hero question his beliefs and remind them of what's at stake while also warning them about where the wrong choice may lead.

So with all of that in mind, your first step toward writing a legal thriller may be to determine what role your protagonist plays in the legal profession. Are they a prosecutor, defense attorney, judge, paralegal, bailiff, or a court reporter as in my novel *Poetic Justice*? Knowing the exact profession will help dictate setting, which you want to vary as much as possible to help immerse the reader into this new world. In addition to attorney's offices, utilize jail cells, police stations, law libraries, jury rooms, judge's chambers, et cetera. These locations can also be used to mirror the injustices your protagonist might be facing such as when a neophyte attorney, whose client has been swindled out of her husband's death benefits, walks into the posh boardroom of an insurance company.

Now, before we wrap up this rather lengthy section, I do want to offer some do's and don'ts regarding the law and courtroom etiquette that will help your legal thriller feel more authentic.

Legal Tips for the Legal Thriller

Know your legal terms and the law. The law can be complicated and vary from jurisdiction to jurisdiction, so make sure to do your research by getting familiar enough with the terms and statutes for your region to simplify them in the way that the audience can quickly understand. Remember, laws and practices will vary from county to state, from state to federal, and from federal to international.

Consider all sides of the case. Regardless of the viewpoint chosen for the novel, the characters in your book should explore the possible motives and outlooks of the other characters when trying to unravel the crime or task at hand. Meaning, if your protagonist is the prosecutor, then have scenes where counsel strategizes about the defense team's theory and vice versa. Exploring the different angles of the crime may provide a point of tension or contention that will raise the stakes in your work.

Show the jurors reactions. Even though the judge calls the shots regarding courtroom behavior and rulings on the law, the jurors decide who wins the case. Most writers new to the legal thriller subgenre overlook the importance of the jury's role because they don't speak until the verdict is delivered, but the attorneys and witness should be playing to them the whole time to lend reality to the proceedings. After all, the jurors are the people the attorneys must convince in order to obtain their desired outcome. But more importantly, the jurors are us — they are an extension of the audience for the scene, so their reactions to the evidence can lend tension, foreshadow trouble to come, or turn the tide for an attorney whose case may not be going so well. You can also use the jury to show the audience how they should feel about the information being conveyed or you can simply use the jury to help steer the pacing, blocking, and tone of a scene by having the attorneys use different tactics to hold their attention and sway their judgement. Regardless of how you use them in a trial scene, don't forget to humanize them. You can use anything from names, juror numbers, clothing, or occupations to describe them individually or as a group, just be sure to show that their presence is significant and carries stakes for all those involved in the case.

Allow your lawyer to make mistakes. While a large part of your story will involve showing the cleverness and mental prowess of your attorney when it comes to her particular area of the law, there should be moments when she fails. This brings a more believable dynamic to the story and demonstrates how the character handles setbacks, disappointment, peril, or any other consequences that may come from the wrong move. It also increases stakes and adds to the *will they or won't they succeed* that is inherent to every thriller.

Know the difference between direct and cross. Work to understand the differences between the direct and cross-examination of witnesses. This will help your dialogue seem accurate and professional to readers familiar with the law. The attorney calling the witness to the stand will start direct examination. During this procedure, she cannot ask leading questions, i.e. inquiries that suggest an answer. For example, "You were standing across the street at the time of the murder, weren't you?" or "Did you agree to meet the victim at Sam's Club after work? Avoid questions that have the lawyer testifying rather than the witness. Direct examination is meant to showcase the witness. The lawyer's role should be more of a background player because the point is to paint a picture for the jury that supports the story their client wants to tell. On the other hand, when the opposing attorney questions that same witness, this is considered cross-examination. Leading questions are allowed during cross, and many lawyers utilize this as a means of directing or controlling a witness's testimony, forcing him or her to deny or agree with the information. This is where the attorney's tactics — waving around documents, punctuating statements was nods to the jury, pacing the courtroom — can come to the forefront as he shapes the narrative he wants to tell through the witness's answers. This is also where you can play around with having the witness's attempts to course correct or fight back succeed or fail.

Avoid having the cops take people in for questioning. Being dragged in for questioning is a movie contrivance that doesn't happen in real life. If the police want to question a potential suspect, that person has the right to refuse and the police cannot arrest them to force that result. An arrest cannot be based on a hunch or a mere tip. The police must have probable cause, which can include the arresting officer's observation of a suspect's behavior but is more often a series of connected eyewitness accounts and investigative techniques that point to the suspect having committed a specific crime. This collection of clues and evidence will be how you make your story interesting — not through the contrivance of an unwarranted interrogation. But with that in mind, be advised that probable cause is a less exacting standard than the evidence needed for a trial conviction, which is beyond a reasonable doubt.

Know the difference between direct and circumstantial evidence. Direct evidence is any fact attested to by eyewitnesses or information stated in documents that affirms the genuineness and veracity of the data. So if that person or paperwork is believed, no further proof is required to verify the specific point upon which they testified. On the other hand, circumstantial evidence establishes a fact from which another idea can logically be inferred. To understand circumstantial evidence, consider the kind of logic we often use against our kids. You put a plate of hot cholate chip cookies on the counter ten feet away from where your nine-year-old daughter is doing her homework. You leave the room for thirty minutes and return to find the cookies gone. Your daughter swears she didn't eat them, but there is chocolate on her cheek and crumbs on her shirt. You didn't see her eat them, but the evidence points to that fact. If we put this in terms of a murder by adding that scenario of circumstantial evidence to a strong motive (i.e. what the person has to gain), a jury could legally choose to convict. Of course, each side is going to work hard to shoot holes through both types of evidence by providing data, forensics, witness with contradictory testimony, et cetera. So quite obviously, one piece of evidence on either side won't necessarily make or break a case. The burden of proof requires that there is enough evidence to convince the jury beyond a reasonable doubt. But it is import to keep in mind that while every attorney would like a case full of direct evidence, the law certainly permits attorneys to use circumstantial evidence as the backbone for a conviction as well.

Let defense counsel defend. Don't waste time depicting a defense attorney who is obsessing over his client's potential (or apparent) guilt. If a lawyer agrees to take a case, they are working under the presumption of innocence and have agreed to force the prosecution to prove their side beyond a reasonable doubt. Failure to reach that burden of proof requires a not guilty verdict. Leave the dilemma of a client's guilt or innocence to the other characters in the story and depict the defense attorney doing his or her job to the best of their ability.

Take a recess. Go beyond the courtroom. Delve into the attorneys' personal lives. Draw correlations between the themes that arise in the courtroom — poverty, classism, racism, sexism — to what's going on with the world at large to give your story scope and resonance.

Showcase the judge's power. In a real trial, the judge runs the courtroom. Even though it is the jury's job to produce the verdict, the judge directs the logistical aspects of the event by declaring the start of trial, reading the jury charge, ruling over objections, et cetera — and that includes admonishing lawyers who get unruly during proceedings. Television and fiction love to show lawyers running around arguing with each other (and the judge!) or badgering witnesses, but the truth of the matter is that attorneys can be held in contempt of court when they get out of line. This can amount to fines or jail time, so if you depict such behavior make sure to show the consequences.

Show the attorney's being respectful. As implied above, a big thing that new legal thriller writers get wrong is that they have attorneys arguing with each other in open court. While, yes, this may occasionally happen at sidebar outside of the earshot or presence of the jury, it doesn't happen during trial because the lawyers aren't formally allowed to engage in conversation on the floor. Concerns are directed to the judge then ruled upon so that attorneys addressing each other directly is avoided.

Keep surprises to a minimum. Every writer wants to create their version of a shocking witness reveal or confession on the stand, but be careful because it rarely happens in reality and often rings false on the page much like the unearned ending of a deus ex machina. Smart legal thrillers find way to illuminate the incongruities between an eyewitness testimony and the truth through the actions and motivations of the full cast of characters in the story.

Focus on the Narrative. At the end of the day, you're still writing a *novel*, not a how-to book. So have fun with your fiction, and don't let all of the legal stuff weigh down your narrative.

Medical Thrillers

Some pioneers of this subgenre include Molière, a French playwright, whose three-act satire *The Imaginary Invalid* (1673) lampoons the medical profession; Mary Shelley's *Frankenstein; or, The Modern Prometheus* (1818), which tells the story of a scientist who creates a hideous but intelligent creature; and Robert Louis Stevenson's *Strange Case of Dr. Jekyll and Mr. Hyde* (1886), which features a medical professional who uses a chemical formula to transform himself. And yet, the rise of the modern medical thriller as we know it can be traced to *Coma* (1977) by Robin Cook.

Cook started his medical career as a general surgical resident and finished with an ophthalmology residency at Harvard, but his literary career didn't begin until several years later when he joined the Navy and wrote his debut novel, *The Year of the Intern* (1972) —an honest look at the physical and psychological toil of being a first-year resident. Unfortunately, this work didn't resonate with audiences the way he'd hoped, which led Cook back to the drawing board.

Five years passed before the publication of his second book, *Coma*. During the interim, he studied the publishing industry to gather suspense techniques. And in the process, he came to the conclusion that he wanted his books transcend entertainment in favor of educating the public about pressing medical and scientific issues. These days several writers have followed in his footsteps with Michael Palmer, Michael Crichton, Kathy Reichs, Patricia Cornwell, and Tess Gerritsen seemingly dominating the genre.

So what makes medical stories so popular? Like most thrillers, their appeal comes from their connection with the truth: We're all vulnerable to illness, disease, and death. We will all need to rely on a doctor one day — and that alone is a frightening thing. *But what if the doctors make a mistake? What if the anesthesia fails to take? What if I am left helpless on the operating table?* These "what ifs" lead to very real fears. Fears that are, perhaps, a little less daunting and a lot more fun when explored through fiction. Not to mention, that medicine itself is mysterious: psychiatric clinics, research laboratories, operating wards, ambulances, morgues, emergency rooms — *What goes on in there? How do doctors know what to look for when curing a disease?* The ability to diagnose and heal is tantamount to magic.

This opens the door to a myriad of possibilities for writers who are interested in the subgenre. After all, the discovery of a disease makes for an excellent opening conflict and a suspenseful story question: *Will the medical miracle be found in time to solve the case and cure the sleuth?* A writer could even use a medical diagnosis as a ticking clock of sorts, motivating an otherwise complacent character to act before his disease takes over. Conversely, a character could use a diagnosis or medication to absolve himself of bad behavior.

However, writing a medical thriller requires a lot more forethought than simply setting your story in a hospital and thinking up a bizarre ailment. Since the main characters are medically trained and the central conflict revolves around medical science or ethics, anyone interested in the genre should have a solid background in the health industry or a penchant for research.

So let's start by talking about some places you can go to both gather story ideas and learn more about the profession. Consider subscribing to research publications such as *Discover, Nature, Science, Scientific American,* and the *New England Journal of Medicine,* or visit some of the news and medical sites on the internet:

- ❖ Centers for Disease Control & Prevention – www.cdc.gov
- ❖ Cochrane Library – www.cochranelibrary.com
- ❖ Healio – www.healio.com
- ❖ MedlinePlus – www.medlineplus.gov
- ❖ Medscape – www.medscape.com
- ❖ PLOS Medicine – www.journals.plos.org/plosmedicine
- ❖ Stanford Medical School – www.med.stanford.edu
- ❖ World Health Organization – www.who.int

Or if you live near a college or medical library, ask if they have user access to PubMed, the National Library of Medicine's Medline subscription database. The site indexes a myriad of biomedical literature published in the United States and around the globe. It also covers a broad range of health-related fields including nursing, dentistry, veterinary medicine, and psychiatry.

PubMed – https://pubmed.ncbi.nlm.nih.gov/

Once you've done some research and found a topic of interest, consider the possible consequences if this medical discovery or issue went awry. Use the "what if" premise creation technique discussed in this book to create a believable and scientifically plausible conflict and plot.

Next, become familiar with the medical aspects needed to tell your story with accuracy. For example, don't have a first-year med student perform a major procedure. Medical school is a four-year journey, and the first two focus on classroom instruction and labs, so this would never happen. The ability to observe and assist in billable procedures (under supervision!) doesn't occur until their residency, which follows medical school graduation and can take three to five years to complete depending on the chosen discipline. At the end of a successful residency, they may then eligible for a specialty certification and may practice medicine without oversight. Making small mistakes in this area, even if they aren't as obvious as my example, can pull your reader out of the story. If you don't have medical training, find a professional to help with the basics. Medical examiners, paramedics, nurses, physicians' assistants, and internists are all great resources if you're not able to connect with an active or retired physician. Have your questions ready ahead of time in written form so as not to waste their time, and it also helps to have something to leave them if they need to cut your meeting short.

Your next task is to work on making your medical personnel sound as realistic as possible through action and dialogue. If you've been in a hospital, you know the language is urgent but calm, rapid and often clipped. No extraneous syllables are uttered. *V-fib! Bagging! He's flat-lining* To keep the pace of the scene, you won't have time to describe the meaning of every term, but you should make it clear what's happening and how its effecting the parties involved through the movement and body language used throughout. Show the anesthesiologist's response to the pop of the epiglottis in preparation for intubation or the scrub nurse's reaction to the smell as the bone saw breaches the sternum. Don't skimp on these details because that's what the readers of these novels pay for — a realistic view of a world they rarely get to visit (without a bill). Of course, you're not required to spend the entire novel in the OR or ER, but a few technical procedures with full-sensory depictions are a must for this subgenre.

To help with this, you may want to talk to a medical professional about the veracity of your work. Also, obtain a copy of Stedman's Medical Dictionary[2] or invest in the online version as well as textbooks on anatomy, infectious diseases, and pharmacology. A good all-in-one resource is *Murder and Mayhem: A Doctor Answers Medical and Forensic Questions for Mystery Writers* (2003) by D.P. Lyle, M.D. The author discusses helpful things like the effect of certain poisons and drugs, the role of the coroner and the crime lab, and the physical manifestations synonymous with traumatic injuries like the gunshot wounds and stabbings we love so much.

The final step is to make your characters human. Doctors and nurses are real-life superheroes, but they are still prone to mistakes, failures, and self-doubt. Don't be afraid to include a misdiagnosis, a surgical error that results in death, or an unethical decision. This is how you develop a protagonist who captures the complexities of the profession and the truth of what it means to be responsible for someone else's life. We should also see them outside the work setting and

---

2.   https://stedmansonline.com/

experience how their mistakes and foibles affect their spouses and loved ones. By placing a character in multiple environments, we can further complicate their inner conflicts and showcase how they may hide or highlight aspects of themselves to better navigate the world.

Medical Thrillers: Recommended Reads

- *The Andromeda Strain* (1969) by Michael Crichton
- *Coma (1977)* by Robin Cook
- *Postmortem* (1990) by Patricia Cornwell
- *Bloodstream* (1998) by Tess Gerritsen
- *Your Heart Belongs to Me* (2008) by Dean Koontz
- *Speaking in Bones* (2015) by Kathy Reichs

Noir

Noir narratives are typically crime stories driven by sharp action and quippy dialogue but are more readily identified by their morally gray protagonists, dark storylines, and grim urban settings. The overall mood is one of disillusionment or desperation — perhaps even paranoia — and the themes commonly reflect some form of moral corruption. Similarly, the main conflicts are often centered on lust, addiction, vanity, greed, or fear and ultimately lead to the protagonist's downfall, making this genre unique from the others discussed in this chapter. That is to say, at the end of a typical thriller, the world may be upended, but the hero has done his best to thwart evil — or at least expose it for others to avoid. In noir, no one escapes unscathed, and when the story ends, there is no coming back from the devastation.

The word "noir" means "black film" in French, yet early uses of the term stem from 1940's Hollywood where the crime drama had exploded in conjunction with its literary counterpart. Films like *The Maltese Falcon* (1941) and *Moontide* (1942), both based on books published in 1929 and 1940, respectively, dominated the silver screen and featured desperate characters trying to erase life's inequities through theft, sex, lies, and murder. Modern noir stories still contain similar elements but the characterizations lean more toward cynicism than desperation.

If you're planning to write a noir, start with the people who will occupy the narrative. Figure out how to turn your seemingly normal characters into scoundrels, willing to compromise their values. *What temptations will they face? What forces will drag them down? What vices will they succumb to?* Their evolution as individuals and the fallout from their decisions will fuel the conflicts you've set up for them. From there, let them sink under the weight of negative consequences and self-destructive behavior. Once again, this is different from how we think about commercial fiction, but don't be afraid to let your characters fail. This may feel difficult at first, but it is ultimately freeing because you have more room to upend the audience's expectations and introduce something unexpected.

Noir also offers writers the opportunity to focus on humanizing someone who in another novel would likely be a tragic hero or antagonist. This genre forces writers to consider what it means to be a compelling character by creating storylines that subvert conventions and our understanding of good and evil. But even with this freedom, we still want the plot to escalate like a normal three-act structure where things go from okay to bad to worse. However, you don't need that moment of redemption, you are free to have a climax that is an utter disaster. You could also opt to have the character achieve what they think they want only to find that they are even worse off. For example, in *The Maltese Falcon* (1929), we have a brooding detective whose partner is murdered early in the narrative, and although he eventually manages to solve that case and several related ones, his efforts are cruelly rewarded with the discovery that his potential lover is the murderer. Talk about your Debbie Downer.

In short, noir endings are bleak, but this may feel more like how things would end in the real world — *despite our best efforts, things are still screwed up*. Just make sure that you're using these defeats and dark conclusions to reinforce the story's theme and overall message just like Hammett's work where the ending speaks to greed and corruption. Remember, noir isn't about suffering for suffering's sake or making tragedy look cool, there is still always an impactful takeaway that speaks to the human condition.

Noir: Recommended Reads

- *Double Indemnity* (1936) by James M. Cain
- *Thieves Like Us* (1937) by Edward Anderson
- *Savage Night* (1953) by Jim Thompson
- *L.A. Confidential* (1990) by James Ellroy
- *Blacktop Wasteland* (2020) by S.A. Cosby
- *Just Thieves* (2021) by Gregory Galloway

Thriller Plot Map

This chapter includes a sample plot map for a standard thriller. If you know you are writing specifically within this genre, use this section to build your outline. However, be aware that plot structures vary from subgenre to subgenre, so you may need to do some tweaking as you get a stronger idea of where you'd like to take your narrative.

As you outline, don't worry about writing full sentences unless you're moved to do so. Simply create bullet points that list the setting, characters, and conflicts for each beat so that you have enough of an idea in front of you to play around with. This can be a quotes or songs or situations — whatever inspires you. Don't worry about fleshing out those ideas until you've had a chance to look at the entire storyline. Until then, the action of the outline should keep the plot moving forward and escalate the stakes as it unfolds.

Once you move toward your final outline, group related scenes or events that happen close together in time or location to form a chapter or overarching story beat. This will allow you to examine any possible problems or address any gaps before getting too deep into your word count (where the resistance to change things increases because that means throwing out precious ideas you've spent months developing).

Whether a plotter or pantser, it's a wise idea to create an outline or plotting framework in advance to avoid plot holes and writer's block. If the idea of prewriting feels uncomfortable, then at figuring out the overarching story question, main conflict, and climax before getting started.

Act I

❖ **Setup** – Establish the ordinary world for the protagonist. This may also include the status quo for the victim and/or the murderer, depending on the type of thriller you're crafting and the number of point of views you're using. Basically, the key is to establish the main characters, set the tone, build a mood, develop the setting, et cetera.

❖ **Disruption** – This is the first moment of change leading into the inciting incident.

❖ **Discovery** – This could be the unfolding of the actual murder on the page if you're writing a thriller or the discovery of the body if you're writing a cozy (or bloodless) mystery. Other possibilities here are the first major indicator that something is wrong or unusual about the world that has been established. This can be a huge clue or a psychological/supernatural event depending on whether the tale you're writing is light or dark.

❖ **Danger Dawns** – Building of suspense, creation of personal stakes, and the establishment of the protagonist's connection to the crime/discovery/disruption and why they want or choose to get involved

❖ **Clash with Antagonist** – This can be the encounter with the dark forces behind the main story conflict or a negative encounter with a nemesis or authority figure the hero must deal with as an obstacle to moving forward. This is the moment when the protagonist realizes the gravity of the situation, and it pushes them into taking action.

❖ **Decision to Detect** – The decision to investigate is typically the final beat of the first act because it marks a point of no return for the characters where they are thrust into the heart of the story — whether it is because of a sense of duty, a physical trap, the loss of a loved one, threat to their life, world in danger, et cetera. But whether you choose to make this the final beat of your act or not, the first third of the story must contain a definitive moment where your hero decides to dive into the danger even though the odds are staked against him.

Act II

❖ **Introduction of subplot** – Often thrillers employ the narrative device of having someone in the protagonist's life that act as a foil, or a mirror, to show what would happen if the hero took an alternate path or approach to their journey or investigation. A foil may also manifest as a nemesis to the hero since narratively to the two characters are different sides of the same coin. If this is too dauting, a simple romance subplot or conniving coworker side story will work just as well. The point is that at some point a secondary plot should be introduced and that story should intertwine with the main one in a manner that complicates the stakes by story's end. Remember, subplots should resolve and/or dovetail into the main storyline by the end of the third act or top of the fourth at the absolute latest.

❖ **Investigation / Red herrings and dead ends / Second clash with antagonist** - These three elements encompass the try-fail cycle of detection where your main character asks questions of potential witnesses who approach the encounter with varying levels of honesty and withholding. The investigation portion will encompass most, if not all, of the second act. In thrillers, this can escalate to include a myriad of things that go beyond questioning like hacking a mainframe, sneaking into a compound, or stealing corporate secrets. The key here is that not everything is going to immediately add up to a solution or lead the hero along a straight line. However, each encounter must still either move the story forward or remind the audience of the high stakes involved. Therefore, some of these encounters should put your hero in danger or show the hero losing something of significant value. As the clues pile up and the investigation gains traction, the main character may find that they'll need to return to one or two of these characters later since, again, not everything will be as straight forward as it initially seems. This is also the portion of the story where the foil, nemesis, authority figure, and/or antagonist will constantly work to complicate, thwart, or overturn the hero's investigation through various means (typically ones that involve death stakes).

❖ **Midpoint** – This is an ideal place to drop a major plot twist, but if your story does not support that structure, a simple turn point for the main character is sufficient. Remember, the difference between a plot twist and a plot turn is that a plot twist is designed to shock the audience making them look at the story differently while a plot turn is a reveal meant for the character, who will learn something new and take the story in a different direction. Regardless of which approach you chose, this beat should change the scope of the investigation either by revealing a dark secret or providing major insight toward the main story question and contribute to the eventual solution. The circumstances surrounding this moment cause the main character to double down on their investigation. Examples include information that invalidates an earlier theory, a secret that casts the victim in a new light, the key witness being murdered, et cetera. Then once the narrative has been infused with this hot piece of information or secret, the pace should pick up as well. Remember, thrillers are so named because they are meant to be page-turners so capitalize on anything that will add fuel to your narrative fire.

Act III

❖ **Renewal of Investigation** – Upon hearing or experiencing the reveal brought on by the midpoint, the characters are forced to change tact and begin a rapid succession of investigative efforts to make up for time lost on their old theories. As with the earlier try-fail detection cycle, things won't immediately fall into place and the antagonist will be working to provide setbacks, but the escalation of the investigation moves more efficiently this round with a clear building toward a major conflict that will act as the climax.

❖ **Loss of Faith** – Because of their renewed push toward a solution, most stories have a beat where the character begins to doubt that they can overcome the odds or they lose faith in the talents or values (or people) that have aided up to this point in the investigation. This could result in them ostracizing themselves thereby exacerbating the danger they already face, or it may mean losing sight of their goal and thus finding themselves or their loved ones at the mercy of a trap set by the villain.

❖ **Partner Becomes a Problem** – Examples include a double cross from the hero's partner or the innocent sidekick falls into danger. Your story may not support those exact concepts, but the purpose of this beat is to provide some type of high-stakes emergency that snaps the hero out of his doldrums and reinvigorates his motivations to take action.

❖ **Third Clash with Antagonist / Moment of Loss** – If you're writing a hard-core thriller, this is where the protagonist's love interest or side kick dies, leaving the hero open and vulnerable to attack. If those aren't options for story structure, just note that this is where the hero endures the worst possible thing that could happen. All is lost externally and internally. Meaning whatever you choose to happen here should not only change the outer aspects of the hero's world, but it should also affect the hero emotionally and alter how he perceives the world moving forward.

❖ **Epiphany or Final Plot Turn** – This is the next big plot twist or story turn that propels your character into the final act. Again, whether twist or a turn, this is a moment of discovery that definitively puts the protagonist on the killer's trail or in the villain's crosshairs (whether they know it or not). Common devices used during this moment include discovering the culprit captured is innocent and the killer is still on the loose. The element must cause the character to regain their focus, establish their resolve, and alter their investigation one final time now that they believe they have all the proper information to thwart the opposition.

Act IV

❖ **Executing a Plan** – The protagonist devises a strategy or makes a decision to deal with the antagonistic forces based on what they now believe is the truth of the matter. In most stories, this involves the main character charging into danger and is often manifested in cinema with the hero going alone to an abandoned warehouse to rescue the victim, whereupon all hell breaks loose. But of course, this beat can take many forms. The key is to remember that no matter what strategy the hero decides to take, whether brilliant or boneheaded, the upshot will not be what he or she expects.

❖ **Love interest or partner becomes suspect** – This is an optional beat that depends on the type of story being written. This betrayal whether major or minor could act as a final plot twist, plot turn, or red herring and be a major part of the plan going wrong that directly pushes the hero into the villain's trap. This usually involves the hero discovering a secret about that person or realizing their partner's motivations for being involved in the case aren't honorable, providing one last bit of doubt that puts yet another wrench in the hero's plans.

❖ **Facing Danger** – This is where our hero either stumbles into a dangerous situation because his plan has gone awry, or he has been coerced into a dangerous one by the betrayal of someone from his inner circle. Either way, he is unknowingly thrust into a high-stakes (i.e. dangerous) situation that he is not 100 percent prepared to face. Once in this situation, this is usually where the protagonist realizes where they have gone wrong and all the random pieces of information gathered throughout the story combine in his brain to reveal the whole truth.

❖ **Impending Doom** – A moment where it truly feels, both to the reader and the hero himself, that he might lose the battle and/or die. This is typically counterbalanced by the character remembering something from the earlier part of the story that didn't make sense then but is now viewed as the clear solution to the trouble at hand — or an unexpected (but well foreshadowed) character comes in to save them. Just be mindful that this moment of impending doom doesn't need to be its own beat occurring in the order listed here, it can also occur as a component of the final battle within the showdown. The key with this beat (and the two that follow) is to exercise creativity. You don't want the final confrontation to unfold too quickly since this is where the reader experiences their catharsis, or the emotional release of all the tension and suspense that's been building up during the story.

❖ **Showdown** – This where the villain is confronted, the evil plan revealed in full, and the two opposing forces battle for dominance. Battles can include chases, explosions, or even the hero temporarily siding with the villain to gain dominance. This beat coincides with the climax so go wild.

❖ **Grand Finale** – Depending on the type of story, this could be the hero stopping the bad guy in time for the cops to make an arrest or the bad guy falling on his own sword rather than being captured. Whatever you choose to do, this should be a grand set piece that speaks to a splashy finish where your hero gets to exercise all they've learned in their quest to catch the villain.

❖ **Resolution** – This is the final moment of reflection before your story closes where any loose ends are tied together. Even though I used the word "moment," be advised that this can span several scenes if you so require. The purpose is to provide a sense of closure to the audience — or as I like to think of it, a palette cleanser that transitions them back into the ordinary world of the story or what the hero may consider his new normal. I say "new normal" because the protagonist should have changed both physically and emotionally over the course of the story and the effects of the villain's presence should have had dire consequences on everyone involved. Therefore, it is important that you take time to reflect this over the course of a chapter or several beats.

❖ **Bum, Bum, Bum** – This is another optional beat that some books (and a lot of horror films) use to give the audience one last thrill. It is one final little surprise that appears in the resolution or the epilogue (if you go that route) in which something that the main character thought to be true is slightly off. A common one is the last-minute discovery that the bad guy wasn't working alone and the cops let that person walk away, so a threat is still out there. The point of this may be to set up another book in your series, or it could just be a way to give your audience one last thrill. As with all of these, experiment and play until you find what works for your tale.

Building Suspense

"Suspense is all about making promises. It's about telling a reader, 'I know something you don't know. And I promise, if you turn the page, I'm going to tell you.'"
~Dan Brown, author of *The Da Vinci Code* (2003)

Picture it. A frantic mother has entered the forest to confront the person who she believes has murdered her son. She knows this is a dangerous prospect as the culprit could be hiding among the trees and spring out at any moment, but she believes this is the only way to bring closure to her despair — capture the threat or die trying. As the author, you'd probably describe her flashlight roaming across the silent depths of the endless foliage. The hiss of her breathing causing her to jump in anticipation of danger. A low-lying fog obscuring her path as heat from the earth mixes with the cool night air and pools around her ankles in gnarly waves. This character stumbles through the dark at the mercy of a fading flashlight and the acuity of her senses, which puts her on the edge of knowing (light) and not knowing (darkness), limiting her point of view and ensuring that anything that slinks out of the shadows will have an immense impact on the events to come.

Meanwhile, the reader focuses wherever you direct the imagery because they are entirely dependent on what you choose to show or withhold. By limiting the character's knowledge and ability to fully perceive the gravity of her situation as well as heightening the minutest details of the sensory input to create an ominous atmosphere, you're building suspense. We immediately attribute much more power to the unseen elements hidden in the dark. You're teasing and tantalizing readers into wanting to know what's hidden and what's next.

We can heighten this suspense and prolong the dramatic tension of the situation by delaying the inevitable and focusing on sensory detail. How does the night air feel on the heroine's skin? What sound does the grass make under her feet? Is there the smell of blood in the air? Slow time by making the characters hyperaware of sights, sensations, and sounds. Turn the mundane into the menacing. Allow the reader access to the character's thoughts and fears. Flood the scene with emotion so the audience can feel the apprehension.

But this is where the technique gets tricky and your story must work overtime to earn its rave reviews on Amazon. Whether the scene is dark and portentous (like the one above) where a character faces the unknown or a nail-biting situation where the audience knows more than the characters (and therefore fears for their safety), we must eventually follow through on releasing the tension of the scenario by exposing the threat. However, that revelation must be done in such a way that subverts the audience's expectations.

Let's go back to our scary forest example. As our heroine moves farther down the wooded path, she may initially encounter something innocuous — the jump scare of a deer bounding through the brush — but each emergence from the darkness must escalate until her problems become life-threatening. Remember, the deal you've made with the audience is that the killer is in the forest and that there will be showdown. So why not have the things that go bump in the night amplify how much our character doesn't know and how unmatched she is for what's to come? For example, to compound the mother's dilemma (and hence, the suspense) perhaps she steps into a steel trap. Her screams now give away her position, and she is beset with the dilemma to cut herself loose before the killer comes or face him while severely injured.

And voila, you've given the audience something unexpected, piqued their curiosity and anticipation about what's next *how can the writer possibly top that?!?!*, made things worse for the character, and heightened suspense.

You can continue to bait the audience in this way as long as the breadcrumbs you give them are grounded in a believable story. So perhaps things get even worse and someone approaches before she's able to make a decision...and that person is *her son*. The same son she thought she lost — who if you plot it right, could be working with the killer or who could be the killer or who could somehow be there to save her. The possibilities are endless, just be sure give the reader something unexpected but believable while raising the stakes.

Of course, you don't want to linger in these suspenseful reveals more than three or four rounds so as not to wear out your audience's goodwill or pull focus from the promise made at the top of the scene (i.e. protagonist's encounter with the killer). But as we will talk about in the section on pacing, suspense is like a striptease where the end result is revealed in small bits designed to captivate.

In literature, suspense is the feeling of unease a reader experiences when they don't know what's coming next. Therefore, a writer creates suspense through the slow release of information, which raises questions and makes readers eager to reach the conclusion. This can be a situation where the reader has the same amount or less information than the protagonist. On the flip side, writers can also build suspense through dramatic irony, which is when the reader knows more than the hero.

Dramatic irony creates a gap between what the audience knows and what a character believes or expects. This creates tension within the text because the reader knows disaster or problems will strike, but they don't know when. That uncertainty causes anxiety which leads to suspense. Now, take the typical comedy. There will probably be some misunderstanding where a character overhears half a conversation and assumes the worst. We as the audience know the truth of the matter and begin to cringe because we realize their faulty assumption will land them in some calamity, embarrassing situation, or troubling scenario. Of course, the cringy tension that builds here isn't the same as the suspense tale because the circumstances surrounding the confusion are humorous. Watch any episode of *Three's Company* or *Raven's Home* to see this comedic form of dramatic irony in action.

But regardless of genre, the tension and suspense are what ultimately drives the plot and keeps the story moving forward. The audience waits on the edge of their seats until the dramatic irony — or rather, the gap in knowledge between what they know and what the character will soon discover — has dissipated. More often than not, especially in suspense stories, the anticipated result by both the reader and the character (whether those ideas are the same or different) are subverted by some reveal or surprise in the narrative designed to both shock the audience and further extend the suspense for all involved.

Consider *Die Hard* (1988) when John McClane meets Hans Gruber near the roof of the Nakatomi building and gives Gruber a gun without knowing he's the bad guy. We squeal and yell at the screen because we think our hero has just written his own death sentence. Even if the scenario doesn't transpire exactly how we anticipate (turns out, McClane gives Gruber an unloaded gun), the technique is used to develop a sympathetic connection between the audience and the protagonist — *will he or won't he get out of the impending predicament* — while reinforcing the readers' desire to see what happens next.

Another useful way to add suspense is to give each character a secret, which can be used to make your characters behave in mysterious ways that cause conflict and tension. These can be secrets that develop and unfold over the course of the story or they can emerge as things the audience knows but the hero does not. Referring back to our scene from *Die Hard*, Hans Gruber's secret is that he is able to do an American accent, which is the element that tricks John into giving him the gun.

Grow Tip: The fiction world is full of possibilities, so work to avoid clichés. If you go with the first solution that pops into mind, then you're probably going to write an outcome the reader has already considered. Endeavor to zag rather than zig. Do the opposite of what's expected. Dig into the backstory and create a credible scenario that aligns with the facts but subverts expectations. This may mean making lists to weed out weak ideas. If you choose this route, push yourself to brainstorm at least twenty different scenarios because it is that last one that's most likely the fresh take that will make your story unique.

Suspense Tips

"Suspense is more enjoyable than terror, actually, because it is a continuing experience and attains a peak crescendo fashion; while terror, to be truly effective, must come all at once, like a bolt of lightning, and is more difficult, therefore, to savor."
~Alfred Hitchcock, filmmaker and Master of Suspense

As Hitchcock implies, successful suspense is an ongoing experience that ebbs and flows. And while every novel has an overarching narrative question that speaks to the main suspense elements, that question should also implicate dozens of smaller suspense possibilities to help sustain reader interest along the way. In this chapter, we are going to focus on how to create some of those smaller suspense moments.

Play with point of view. Consider using multiple viewpoints to add dimension to your suspense story. For example, you can use third-person omniscient if there are certain moments in the narrative when you want your readers to see what's coming before the protagonist, thus building suspense through dramatic irony as discussed earlier. On the other hand, if you prefer the reader only discover things when the hero does, use first-person or third-person limited. Moreover, if your story uses the viewpoints of several characters, you can control the flow of information to the audience by shifting from one point of view to another. This has the potential to limit the quantity and type of information provided to the audience, essentially enabling you to misdirect their attention while still playing fair.

Foreshadow future events. Suspense stories can both justify plot twists and create anticipation through foreshadowing. We'll talk about this more in subsequent chapters. But basically, hinting at future events creates anticipation in the reader who grows eager to see how that implication will develop into a problem or solution for the protagonist. The pitfall is including clues that are too obvious, so make sure that you're practicing subtly and hinting at several possible outcomes that could misdirect their attention. That way, there is room to eventually subvert the reader's expectations with something unexpected.

Raise the stakes. If you've created a protagonist that readers care about, create a scenario where he loses something meaningful, like a loved one or his freedom. High stakes lead to a more satisfying ending.

Make it personal and specific. Look for ways to give validity to the threat by putting those emotions and consequences in context. For instance, if your story is about the risk of a nuclear explosion, introduce the reader to a set of sympathetic characters who will be in the line of fire when the device detonates. We see this all the time in superhero movies even though many of them botch the execution by playing those moments of laughs — e.g. the last act of *Justice League* (2017) where The Flash, amidst destruction of the planet, saves the Russian family in the pickup truck. In contrast, other films have successfully used this tool as a means of reminding the audience of the stakes while also fleshing out setting and providing additional characterization. Consider *Independence Day* (1996) where Jasmine Dubrow (Vivica A. Fox) helps injured survivors as she escapes evisceration during the alien attack on Los Angeles.

Isolate the hero. Cutting the hero off from his resources is a great way to create suspense because the audience automatically assumes the worse and worries that the hero may finally fail. When isolating the hero, think about the ways this can be done both physical and socially — whether you start by eliminating his access to tangible items like weapon, allies, and shelter or intangible items like intel or social interaction.

Play with silence and noise. Remember that scene from the film version of *Jurassic Park* (1993) when the T-Rex breaks out? Even though the initial sound of his approach is imperceptible, that tight shot of the water cup jiggling on the jeep's dashboard, puts not just the characters, but the audience on edge. You can do this with your fiction by playing with silence and noise in ways that hint at danger to come. Consider: The creak of floorboards in an otherwise silent house. Light flickers from a burnt out blub. A loud crash echoes from an empty room overhead. All of these sights and sounds lead to questions that put the reader on edge. *How'd that happen? What does it mean? What will happen next?* This is a quick and easy suspense technique that you can implement at will.

Avoid writing Mary Sue's. Perfect people are rarely fodder for suspense because their inability to fail removes the element of doubt from the equation. Remember, suspense is built on the audience feeling anxious about what's going to happen next, and its main purpose is to ingratiate the reader to the characters through the uncertainty of their situation and the characters' vulnerability. Therefore, to create suspense, your characters must fail and have flaws.

Allow the setting to add to the drama. There is a reason why *Speed* (1994) is set on a bus. You know the premise: Bus #2525 will blow up if it drops under 50 miles per hour. And what makes that scenario so awesome is that the setting immediately complicates the story problem because a bus is an impractical vehicle for maintaining high speeds! Every situation in that film, from the elevator full of hostages in the opener to the driverless subway car at the end, uses its setting to help define stakes and establish consequences for failure. You must do the same.

Change the order of things. One way to create anticipation is to start with the outcome or consequence of a dreaded event. This hooks the reader through an intriguing action or something that will have a long-lasting effect on the main characters moving forward. The reader then wonders: *Why did this happen? What started the hero on this path? Can he ever recover?* The story will then need to flashback to the events that set this disaster in motion. If done correctly, this will make the reader feel even more intensely about the character and his plight. But a word of caution: Do not do this too often or put such flashbacks too early in the story. You don't want the audience to feel like you are deliberately playing with their emotions, and you don't want to do this at a point when the reader has yet to connect with the protagonist.

Checklist: Building Suspense

❖ Have you utilized sensory and emotional descriptions?

❖ Have you slowed the pace and focused on making the mundane feel menacing? (Or if you're dealing with a situation that contains a chase or ticking clock, have you established elements to show immediacy and urgency?)

❖ Have you used foreshadowing to hint that there may be something strange about the situation?

❖ Have you teased the audience with an unexpected outcome?

❖ Have you incorporated internal and external dialogue to convey the POV character's fear?

❖ Have you delivered on the promise for the sequence?

Grow Tip: When it comes to developing suspense, word choice is paramount. Choose wisely. Avoid cliched phrases — *It was a dark and stormy night* — or obvious verbiage. Strive for words that jump from the page and move the reader from horror to delight to bewilderment and back again. Grab a thesaurus, and find strong verbs and adjectives to improve your diction.

Are Tension and Suspense the Same?

In 2022, a national cable company ran a very effective series of ads about their services for the hearing-impaired. In one commercial, a television viewer stops the action of her favorite show to ask the characters to speak up. This prompts them to hold up signs that eventually turn into closed captioning as the commercial reaches its final pitch. But while the characters create their signs, a brief argument ensues over the description of the music as "tense" or "suspenseful," prompting one character to ask: "Aren't they the same thing?"

Surprisingly, no! We tend to conflate the terms because their narrative purposes are connected and it could be argued that one is a byproduct of the other. However, when we look at their definitions, there is a clear distinction. Suspense is our minds grappling with an uncertainty while tension is the feeling we experience when those worries manifest.

Let's place the full definitions side by side and see if we can spot the differences.

Suspense is the feeling a person has when they want something to happen in one character's favor and it doesn't. Think of this as the anxiousness, apprehension, or anticipation you have about something potentially happening or the psychological uncertainty that manifests in a *will-she-or-won't-she* scenario. This can also take the form of an unresolved situation where something is at stake, but the outcome is temporarily delayed, causing worry and doubt. In addition, suspense is the miscommunication or misdirection brought about through dramatic irony when the audience knows something the character doesn't thus changing how both parties interpret what's happening on the page.

In contrast, tension is the reader's anticipation of conflict rising, or the physical realization of suspense unfolding. In essence, tension is the immediate feeling of discomfort that occurs when a dreaded or anticipated action or event comes to fruition.

Does this mean you need to drastically alter how you speak about these terms? Maybe. I will fully admit that I use them as synonyms throughout this book. However, I believe it is important that you are aware of the difference in execution because that knowledge will help you develop a more successful novel.

You will need to work much harder to build suspense because that's a matter of changing the audience's mindset and making them willing (or rather, eager) to wait through a series of slow reveals throughout the length of the plot, e.g. *Will John Constantine save the world from being overrun by demonic forces?* That's an example of suspense that spans the entire story. Of course, it is best if your novel has multiple sources of suspense to keep the audience invested — and yes, those additional challenges should still be tied to the overall narrative question: *Will John Constantine save his partner Isabel from possession? Will John Constantine find a way to earn his place in heaven?* Bottomline, consider suspense a series of conundrums or problems setup early in the story that keep readers (and/or the characters) worrying and wondering but whose answers aren't provided until much later.

Meanwhile, tension is much more immediate and can unfold in every scene because its effectiveness simply depends on the direness of your conflict and stakes. For example, a scene with two adversarial characters threatening to punch each other's lights out is tense because we know by scene's end one of them will be attacked. But if something happens too easily or without conflict, you've lost tension. If characters act implausibly or unrealistically, you've lost tension. Remember, tension helps fuel the narrative, so you want tension in every part of the story right down to the sentence level.

Checklist: Mastering the Art of Suspense

Opening Hook and Establishing the Scene

❖ Create an empathetic or relatable protagonist.

❖ Devise a credible and clever villain.

❖ Build setting(s) that can contribute to the story's main conflict and allow the audience to experience something new.

❖ Develop a high-concept premise that outlines the main story question and points to a significant conflict with high stakes and serious, lasting repercussions for the protagonist.

❖ Choose a central viewpoint that gives the reader a personal bond with the protagonist or at least in-depth insight into his/her problems and motivations (alternate viewpoints are optional, but they should be separate scenes or chapters).

❖ Use sensory descriptions to show (rather than tell) how your character reacts both internally and externally to his/her environment and challenges.

Introduce Conflict and Danger

❖ Draft a strong opening hook that immediately entices the reader with an active glimpse into an extraordinary moment in their lives.

❖ Craft the scene containing the inciting incident, which should drive the novel's overall story question.

❖ Introduce the mantle of responsibility that will force your protagonist to move forward and accept the challenge presented by the main story conflict.

❖ Raise the stakes for your main character.

❖ Add surprises, reveals, dangers, and tough moral decisions throughout each act so that the journey to success is difficult for your protagonist.

- Use slow reveals to stretch the release of information and build tension.

- Pump up the tension and suspense by isolating your hero from help or incapacitating him/her. If this is not appropriate for your genre, add a ticking clock, harrowing chases, or life-threatening obstacles.

- Add reversals, twists, epiphanies, or turns at the end of each act to help develop character and reveal secrets.

Structure and Pacing

- Start every scene near the heart of the conflict.

- End every scene with a problem or dilemma.

- Format scenes and chapters so there is an occasional cliffhanger.

- Summarize unimportant scenes or passages of time (i.e. greetings, travel, transitions, et cetera). Scenes that are essential to the plot should unfold in real time and convey the characters actions, reactions, and dialogue.

- Foreshadow plot turns, twists, and reversals. Ensure that essential plot points have been clearly justified by the narrative.

- Ensure that you've obeyed the philosophy behind "Chekhov's Gun."

- Strive for immersive fiction that develops sensory imagery for the reader.

❖ Remember to vary the pacing and tension to take the reader on a roller coaster ride. A novel constantly in high gear runs the risk of exhausting the reader and making them numb to the action.

Showdown/Climax

❖ Devise a battle or showdown between the protagonist and the antagonist.

❖ Incorporate something new — a different approach to success (or failure) against the antagonistic force than previously seen in the novel.

❖ Divulge a final twist that clarifies the conclusion. For example, in Sue Grafton's *A is for Alibi* (1982), the novel's protagonist successfully completes the case she was hired to investigate, but in the end discovers she had overlooked the motive for a hidden killer.

❖ Ensure good defeats evil — or at least gets the upper hand. Unlike traditional mysteries, suspense stories tend the muddy the lines between good and evil so that there is a gray area where sometimes stories don't end on the side of "good" as much as they land on the "acceptable" side of two evils. Even if the story doesn't end happily, it should resolve in a manner that suggests the conflict has been given sufficient closure.

❖ Show the hero's growth, i.e. a discovery about himself or the world at large.

Thriller Tropes

Below you will find a list of literary and thematic conventions that are common to the thriller or suspense genres. Some of them are quite worn to the point of overexposure. So if you decide to include any of these elements, make sure you are subverting expectations and adding your own twist so that your narrative stays ahead of the savvy reader.

- The badass but debonair male lead (think James Bond)
- The young, idealistic rookie (think Clarice Starling)
- Stories about identity swaps or amnesia
- Evil twin versus good twin
- Trapped or close proximity stories
- Everyone's a suspect
- The innocent suspect is not what they seem

How to Write Contained Suspense

Contained suspense refers to a narrative whose primary action takes place in a single setting. These stories emphasize the confinement or physical limitations of its characters — usually one or two but no more than five or six — and their spatial limitations are meant to build anxiety in the audience by preying on one's fear of being trapped without the hope of help. The plots are often a variation of the protagonist attempting to escape or overcome the antagonist's scheme, riddle, murderous device, or supernatural element without the proper resources or information. And interestingly, the setting for most contained thrillers act as both the defining element for the conflict and the main narrative hook. Some recent cinematic examples include *Panic Room* (2002), *Phone Booth* (2003), *Buried* (2010), and *The Guilty* (2021) — a remake of the 2018 Danish film of the same name. As you will note from the list above, horror and thrillers are the most notable genres for this technique since the former focuses on building dread and the latter centers on the creation of tension. Contained suspense, however, takes those ideas to the extreme.

For that reason, structure is essential. Unlike stories with a larger narrative landscape, contained narratives rarely stop to develop subplots, moral dilemmas, or character self-discovery. Instead, they use a tighter story structure to force the tension to simmer at a much higher level throughout. Use the following elements in combination to create contained suspense, for none of these elements will succeed on their own.

Conflict: How do you keep conflict and tension high while in one confined location? Make confinement one of the key issues or themes of the story. For example, in *Buried*, the protagonist awakens in a coffin with only a Zippo lighter, a pen, and a cellphone that has a weak signal and dwindling power. This immediately piques our interests as we wonder how he will use them to escape. Later, we learn that he is an American civilian who has been captured in Iraq, which further compounds the problem and complicates the story question. *Will he escape alive?* So if you choose to incorporate this technique, make sure that conflict remains at the forefront throughout.

Foreshadowing: You must provide your protagonist resources that aren't immediately obvious to the audience. So ask yourself, what can I plant in the environment that will benefit (or hurt) my hero's current situation? This may mean using traditional objects in nontraditional ways or hiding a big clue to the conclusion in plain sight. In *Buried*, many of the protagonist's resources stem from his backstory and the people he can call for rescue, but he is later informed by his captors that at the foot of the coffin that he occupies are additional supplies: a flashlight, a glow stick, a flask with alcohol, and a pocket knife. Be creative with your environment to keep the audience invested since physical movement and changes of scenery will be limited.

Tension: The idea of escalating tension, stakes, and conflict will be a repeated throughout this text, but it is doubly important for this type of suspense story. To do this, start by creating a narrative question or problem, provide clues or situations that build to a climactic moment, then devise an answer or temporary solution that releases tension — during which another problem arises to reignite the tension and drive toward another climax. These mini conflicts should become increasingly difficult or dangerous so that the story stakes (i.e. consequences for failure) are rising throughout. This is known as "escalating complications" and will keep the audience engaged and turning pages to find out what will happen next. You don't want the story to get stale or the problems to stall. Make sure that things keep changing despite the setting's limitations.

In each act, ask the following questions as a way to build upon the action that came before so that the conflicts and their consequences are increasing in severity as the story progresses:

❖ Does the meaning and purpose of the story's setting change as the dangers increase?

❖ What aspect of the setting can be used as a weapon or defense mechanism?

❖ What about the setting is becoming increasingly dangerous?

❖ Is the setting isolated (or can it become isolated) so that outside help is unlikely?

❖ Are there dangers afoot besides those from the antagonist (like loss of electricity, animal attack, bad weather, et cetera)?

- ❖ What tactics will the protagonist use to overcome her current obstacle? What special skills does she have that will help with (or complicate) this particular problem?

- ❖ What's at stake if she fails to overcome her current obstacle? What will she sacrifice?

- ❖ How will this sacrifice alter the conflict and thrust her into a new challenge?

In *Panic Room*, the complications build from the initial home invasion to the robbers pumping propane into the panic room to flush out the protagonist and her daughter to the protagonist being forced leave the panic room to retrieve her daughter's diabetes medication. But regardless of what obstacles you choose, the point is that we must always find new ways to change the lead character's circumstances and thus their thinking about the situation, which forces the hero to adapt new and increasingly risky strategies for reaching their goal. Each new challenge should be something she must endure — something from which she cannot back down. In other words, if she refuses the challenge, the alternative must be a fate worse than death — and so, she's pushed forward to confront the new challenge whether she's ready to act or not.

Plot Turns: Plot turns or plot reveals are when the protagonist receives important information that drastically changes his situation. This is different than a plot twist in that this information is new to the character and effects their decision-making but may not necessarily be new to the audience. This narrative element is no different than that of a mystery or any other story hinged on suspense. However, it is super important in a contained thriller because new information can create new problems and escalate conflict without the author having to introduce new characters or pull the existing characters from their environment. Use plot turns at the end of each act to thrust the characters into a new cycle of tension.

Transparency: While deceptively simple, this last point is key to making the whole process work: Always be clear with the audience about your story's main conflict and the problem(s) your characters encounter. This is essential for creating tension. Otherwise, your reader won't know what to be on edge about or why certain story events are important or devastating to the characters or what the fallout means for your protagonist when she fails or succeeds. Basically, the key to keeping your audience hooked is clarity.

Checklist: Contained Suspense

❖ Brainstorm a unique location for confinement that can, as the story develops, become increasingly dangerous.

❖ Develop a strong main character whose internal conflict is just as strong, if not stronger, than the external dilemma that he's currently facing.

❖ Build problems into the environment so that the audience doesn't become bored with the locale and the narrative has numerous emotional highs.

❖ Raise the stakes and increase the difficulty of the obstacles.

❖ Foreshadow the ending with clues.

❖ Subvert the anticipated ending to give the audience a final twist.

Opening Hook

In *The Basic Formulas of Fiction* by William Foster Harris, he defines the hook as "...the first brief, potent statement of what is the matter with the central character, what his problem is, what difficulty he is facing." Every successful suspense story contains a powerful hook —something memorable that catches the audience's attention and demonstrates that the story will be worth their time. An effective hook not only arouses curiosity but doubles it as things unfold. In short, the primary objective of the first scene is to set up dilemmas, questions, or scenarios that immerse the reader in the protagonist's problems and make them curious about what will happen next.

Thrillers and other suspense-filled stories traditionally open with an action sequence or dramatic scene that speaks to the overarching story question the narrative will answer. This event is usually something that's out of the ordinary for your main character or a groundbreaking occurrence outside your main character's orbit that will act as an inciting incident or call to action once her ordinary world is introduced. When crafting these opening scenes, make sure to provide enough information that the audience has a basic understanding about what has occurred. You can mislead them about people's motives or even the importance of the situation, but don't confuse them on the general elements such as the *who* is the main person, *what* is happening in the moment, and *where* or *when* things are happening. You don't want to alienate your audience on the first page. Readers expect to be introduced to the main character and form a bond with him or her, so start in the point of view of that character or introduce them as soon as you can. Meanwhile, the scene's *why* can be a bit more allusive since it is often attached to the main story question, which will develop and deepen as the story progresses.

That said, work to get the audience emotionally involved from the start. That first scene should be designed to hook the reader by introducing the key elements of the story in a dynamic manner. Strong openings grab readers' attention by starting "in medias res," which is Latin for "in the middle of things." The key is to introduce an early problem or conflict. Your hero wants something and has now encountered several obstacles to that goal. Their response to this dilemma should be active. Don't open with your hero alone, quietly pondering the meaning of life. That lacks the movement needed for an enticing opener. Toss the audience into the action and generate curiosity by introducing intriguing characters, an unusual situation, compelling dialogue, high stakes reactions, or an important question. That way, the reader can experience the characters' personalities and understand how they view their world.

Advice books often suggest opening a story with the ordinary world or by showing the status quo, which to some writers may imply that they must depict a character's static or boring existence. However, with fiction, we don't need to equate "ordinary" with "tedious" or "dull." Depending on the character and the circumstances, a character's typical day can still be filled with excitement, wonder, or even action. For example, take the introduction of Jack Traven (Keanu Reeves) in *Speed (1994)*. The film briefly opens on the bad guy who sets off a small explosive that puts an elevator full of innocent bystanders in jeopardy.

Then we quickly cut to Jack and his partner as they drive onto the scene to handle the hostage negotiation. Even though this is a tense moment that is made even more suspenseful once their boss points out they have only 23-minutes to find a solution (ticking clock!), we can still consider this part of Jack's ordinary world because he's a police officer. The opening event also sets the scene for the type of work he does — i.e. he's a member of SWAT's bomb division — and that he's an innovative thinker, an adrenaline junkie, and a loose cannon when it comes to following standard police procedure.

Admittedly, the upshot of the opening sequence becomes the bad guy's motivation for revenge and sets in motion the series of disasters that constitute the bulk of the film; however, this peek into Jack's "ordinary world" tells us almost everything we know about him, his partner, and even foreshadows how he gets out of his first scuffle with the bad guy. That's the magic of a powerful opener.

So when we say that a story should start with a character's ordinary world or reflect the status quo, what we mean is that the story should start in the middle of that person having an extraordinary day — whether that be stellar or stinky one — and it must be a day that puts them on the cusp of an even bigger problem.

But with that said, be careful about putting your main character in a situation that is overly precarious. Starting the first paragraph or prologue in the middle of a moment when the hero is already battling through a life-or-death, climax-level situation may not only be jarring for the reader, but puts you in a tough spot as an author. After all, how will you top it? Remember, a story must have escalating conflict *and* stakes. But more importantly, opening in the middle of a highly harrowing moment doesn't give the audience an opportunity to learn about the hero. If we don't know anything about him, it is hard for us to care whether he lives or dies. So strive to strike a balance between introducing the status quo in a compelling manner and setting the stage for the inciting incident that changes everything.

Invent a situation that throws your protagonist off guard and upsets his world — even if he doesn't immediately understand how or why. Use a close viewpoint to show us his anger, confusion, or determination. Force him to make horrific decisions or tap into talents/courage that was otherwise dormant or faulty as he confronts the threat and scrambles for solutions. All of this creates worry and uncertainty in the reader who wonders if the hero is actually capable of overcoming the challenge. And of course, that feeling you've just created in the audience is suspense.

The other feeling you'll want to start building in the opener is empathy. This is the ability to understand or be sensitive to the experiences and feelings of another person. That's why it is so important that your hook include the protagonist or one of the other primary characters. You want the audience emotionally connected to the story via the problems that arise from the internal and external conflicts of those people. You want the reader to *share* some of the hardships your characters face. This goes beyond sympathy, which is more about a person having their own reaction to someone else's hardship. Creating one or two empathetic characters or situations links the reader to the story and gives them something or someone to care about —or should I say, worry about — which leads to a vested interest or what we might call a page turner.

However, notice I said "empathetic," not "likeable." In many ways, likeability is relative, but if you give your key characters at least one redeeming quality or one moment when they finally do the right thing for the right reason or if you put them in a dilemma where they are making the best choices they can under the circumstances, then the audience will start to identify with them. This level of relatability is far more powerful than a mere "like" and can help evolve the suspense in your story.

Your hook should also challenge the reader to keep their eyes open for additional information and encourage them to read further. Strong opening hooks may also have some symmetry with the novel's final image, whether a direct reflection or a polar opposite. *Memento (2001)* is a fantastic example of the former, giving the film the feel of a continuous loop just like protagonist's memories.

There are a number of approaches one can use to create a successful opening scene, but consider these elements before getting started:

❖ Who is the POV character for the scene?

- What's the current setting, and how does it influence the action? How can I use this setting to develop one or more characters?

- What event unfolds, and what's the disturbance in the ordinary world that hints at the inciting incident or problem to come?

- How will what happens here affect the protagonist? (Although preferred, the protagonist doesn't always need to occupy the first scene. Some writers start from the viewpoint of the villain or another character, but you still must be aware of how this will eventually shape your hero.)

- How can I use the first line to set the scene and indicate the genre?

- What phrasing, literary techniques, or imagery can I use to emotionally target the audience in the initial paragraph?

- What will the completed opener imply or promise about the plot moving forward?

Once you've decided how to shape your scene, use one or more of these techniques to pique the audience's curiosity and introduce the story's theme or narrative question.

- Start in medias res with a dilemma, challenge, or conflict.

- Introduce flawed, morally ambiguous, or opinionated characters to drive the action.

❖ Use dialogue to introduce a character and quickly establish the setting. Conversation thrusts the reader into the scene's conflict without delay. This technique is a creative way to start while putting the audience's interests first.

❖ Write tight. Wordiness dilutes the impact of your scene. To heighten the power of your opening and develop the feeling of brisk pace, keep sentences short. Limit description and background to just a few words or reveal it through dialogue and action, which are the two narrative forms that best capture reader interest. In contrast, if your goal is to create the mood or feeling of foreboding, danger, and intrigue, longer more descriptive sentences may prove effective. But in either case, omit needless words. Avoid excessive backstory. Describe only the necessary elements.

❖ Add questions as an additional way to get things started—but keep in mind, they must be supported by the text that follows and they shouldn't merely be there for shock value or window dressing. For example, *Something in the Water* by Catherine Steadman opens with the question: "Have you ever wondered how long it takes to dig a grave?" The story's protagonist, Erin, continues on to explain the troubles she had while digging one and in the process hints at a troubled relationship that may or may not be the reason for her digging. Of course, the question raised doesn't need to be literal. It could be a statement that raises a "what if" question as with *Peter and Wendy* by J.M. Barrie: "All children, except one, grow up." Within a single opening line, we have the story's theme and premise — *What if there was a boy who never grew up?* By hooking us with an unusual query, an intriguing picture is painted and the audience's curiosity is raised.

❖ Be clear about the tone. By definition, this is the attitude the work takes toward the material. In fiction, this often reflects the protagonist's feelings about the story situation and leads to mood, which is the emotion a scene evokes in the reader. So you want to set the tone as soon as possible to help the audience understand what type of story is on the horizon. A humorous opening should signal a light-hearted or romantic story while a brooding or bloody one implies a tale that's horrific. A large part of writing commercial fiction is about meeting audience expectations, and your hook is where those promises are being made, so be sure to follow through.

❖ Develop a contrast or contradiction by delivering the unexpected or having an event take the viewpoint character by surprise. For instance, in *Turn Coat* (2009) by Jim Butcher, the protagonist receives an unexpected visit from his nemesis:

The summer sun was busy broiling the asphalt from Chicago's streets, the agony in my head had kept me horizontal for half a day, and some idiot was pounding on my apartment door.

I answered it and Morgan, half his face covered in blood, gasped, "The Wardens are coming. Hide me. Please."

This is an unpredictable contrast because Harry Dresden and Donald Morgan are mortal enemies at this point in the Dresden Files series. The fact that Morgan would go to Dresden for help is a bit of a contradiction for the audience because we know he thinks that Dresden is one of the bad guys. But with nowhere else to turn, Morgan has to trust someone, and Dresden is the only one who won't turn him over to his superiors, who are in hot pursuit.

In general, avoid cliched openers that focus on things like the weather. *It was a dark and stormy night...* If you must use the setting as the opener, tie it into the action and attitude of the narration to help set mood and tone. In other words, let the character experience the weather. Show us the conditions by describing the hero's reactions and emotions. Also, ask yourself: How is the environment connected to your plot? Is it a sign of things to come or mere background? Do readers sense what the character is feeling both physically (through their senses) and emotionally (through mood, tone, and anticipation of what lies ahead)? Use every color on your palette to create a rich scene.

For example, rather than say, "It was a long, hot, crazy summer," follow the approach of author Liz Jensen's *The Rapture* (2009):

> That summer, the summer all the rules began to change, June seemed to last for a thousand years. The temperature was merciless: ninety-eight, ninety-nine, then a hundred in the shade. It was heat to die, go nuts, or spawn in. Old folks collapsed, dogs were cooked alive in cars, lovers couldn't keep their hands off each other. The sky pressed down like a furnace lid, shrinking the subsoil, cracking the concrete, killing shrubs from the roots up.

Jensen's opener, not only paints a picture, but tells us volumes about the potential trouble the main character will face — *all the rules began to change.* The ordinary world has been turned upside down and conflict brews on the horizon. While we aren't given the "I" voice of the protagonist until the second paragraph, this use of weather is filtered through how it affects people. This is not merely description for description's sake. This is designed to make us wonder: *Why is this happening? How dire will things become? What role will our protagonist play in all of this?*

You will notice that all of the top techniques used to hook the reader have one thing in common: They force the audience to ask questions. A strong hook — whether it uses action, emotion, or dialogue — should have your reader guessing about your characters' motivations, backstories, and more. This is key because the more questions raised means the more that the storyline, and hence the reader's interest, can be deepened and drawn out. That's the job of an effective opener — to keep the audience invested. The reader hopes to find the answer in the next line only to find something else that piques their interest. They acquire just enough knowledge to realize that there is an even bigger picture. In essence, that first line or opening paragraph that we call the hook raises the who, what, where, when, why, and how questions that help lay the foundation for the story and the conflicts to come. The goal is to draw the audience forward and keep them turning pages.

Suspenseful Opening Hooks

You might open with the villain on the prowl committing dastardly deeds. This is an excellent way to set up an immediate story question while inducing audience worry. The pitfall to this approach occurs when the hero is introduced and he slowly and painfully discovers the same clues the audience has been privy to for several pages. Tread carefully if choosing to start with the villain because you don't want the audience to grow frustrated while the protagonist finds his bearings.

Alternatively, the opening that should be absolutely avoided is the dream sequence. The moment the audience realizes something isn't real they either analyze its purpose or question its existence. Either way, their head and hearts are removed from your story. The key to a strong opener is to immerse the audience into the present conflict and stakes of the story. To begin by presenting something false, puts them at a distance...a pitfall that your story may never recover from.

Basically, writing an opening scene is like making cookies from scratch. The conflict, action, and dialogue are your base ingredients — the flour, baking powder, and sugar, if you will. It isn't until after you mix those three things together that you add in the setting, like folding in the eggs and butter, which work to hold things together. Once your main mix is complete, you lightly sprinkle in the chocolate chips, or backstory, as needed.

Analogies aside, the point is that you want to focus on the main ingredients in the early stages. Don't overwhelm the audience with background information when it isn't needed. Lay the foundation first. Give them the stuff that the story can't live without before burdening them with exposition.

Now, pull out your work in progress. Read the opening. Does it start with something disastrous happening in real time to a major character? Does it hint at problems to come? If so, you've created a great opening. If not, consider the following:

❖ Start the story at the moment when trouble is brewing on the horizon. In other words, a couple beats before the person or element that disturbs the ordinary world is introduced.

❖ Foreshadow the story conflict by hinting at trouble on the horizon. Set up the ordinary world so that there are cracks in the façade. Maybe your hero isn't happy with his life or perhaps things aren't as perfect as they seem or that task isn't as simple as described.

❖ Open with action. Avoid info dumps or an abundance of backstory. While you want to acclimate the audience to the scene, this doesn't need to be done immediately. Focus instead on getting them hooked on what is happening and why.

❖ Focus on the main characters. If you've started with minor characters, place that scene later in the story and begin with the protagonist. Make it clear to the audience who to root for and what he hopes to accomplish.

❖ Avoid flashbacks in the opener. We don't have enough information about the characters for the audience to find value in depicting some aspect of their history. Build interest in the characters first by creating real-time scenes with immediacy. If flashbacks are needed in your manuscript, save them for a turning point in the plot such as at the end of an act.

Inciting Incident

Sometimes a story falls flat because the inciting incident isn't compelling enough. Remember, the inciting incident is different from the opening hook, which refers to the first few paragraphs. The inciting is the unexpected story event that occurs within the first few chapters and upsets the normal world, thrusting the protagonist into a series of complications attached to the narrative's main story question. If we return to the *Speed* example from earlier, the inciting incident is when Jack receives a call from the bad guy telling him to find Bus #2525, which has a bomb on board. As you can see from this brief description, the inciting incident should have the power to drive the story forward immediately. If you find yourself overexplaining things in the first quarter or doing flashbacks, you probably have a weak inciting incident or may have started the story in the wrong place. Here are some questions help find the inciting incident:

❖ What is the actual event that kicks of the action of your story?

❖ Does this event force your characters into a choice or cause them to leave something behind?

❖ Does this event come with mixed emotions, fear, uncertainty, or excitement?

❖ Is the main character actively involved?

❖ Can your protagonist go back to life as it was before the incident? IF SO, the event is not strong enough!

Exercise: Opening Hooks

Collect four of your favorite books that fall within the genre you plan to write. For the sake of staying abreast of industry standards, make sure none of the books are more than four years old. Read the opening of each book. Which openings grab your attention and inspire further reading? What techniques does each author use to hook and maintain your interest? Which openings are the most memorable and beg for a second look? Apply the same critical eye to your own work. Based on what you've learned from the experts, what can you do to improve?

Checklist: Opening Hooks

For your opener, avoid rambling descriptions, information dumps, cliched lines about the weather, or shocking statements that don't align with the main story question. Create an opening built on action and dialogue that develops into the backbone of your text.

❖ Does your opener introduce the main character?

❖ Does your opener lead the reader to feel for the main character or find them relatable?

❖ Does your opener start in medias res?

❖ Does your opener have a clear mood and tone that speaks to genre?

❖ Does your opener spark interest about the story's 5Ws without resorting to cliches?

❖ Does your opener begin with a threat, contradiction, dilemma, conflict, predicament, and/or change in attitude or environment?

❖ Does your opener avoid information dumps?

❖ Do the events of your opener lay the groundwork for the larger story question and build reader interest that will be further sustained throughout the text?

Prologues

A prologue is the section of a literary work prior to the first chapter meant to provide context to the main story even though the purpose or importance of the information may not prove immediately obvious. This is not to be confused with the preface, which may also be found at the start of a novel but is a nonfiction statement written by the author to introduce the subject or to define the book's purpose.

A successful prologue consists of a scene that takes place *before* the novel's main action and establishes a problem or ghost from the character's past that he will need to unravel as the story's conflict unfolds. **Not every fiction text needs a prologue.** But if this is something you're considering, remember the best prologues stick to the purest definition of the word.

According to the *Etymology Dictionary* online, the term derives directly from the Latin *prologus*. "Pro" means "before" and "logus" means "discourse or speech." The site further defines the full dramatic term as "a preliminary act or event." Similarly, *Merriam-Webster* online notes the word also derives from the term "prologos," used in ancient Greek drama, wherein a speaker would "set the scene" with "a speech beforehand." Unfortunately, modern writers have failed to unearth the original purpose of this literary device.

Some writers rip a high-octane scene from the middle of the book and stick it up front to give the illusion of starting with a bang. Authors who do this often claim it is a fast way to hook the reader, introduce the story in a dramatic fashion, foreshadow the main story question, and offer the audience temporary insight into the villain's or victim's mindset. They also believe the stakes are foreshadowed in such a way that the reader begins to draw a conclusion about how the situation could have gotten so severe and thus becomes more invested when the story reverts to the quiet confines of the ordinary.

The problem is that this is a hallow way to build suspense because you're giving away critical plot points too early. Suspense by definition is the anxiousness, apprehension, or anticipation the audience has about something potentially happening. If you put the reader in a situation where they think they have everything figured out, there's no suspense. You'll need to work ten times harder to rebuild that feeling or implement a twist that truly surprises.

But the bigger question is this: How much does a middle pull really move the start of your story forward, especially if the next move is to jump backward to square one? No matter how you choose to justify it, this approach does nothing to flesh out the larger thematic world of your story, which is what the start of your book needs most. In fact, if you have to pull something from the middle to jumpstart the beginning, that's a clear sign that you haven't paced your novel correctly or may need to start closer to the inciting incident.

Furthermore, opening with a middle scene or glimpse into the future is a confusing prologue because the audience is working so hard to understand the potential behind the stakes, the risks, the character motivations, who they should root for, and the setting that they're probably not as invested in the scene as the writer believes. The reality is that the audience cannot make an emotional connection to the story or the characters if they are confused about what is happening or whose agenda holds the highest importance. Remember, our goal is to immerse the reader in the story, not pull them out of it.

Not to mention, the people who evaluate prologues — i.e. agents, publishers, and Amazon reviewers — often find that the disconnect between the "makeshift prologue middle" and the first chapter (which will inevitably be a downturn in tension) wrecks the novel's structural unity. After all, the book's opening hook should be able to stand on its own without such rudimentary tricks.

Now, this doesn't mean you should never write a prologue that contains a heart-wrenching moment or pulse-pounding action. My point is simply this: If opening with an action prologue, it is always better that those events are self-contained moments that don't happen elsewhere in the story. The scene can be an unforeseen (but detrimental) element of the present like we see at the start of every James Bond movie or it can depict a far-removed past event/problem that haunts your hero as we then zing forward to the present in the first chapter. But as noted in the initial definition, the key is to give the reader something that will clearly set the novel's scene through a *preceding* event or development whose existence somehow sets the story in motion. Prologues work best when used to introduce something that happens outside the timeline of the story or a seemingly random fact that absolutely needs to be known before the story is told.

Basically, a strong prologue acts as a foundational moment that instills doubt in the reader about the main character's ability to deal with the stress and complications of the conflict to come. The prologue should inform the story and the protagonist from the very start, allowing the audience to anticipate how the rest of the book will shape the characterizations, situations, and dilemmas to come.

Therefore, the most justifiable type of prologue is one that works to provide a short backstory. This can be a brief dramatization, correspondence, a dairy entry, or even a news article. You can adopt an unusual viewpoint, travel back in time, or deviate from the main setting. Your main aim is to keep things as active and as short as possible. Slowly weave the bulk of the backstory into the main narrative over the course of several chapters. Be advised: This is not an endorsement for using the prologue as a massive information dump. Avoid having your prologue become a place for bloated exposition. If you use the prologue solely to give the reader background information or historical research, you are apt to alienate them — even if you have an active or interesting way of revealing this information such as a dream, a precognitive heroine, or a possessed video game. Going overboard with background detail is the quickest way to lose an audience since such paragraphs of dense text are often hard for the reader to consume so early in the novel's development. Instead, opt to give just enough background to hook the reader's interest as you string them along to the next section of the book.

When deciding whether to insert backstory into *any* portion of your text, ask yourself: Does the reader need to know this fact now? Is the detail crucial at this point in the story? Will the story collapse if I withhold this information for another scene? Is there a point in the story where such background information may be better served? Or can I accomplish the same effect more subtly using hints, innuendo, and/or dialogue thus allowing the audience to use their imaginations to fill in the gaps and participate more fully in the present story?

Similarly, avoid using a prologue to summarize story events — whether it's a catastrophic world-ending disaster or a critical moment in the protagonist's life. Why? Because a summary lacks the conflict and real-time action the audience wants from a scene. In fact, a summary is not a scene. It's the more handsome brother of the information dump and should be used sparingly and strategically.

In stories packed with suspense, summaries work best as a transition between scenes like when there's been a large passage of time or when a character must share the same information with different colleagues over and over again. And if you insist upon using summary detail at the start of a narrative, it may be better for it to unfold as an active prologue sequence or be discussed by characters during the main narrative portion of the text. In both instances, the reader will receive a more well-rounded impression since action scenes and dialogue allow for perspectives and opinions that are impossible in a summary.

So if the first big no-no of prologues is stealing from the middle, then the second is using the device solely for exposition and the third is using the prologue to summarize past or future events. Remember, a prologue should be an active and compelling scene that's relevant to the main plot. Work to include a character who the audience will care about and who will be directly affected by the events. When considering whether to write, keep, or ditch a prologue, consider the following:

❖ What information is being provided?

❖ Why is it important to open the story with these details?

❖ Does the information support the primary narrative and play a vital role in the understanding of the overall work?

❖ Can I sprinkle this information throughout the story and still achieve the intended impact?

❖ Is the viewpoint character used in the prologue also used elsewhere in the story? If so, is it possible to turn the intended prologue section into part of the first chapter?

Now that you have a clear understanding of prologues, here is a complete list of pitfalls to avoid. Since prologues are such a loaded subject for some writers and their publishers, use the next section like a checklist to tweak your technique.

Prologue Pitfalls

Don't create a prologue for shock value that has no connection to the main text. While a prologue doesn't need to be a true standalone or have the same structural fortitude as the book's first chapter, it does need to do more than be a click-bait type hook or gimmick. A poorly formed prologue will be quickly ferreted out by the reader. After all, it is the first thing the audience encounters when they open the book. Even if it is not immediately apparent, the prologue should *always* tie back to your main plot and propel or impact the action therein — this could mean unveiling the catalyst for a character's emotional journey or foreshadowing the story's stakes. Seek to create something that has a long-term or meaningful affect.

Don't default to violence. Raw emotion works well too. While starting in the middle of an action sequence is an interesting way to open a narrative, consider whether the event is essential to the plot and if the action really indoctrinates the reader in a manner that's clear and relatable. You may find that a cornerstone scene from the hero's childhood or a moral-bending turn in the villain's previous relationships may prove equally as powerful when it comes to helping the audience understand why your story's problem starts where it does.

Don't write a prologue if you don't need one. I give this advice not as a hater of prologues — because they aren't a bad thing when approached properly — but as someone who believes that we should never fill our work with extraneous details or superfluous techniques. By the end of an effective prologue, the reader should be excited about the upcoming story and eager to learn how the event play into the overall plot. To prepare for this, ask yourself (and be honest!): Does this prologue unfold in a time, place, point of view, or manner that makes it far enough removed (or different) from the first chapter that it should be its own section? Does a prologue improve the story? If the answer to both questions is "yes," then you can set it aside as a prologue. If not, sprinkle the material throughout your first act — or perhaps, trash it altogether. In fiction, readers often skip the front matter (i.e. the introduction, dedication, contents, et cetera), so why run that risk happening with a poor prologue? When possible, start your story with the standard first chapter hook instead. That way, your work and the reader are in sync from the first page.

Don't create a prologue that delays introducing the protagonist. This is tricky because sometimes prologues are better suited for introducing the villain or sympathizing with the victim. However, the point of this tip is to remind you that even if the protagonist isn't in the prologue, the upshot or meaning of the event should eventually affect him in some manner or point to his existence. In other words, allow some aspect of the prologue to inform his characterization whether it's as big as his childhood fear or as small as what he does for a living and why. We want all roads to lead to the main character because that's the person the reader needs to empathize with and who they will follow over the majority of the story — establish that connection as soon as possible.

Don't bog the material down with description for description's sake. Although the prologue may seem like the perfect place for worldbuilding, this doesn't mean you should use the space to outline the novel's magic system or wax philosophical about the layout of the hero's village. Like an abundance of backstory, too much detail too soon can be a reader turn off. Keep the details light so your scene can move at a brisk pace. Any and all information provided during the prologue should build toward something meaningful — and that includes the imagery focused upon during the scene. So select details that will highlight the difference in time or location if the prologue is far removed from the first chapter setting, or invest in descriptions that juxtapose conflicts, problems, or dangers if the era and locale are similar to the primary setting. This will help readers acclimate themselves as they transition from prologue to page one, and it ensures that you've created some thematic connection with the main text.

Don't drone on forever. Keep your prologue short. This is an area where less is more. The goal is to hook the reader and propel them into the main text, not trap them in the muck of early idealism.

Don't saddle the prologue with extraneous exposition. Show, don't tell. This one can't be overstated!

Point of View

Unlike traditional mysteries, where we typically stick with one character's point of view, suspense stories have the option of using several viewpoint characters and multiple points of view. You can follow both the protagonist and the antagonist by putting the main character in first person to build audience comradery and the villain in third-person objective to provide some distance between the reader and that dastardly dude. The choice is yours. Suspense tales use viewpoint to shape the story and keep the audience guessing, so choose wisely, but don't feel confined by any one convention.

When choosing the viewpoint character for a scene, select the person who has the most to learn or who faces the highest stakes. In the former situation, you're choosing the character who will help educate the audience and act as an avatar for the reader's immersion into the story. In the latter instance, you're building tension by ensuring the scene has a significant conflict and have selected someone whose plight may draw empathy or disdain from the audience. Finding a character's voice is about determining what they decide to tell you and how they decide to tell it. The key is to figure out **whose point of view will best heighten the audience's interest in your narrative,** and whatever approach you choose should add emotion, depth, and suspense to the tale.

You may need to play around with viewpoint initially to figure out what works best, so feel free to write a scene from multiple perspectives to figure out which one provides the most tension and suspense. Maybe you'll find that you need to split the scene up and tell one half through one character and the back half through another. That's fine. Just be sure to make a visual distinction either with a chapter, section, or paragraph break to indicate that a change is being made in the perspective.

As you switch viewpoints, find immediate ways to make that indication clear through the words and attitudes chosen for the text. Switching point of view is a plausible way to misdirect or withhold information from the audience without the act feeling like a cheat. After all, you can only describe things that your viewpoint character would know through their own senses and experiences. By moving to another character, you temporarily shift the base of knowledge from which the audience will draw their conclusions.

Some narratives choose to tell the story from the viewpoint of a secondary character or someone who is adjacent to the main action. The Sherlock Holmes stories are perfect examples since they are told from Dr. Watson's viewpoint rather than the titular character. Perhaps, like Holmes, your main character is extremely clever or knows information you want to hold from the reader. This is where the use of your secondary character's viewpoint comes in handy because that person's genuine confusion or curiosity will help usher the audience toward the questions you want them to consider. And yet, since the secondary character isn't privy to the story's higher levels of information, you as the writer can again obscure data from the reader in a manner that feels natural.

Most suspense stories written either in first-person past tense or third-person past tense. I won't get into the nuances of writing in present tense even though it is has become increasingly popular in the young adult and romance genres. However, for the sake of thoroughly covering viewpoint, we will discuss the five major point of views.

First-Person Viewpoint

First-Person Strengths

- ❖ Creates intimacy between the reader and narrator
- ❖ Allows for a distinctive narrator voice

❖ The preferred POV for the unreliable narrator
❖ Easy to write and plot

First-Person Pitfalls

❖ Unable to depict situations where the protagonist is absent

❖ Narrative flexibility is limited because backstory is restricted to what the narrator knows

❖ Audiences may tire of a single narrative voice that's prone to lecture-like introspection

❖ The speaker is inherently biased

First-person viewpoint is identified by the use of "I," "me," and "my." Through this viewpoint, we experience a single character's thoughts as if we are that person. We take residence inside the narrator's head and experience the world as they see it. Thus, character intimacy is immediate, and the author has an opportunity to create a unique voice for the narrator since there is no filter between the speaker and the audience. However, because the reader never gains the opportunity to learn something that the viewpoint character doesn't know, this technique leaves very little room for dramatic irony, a staple in suspense. This becomes a significant problem if the point-of-view character is the protagonist because the audience loses the opportunity to worry for the hero if he walks unknowingly into a trap.

As alluded to earlier, you do have some flexibility in this regard if your narrator is the protagonist's sidekick like Dr. Watson, whose position as foil often meant that he missed information that was obvious to Holmes. By choosing an uninformed narrator who is slightly behind the events of the narrative, we allow space for the reader to draw their own conclusions. This also obligates the two main characters to update or debate each other on the pertinent issues of the case, allowing for the audience to form alternate theories that they can use to decode the narrative.

There are, however, pitfalls to this approach of sidekick as narrator. If this person is too slow or bumbling, he may cause the audience to lose interest. The author also runs the risk of creating a viewpoint character who becomes a mere conduit for exposition or a narrator whose sole purpose is to ask naive questions of the superior sleuth. Both of these problems are tedious and make the audience aware of the filter through which the story unfolds.

Another way to utilize suspense techniques in first person is to have the narrator telling his story from the position of authority as if the events have occurred in the recent past rather than real time. We see this with frame stories, which are discussed in detail in the chapter on flashbacks. This often infuses a small but potent level of unreliability since the speaker now relays the events with the power of hindsight and may want to downplay an event that makes him appear foolish or embellish things that make him look good.

Now, in case you're wondering, the reason why most thrillers aren't written solely in first person is that the singular viewpoint limits the scope of the story and the audience's ability to see the threat from multiple angles. However, you can continually create suspense in first person simply by having that character overly aware of the odds stacked against them such as the ticking clock that comes with solving a major crime or by having the hero inadvertently misinterpret the initial actions of a character who may be attempting to help rather than harm him. You can also create heightened suspense by delving into the psychological aspects of being in first person. A character may question their own perception, capabilities, or sanity, which creates a level of uncertainty and vulnerability that the audience finds relatable while maintaining the *will he or won't he succeed* dynamic that's essential to thrillers.

In addition, suspense stories have a little leeway in their use of the first-person viewpoint because they don't necessarily need to play fair with the audience at all times. While it is usually safe to assume a suspense story's first-person narrator is honest, there is still room for some misdirection. In other words, it is acceptable for a thriller's first-person narrator to simply hint at a danger that's on the horizon without describing it in full to the audience, thus stringing the reader along in a way that builds tension because the protagonist knows something we don't. Of course, this isn't the same as the unreliable narrator, which is its own literary device and an exception to the rule that we will discuss in future chapters.

On the other hand, a thriller author can keep their first person as traditional as possible adhering to the rules of fair play that are often attributed to cozies, sharing everything they see and hear with the audience. This can add suspense too. Because if the writer excels at their craft, the audience is not only listening to a uniquely crafted voice full of lively idiosyncrasies — see *Hostile Witness* (1995) by William Lashner as an excellent example — but they are also viewing the action through an empathetic character, which amplifies any perceived danger.

Second-Person Viewpoint

Second-Person Strengths

- ❖ Creates intimacy with the reader
- ❖ Allows for a unique storytelling experience
- ❖ Forces the reader to participate in the narrative

Second-Person Pitfalls

- Difficult to write and plot, especially over the long term
- Some audiences may find it distracting, alienating, or difficult to read
- Not commonly used, so very few examples to follow

Second-person viewpoint is distinguished by the use of "you" as the narrative device. While this approach seems easy and appropriate when giving directions or drafting instructions on how to bake a cake — *You want to make a right on Doheny;* or *Place the tin at the center of the rack* — it becomes a difficult conundrum for fiction. Many writers and readers unfamiliar with this technique often question who is the "you" in these instances. Does "you" refer solely to the reader, or is this the reflexive act of the narrator addressing himself? The answer depends on the topic and structure of your novel. But in general, using "you" as either an omniscient narrative voice or the main character forces the reader to participate in the creation of the plot by drawing them into the action of the story. The risk you run here is that the reader will reject the "you," not wanting play the lead or ride along with the persona of your narrator.

However, if this point of view appeals to you, the easiest way to incorporate this technique is to use "you" as an alternative to "I" in a story where the narrator is too self-conscious (or guilty) to face the painful truth. They are telling their own story in a manner that allows them to distance themselves from actions they may deem unconscionable thereby enabling them to appear more palatable and perhaps even sympathetic to the reader. On the other end of the spectrum, the narrator may use "you" as a way to draw attention to what he mistakenly believes is a universal experience or idea. His goal is to force the audience into looking closer with the hope that, by immersing them in his world, they will start to identify with his outlook. In both instances, there is an appeal that hints at unreliability, which is a stellar suspense technique when used properly as discussed in the next chapter.

But be forewarned, this isn't to suggest that the approach is as simple as changing a few pronouns. You will need to create a premise where such an approach is necessary as with *Bright Lights, Big City* (1984) by Jay McInerney, which includes a narrator whose distancing is meant to hide his inability to deal with his mother's death, or *You* (2014) by Caroline Kepnes, which features a narrator who periodically uses the "you" form to justify his obsessions.

Third-Person Objective Viewpoint

Third-Person Objective Strengths

❖ Because the narration is neutral and removed from its characters it is considered the most unbiased form of narration

❖ Useful for conveying factual information

❖ Allows the author to reveal character action without having to include personal details

Third-Person Objective Pitfalls

❖ The distancing effect and neutral voice undercuts the narrative's humanity

❖ Doesn't tap into the thoughts or emotions of its characters

❖ Doesn't provide interpretation for facts offered

❖ Less effective for character driven stories

There are three main types of third-person narration: limited, omniscient, and objective. We are not going to spend a lot of time discussing the objective form in this book because this technique utilizes a neutral narration that merely observes its characters without providing insight into their thoughts or emotions. When you write in this viewpoint, you are merely describing the action in a factual manner. And as we've discussed throughout this text, we need the audience to empathize or relate to the characters if we want to whip up suspense. Obviously, that task becomes much more difficult if we are never able to truly understand what those people are thinking or feeling.

However, objective can be helpful technique for small sections of your suspense tale. For example, if you'd like to unveil your villain early in the story and include a scene that gives us a glimpse of him in action (without revealing his motivations), you can use the objective viewpoint because it won't ruin the ending by telling us what he's thinking. This point of view allows us to observe him from a distance, which maintains the menace and signals to the audience that they shouldn't get attached to this person — an important perk if we decide to open the book with the villain rather than the hero. Such scenes raise a number of suspenseful story questions that you can then carry over to the main point of view which will be your protagonist in first or third-person limited.

Third-Person Limited Viewpoint

Third-Person Limited Strengths

❖ Provides access to the character's thoughts similar to first person but also allows for some distancing since the character's adventures are conveyed through a narrator

❖ Easy for the audience to understand without having to jump directly into the main character's shoes

❖ Because they're following one person, the reader gains information the same time as the character

Third Person Limited Pitfalls

❖ The narrator can only convey what the POV character knows

❖ Because of the built-in narrator, the text often becomes filled with "telling" language rather than "showing" personality and action through behavior

Third-person limited — sometimes called "restricted," "subjective," or "close" third — is the viewpoint most often used in suspense stories. It shares some similarities with first person in that it follows one character and gives us access to their thoughts and observations. The audience can move through the fictional world with that viewpoint character experiencing only those sensations in her vicinity without knowing what the people around her are thinking — that may be why this perspective is often referred to as "limited" because the reader is limited to what the character knows.

However, this technique still allows the author the opportunity to write from a broader perspective since the story is being narrated rather than dictated by the main character (as with first person). Therefore, the narrator can follow this single person throughout the novel or switch to a different character as the story moves from scene to scene or chapter to chapter. As discussed in the introduction to this section, switching points of view is a plausible way to fool or misdirect the reader without the act feeling like a cheat.

To draw the audience into your story, write in what authors refer to as "deep" third. Show the protagonist's darkest fears and loftiest dreams as well as how she feels when placed under pressure so that the worry and uncertainty synonymous with suspense arises in the audience. Basically, this involves writing close to the viewpoint character and allowing their personality to shine through so that the audience is less likely to notice that their experience is being filtered through a narrator.

Third-Person Omniscient Viewpoint

Third-Person Omniscient Strengths

- ❖ Powerful way to convey stories with large casts and multiple settings

- ❖ Allows the narration to move smoothly between events, topics, and places

- ❖ Gives the narrator a unique voice from the characters

- ❖ Helps the story achieve a larger scope because narrator can relay different places and times

Third-Person Omniscient Pitfalls

- ❖ As a typically distant point of view, this leads to less intimacy with characters

- ❖ With such a powerful narrative persona, head-hopping becomes more prevalent — which can be confusing to readers

❖ Due to the wider scope, sometimes the focus is pulled to frequently away from the main characters and settings

❖ In theory, since the narrator knows all, nothing can be left secret

Third-person omniscient is the God-like or bird's-eye view perspective — wherein the narrator knows each character's past, present, and future. The narrator can also follow any character at any time and can even enter a person's thoughts, moving from place to place and character to character as the story sees fit. On the surface, this has massive potential for suspense since you can cut from scene to scene to create the dramatic irony of having the audience know something that one character doesn't. However, all that head-hopping may become confusing for the reader and diminish the opportunity for them to identify or empathize with the main character.

Therefore, with this viewpoint, you may need to work doubly hard to maintain interest in your hero. One remedy is to make sure that he holds the largest portion of the narrative focus and that most of the internal work revolves around this character's faults and fears. You can also share the character's own interpretations or predictions of events to help shift or influence the reader's opinions.

Now that we have discussed each mode of narration, a word of warning: Regardless of the viewpoint, avoid stepping in as the author and interrupting the narrative to address the reader about events, characters, or your intention. This may seem obvious, but writers do it all the time with lines like this: *He had no idea that accepting that glass of whiskey would change his life forever.* As fiction writers, our goal is to immerse the reader in our imaginary world. Don't intentionally do anything that will pull them out of it.

Point of view plays a crucial role in determining the overall effectiveness of the narrative by providing the filter through which the audience determines characterization and experiences the events of the story. But how do writers develop a plot and maintain that rich connection with the audience when confined to a first-person narrator, especially one who isn't the protagonist or one who provides misinformation? Let's talk about it in the next chapter on unreliable narrators.

Unreliable Narrators

We love unreliable narrators like Tyler Durden from Chuck Palahniuk's *Fight Club* (1996) or Amy Dunne from Gillian Flynn's *Gone Girl* (2012), but we rarely talk about how such narrators are written and what makes those characters so memorable. After all, what purpose do unreliable narrators serve in fiction? What are the benefits of using an unreliable narrator to tell a story? And how do writers reveal the unreliability of their narrators without cheating the audience?

We'll answer all of those questions and much more. But first, what is an unreliable narrator?

An unreliable narrator is someone whose storytelling lacks some level of veracity or credibility and whose inaccuracy produces a void between the story's reality and the narrator's reality, which the reader must then bridge and eventually fill. This narrative device can take many forms but is often a first-person narrative that unfolds in one or more of the following ways:

❖ The narrator breaks the unspoken pact of honesty with the reader and deliberately misinforms

❖ The narrator tells the reader one thing while showing the reader something completely different

❖ The narrator tells the story but inadvertently hides the truth from himself and others

Because unreliable narrators blur the lines of reality, this technique forces the audience to question their perceptions and catches the reader off balance in a way that allows the author to build suspense by playing with moral gray areas. However...

A Word of Caution: Don't confuse an unreliable narrator with any person who lies. All characters lie — out of fear, appeasement, or shame — but not all are unreliable narrators. The difference between a standard liar and one who is an unreliable narrator is that the latter is omitting something that ties into the overall story question. Their misrepresentation or misconception (and the eventual correction thereof) changes the way the reader views the narrative. This also means your unreliable narrator isn't necessarily a villain or a bad person — they could simply be someone with a skewed viewpoint.

For example, in *Training Day* (2001), Detective Alonzo Harris (Denzel Washington) is clearly a liar. We watch him steal, double cross his partner, and murder, but his lies and duplicitous actions don't tie into overarching plot in a way that alters our basic understanding of the tale. He is not an unreliable narrator. In contrast, consider *The Usual Suspects* (1995). Verbal's lies initially fool Detective Kujan — and by extension the viewer. But once his lies are revealed, we question the entire narrative and gain a fresh understanding of the film's underlying lesson: It is never wise to underestimate an adversary.

Furthermore, this technique is not a requirement for a suspenseful story. However, it is a powerful tool for your arsenal since no one has more control over the plot — the who, what, where, when, and why — than the narrator. Remember, the narrator controls the story's moral compass and who to root for as well as the pacing, diction, and attitude the audience should take about what happens. So, select your point of view with care.

Think carefully about how to use the technique to improve your story. An unreliable narrator is a sophisticated addition to any text, but you shouldn't do so without having a specific reason in mind. Will using an unreliable aid in tying together an intricate plot? Will it help explain the complexities behind a character's competing motives? Will it help drive the overall story question? In other words, your unreliable narrator should still enhance the story.

On the other hand, the reliable narrator — i.e. the type most writers strive to incorporate — uses his personal perspective to tell readers all the information they need to know and does so as accurately as possible. Yet, the reality is that a single character's subjective perception prevents the reader from ever having a completely accurate picture of events. In other words, no one ever see things as they genuinely occur. Most people tell stories through the lens of their past experiences, which often contain bias, and memory itself is a faulty illusion filtered through the ego. A person's perspective changes the further removed they are from the problem, whether that's via distance (e.g. rank or class) or time (e.g. maturity or age). And more often than not, the degree a person is honest or dishonest about something is in direct proportion to their involvement in the story being told.

This means your job as a writer is to decide how trustworthy or untrustworthy to make your protagonist. Luckily, the rating system for unreliability runs on a large scale from inconsequential to heavy duty. You can even develop characters that have layers of unreliability (e.g. they're unreliable only about things related to themselves but honest otherwise). In fact, a story or a character doesn't need to tell the whole truth to still be true.

For instance, in *Harry Potter and the Prisoner of Azkaban* (1999) by J.K. Rowling, Harry feeds the audience misinformation based on what he thinks he knows about the escaped prisoner who aided in the murder of his parents. But later, Harry and the reader discover the entire story is a lie. Now, I would in no way define Harry as an unreliable narrator, but I do think Rowling implemented some of the techniques we'll discuss later in this chapter. And her usage here is worth noting because even if your lead character is kindhearted, you can allow them to have *unreliable moments* to make them slightly flawed — and thus, more realistic. You can also see how one character's naivete can change the meaning or interpretation of the narrative in a manner that adds drama and suspense.

Not to mention, when you use the unreliability technique to its fullest extent, you can reveal that device to readers at various times to achieve different effects — immediately, gradually, or late enough for a major final act plot twist. Consider the examples below, but please note that these aren't the only ways or reasons to employ the technique.

Immediately – In *The Perks of Being a Wallflower* (1999) by Stephen Chbosky, the narrator admits his manipulation of the story from the very first page. "I will call people by different names or generic names because I don't want you to find me." His desire to remain a mystery makes him unreliable and acts as a way for him to distance himself (and us!) from the story of his painful freshman year. His reliability is also further minimized throughout the book by drug use and an implied mental illness. Now, we talked about unreliable narrators falling on a scale from mild to heavy. And yes, this is what some may call a mild variation of the form since the protagonist's misdirection or misrepresentation isn't a duplicitous effort to deceive the audience — rather, it is an example of unreliability manifested due to the narrator's abusive past and socially awkward present. That's why even though he admits his unreliability early, the audience still empathizes with him. He sincerely wants to get to the bottom of his own experiences and discover where things went wrong.

Gradually – Author Gillian Flynn takes a different approach with her novel *Gone Girl* (2012). The truth about Amy Dunne's false narrative created through the dairy is revealed slowly, not only to shock the audience, but to show the methodical nature of the character's plan and to make us reevaluate everyone's motive. If you really want to get picky, since the book is broken into sections, we get three unreliable narrators — Amy's Dairy, Nick, and Amy. The tangle of lies their collective narratives create mirrors their bitter marital struggles and puts the audience in the same situation the characters find themselves — unclear of what's real and who to trust.

Late – In Agatha Christie's *The Murder of Roger Ackroyd* (1926), the reveal of the unreliable narrator arises as a major final act plot twist. While there are many ways to do this, Christie very subtly creates a frame where the story is being told via the memoir of Dr. James Sheppard. As the story unfolds, she places Sheppard alongside the famed Detective Hercule Poirot. From there, our own biases take over, and we miss the signs that the narrator is evading the truth. By placing Dr. Sheppard alongside the detective, we *assume* the physician is going to adopt a Watson-like role where his narration is meant to highlight the sleuth's investigation. However, upon the final reveal, we discover Sheppard's entire narrative was his memoir — a clever coverup to hide his role as the guilty party.

Note that in each of these examples, we have different types of unreliable narrators. Some are purposefully engaging in a duplicitous deception to avoid detection (Verbal Kint) while others unintentionally misconstrue the facts due to naivete or having the wrong information (Harry Potter). Being able to clearly articulate this distinction will help you decide what type of unreliable narrator is most appealing to you and how to successfully incorporate their traits into your story. So with that in mind, let's break our narrators into categories.

Types of Unreliable Narrators

In *Pícaros, Madmen, Naïfs, and Clowns: The Unreliable First-person Narrator* (1981) by William Riggan, the approach to unreliable narration is divided into five types: Pícaro, Madman, Clown, Naif, and Liar.

Pícaro – one who exaggerates or misrepresents events for the purpose of bragging

❖ An early example of a pícaro is in the comedic play by Roman playwright Titus Maccius Plautus (254-184 B.C.) called *Miles Gloriosus*. The title can be translated to "The Swaggering Solider," and the play is essentially about a coward overstating his prowess.

❖ A modern pícaro example is *The Wolf of Wall Street* (2007) by Jordan Belfort, who in the prologue describes the story that follows as "a satirical reconstruction" of his time on Wall Street. Although marketed as a memoir, the book reads like fiction — so much so that it became the inspiration for the splashy 2013 film directed by Martin Scorsese, starring Leonardo DiCaprio.

❖ Because of the narrator's absurdity, the audience usually catches this type of unreliability early in the story, allowing for a laugh and lesson of what not to do when caught in similar circumstances.

Madman – one who is dealing with trauma, mental illness, or emotional flaw that makes it difficult for them to interpret events accurately

❖ An early example of the madman is the narrator in "The Tell-Tale Heart" (1843) by Edgar Allan Poe. In this short story, we have a narrator whose unreliability stems from a mental illness that make it difficult for him to discern falsehood from reality.

❖ A modern madman example is Bret Easton Ellis's *American Psycho* (1991), which follows the psychological unraveling of Patrick Bateman, a Manhattan investment banker and potential serial killer.

❖ *The Girl on the Train* (2015) by Paula Hawkins is a modern madman example that leans more toward trauma or an emotional flaw — specifically in the character of Rachel Watson, whose recollections are impaired due to the alcohol she uses to dull the pain from her broken marriage.

❖ The madman approach adds suspense because people who are dealing with emotional instability are often as unclear of their own truth as the reader, creating a sense of discovery that potentially results in satisfying plot twists.

❖ When drafting this type of narrator, consider what social or political themes your character's psychological difficulties will help the reader explore (e.g. in *American Psycho* it's consumerism, capitalism) and give the character some personal dimensions outside their issues to avoid solely using depression, trauma, or illness as a plot point.

Clown – one who doesn't take things seriously and thereby toys with the common narrative conventions

❖ An early clown example is *A Clockwork Orange* (1962) by Anthony Burgess. In this instance, the protagonist considers himself a master manipulator and tells much of his tale in a state of inebriation.

❖ A modern implementation of the clown is *Gone Girl*, which as we discussed, uses Amy's fake diary warp normal narrative conventions and alter audience expectations.

❖ This narrative approach works because we often don't know they're unreliable at first, but the shock of the realization forces us to reevaluate everything we thought we understood.

Naïf – a naïve or inexperienced narrator who views things from an innocent perspective

❖ An early naïf example is *The Adventures of Huckleberry Finn* (1884) by Mark Twain. Huck's naïve misreading of situations creates dramatic irony, which contrasts Huck's good heart with adult hypocrisy (thus shining a light on racism!).

❖ *The Curious Incident of the Dog in the Night-Time* (2003) by Mark Haddon is a modern naïf example because the narrator is a fifteen-year-old boy with autism, which means his interpretation of events comes from a unique perspective.

❖ This category can also be defined to include the innocent, the uninformed, the confused, the misunderstood, or the unknowing, so don't let the term "naïf" lead you to believe this distinction only includes children. On the contrary, the category includes anyone (adult or child) dealing with unfamiliar surroundings or misinformation. This also includes developmentally disabled adults as found in Winston Groom's novel *Forrest Gump* (1986) or the Christopher Nolan film *Memento* (2001).

❖ This narrative approach allows moments for the reader to understand what's going on better than the main character, lending depth to a story that seems simple on the surface. And yet, this category is tricky because the narrator's embellishments should mainly come from a place of innocence or unintentional misdirection with no overtly malicious motive. Therefore, this isn't the best choice for an author looking to create a huge last-act twist.

Lair – one who deliberately lies about events or hides important information

❖ As discussed earlier, Dr. Sheppard in *The Murder of Roger Ackroyd* by Agatha Christie and Roger "Verbal" Kint from the film *The Usual Suspects* are prime examples.

❖ These are characters who lie to deceive or to hide old transgressions, and their motivation is often self-preservation or self-aggrandizement.

❖ The deliberate nature of their lies often leads to stories where the narrator does indeed have a malicious intent for their deception.

Please note that even though we can place most unreliable narrators into one of these categories, these classifications aren't black and white. As with many things in fiction, shades of gray exist, and you can take advantage of that by using two of the five types to make your characters more complex. For instance, it could be argued that Alex from *A Clockwork Orange* is both madman and clown.

Or you may find yourself mashing up the categories or breaking them into new chunks. I have had many colleagues argue that there should be a category for "the supernatural" where the narrator's unreliability comes from some sense of magic or otherworldliness. An example of this could be the character of Eleanor from *The Haunting of Hill House* (1959) by Shirley Jackson although I would still place her under the madman category. Or perhaps, you'd like to include a category such as "the outsider," i.e. someone whose view is skewed because they've been scorned over personal issues such as race, class, culture, or gender — think Ralph Ellison's novel *The Invisible Man* (1952).

Or it may simply help to think of unreliable narrators as one of two types: **deliberate** (ones who know they're deceiving and why) versus **inadvertent** (ones who believe they are telling truth or are doing their best despite shortcomings). This will free you from having to worry about how to bring nuance to a stock character.

DELIBERATE	INADVERTENT
•Liars	•Mental illness
•Shit stirrers	•Trauma
•Braggarts	•PTSD
•Twisting truth for self-preservation or self-aggrandizement	•Naiveté
	•Immature or uneducated
•Breaking the fourth wall or playing with convention to give us "truth"	•Wrong assumptions
	•Misinterpretation due to lack of knowledge
	•Personal bias
	•Bad information given from faulty sources

History of Unreliable Narrators

Literary critic Wayne C. Booth is given credit as having first coined the phrase "unreliable narrator" in *Rhetoric of Fiction* (1961), but the technique has been used throughout history.

For example, in Book 9 of Homer's epic poem *The Odyssey* (725–675 B.C.), Odysseus tells a story about the Cyclops Polyphemus that is not only later proven in the text as inaccurate but also shown to have gained him favor with the Phaeacians in the process — which is often how we think of unreliable narrators today, one who twists the narrative for personal gain.

Now, since dramatic works (plays) by definition are presented mostly in dialogue and don't typically have a narrator, we can't wholly tie the concept of unreliable narration to the Old Comedy of ancient Greece, but it would be careless of me not to mention how this technique was used in the work of Greek playwright Aristophanes' during the 5th century B.C. — *The Clouds, The Birds, The Frogs,* et cetera. These plays often commented on the ridiculous aspects of society through inconsistent and often contradictory portrayals of public figures (Cleon, Socrates, and Euripides) and through the use of the chorus speaking for the author via the parabasis. The parabasis is an interlude from the main action where the chorus addresses the audience to express the author's intent but often in a way that exposes the truth or shines light on the misrepresentations offered during the main action. We laugh at the characters and their vanity while deftly decoding the truth and learning from their misfortune — a common occurrence for many of the early uses of the unreliable narrator technique.

Another early example can be found in the work of Medieval poet and chronicler Geoffrey Chaucer (1342-1400), who used various unreliable narrators in *The Canterbury Tales*. A specific example is the bragging and exaggerating titular character in "The Wife of Bath's Tale."

But the first-person unreliable narrator really became popular in Western literature during the Modernist period starting in the mid-19th century with such works as "The Tell-Tale Heart" (1843) by Edgar Allan Poe, whose narrator who attempts to convince the reader of his sanity and thus buries the truth. We can also look to *Wuthering Heights* (1847) by Emily Brontë since it has two tarnished narrators. The first is Mr. Lockwood's whose unreliability comes from his status as an outsider, so his knowledge of the situation contains a narrow-minded naivete. The second is Ellen "Nelly" Dean, who is unreliable due to her gossipy lack of sympathy and hate-fueled bias.

These days unreliable narrators are popular because they allow for twists and turns that shock and challenge the audience's sensibilities, leaving them feeling more engaged. And even though we read fiction to escape our ordinary word, it is sometimes fun to have books that turn the conventional happy ending on its head and instead mimic the uncertainty of everyday life.

Benefits of Unreliable Narration

Applying this literary technique allows you to surprise your readers through the reorientation of perspective and is a clever way to incorporate twists and build suspense. As we've seen from our earlier examples, this technique is especially useful in the horror, thriller, and supernatural genres for writers who want audiences to question what's real and what's imagined.

This gap between the reader's initial perception and the narrative's reality can even be used to amplify the story's overarching theme. For example, if we were to consider the lead character in *The Sixth Sense* (1999), Dr. Malcolm Crowe, an inadvertent unreliable narrator, we'd notice that the film's final revelation not only changes the story's meaning for him (and us) but also shines a spotlight on the film's themes of communication and coping with trauma. Along with the shocking conclusion, we experience a sense of growth for Dr. Crowe, who realizes that, despite his previous failures with his patient (the murderous Vincent), he was able to help young Cole.

In this instance, the unreliable narration is not intentional since Dr. Crowe is unaware of his condition until the end of the story, but the director's use of the technique (and our eventual dual understanding of the story) is the same as it would be with a more deliberate narrator like Verbal from *The Usual Suspects*.

In dramatic novels with inadvertent or naive unreliable narrators as with *The Adventures of Huckleberry Finn*, the reader understands the circumstances of the world the character occupies better than the characters themselves so the fact that something is amiss in the narration only leads to highlight the importance of a greater understanding — perhaps even a lesson or moral learned — by the audience rather than a misinterpretation or misconception. In other words, because we view the story not only through the narrator's perspective but more accurately through our own, we get to judge the good alongside the bad and that juxtaposition clarifies what it is about our perspective (i.e. the truth) that's worth adopting.

With those examples in mind, here are some ways unreliable narration can improve your manuscript if handled correctly.

❖ Teaches reader a lesson or moral

❖ Delivers a powerful emotional punch

❖ Forces the audience to question their interpretation and the line between fantasy/reality —what's happened vs. what being shown vs. meaning

❖ Creates twists and suspense by delaying or concealing the truth

❖ Adds conflict and intricate layers to characterization through the narrator's reasons for concealment

Tips for Creating an Unreliable Narrator

The key to developing an effective unreliable narrator is foreshadowing. Provide clues throughout to indicate the truth about your narrator and to show (in retrospect!) how and/or why they misrepresented events. This is doubly important when using an inadvertent unreliable narrator who may never have enough information to reveal the misconception on his own.

You can provide these clues by using the characters or the environment to draw attention to the portion of the narrative deemed most credible. Failure to do this will leave the reader feeling cheated upon the reveal because they want to look back and see how the narrative arrived at this new place. Remember, if a character is unreliable and there isn't a method for distinguishing the truth, the technique serves no purpose. Spotting that thin line between truth and lie is what makes your story memorable, helps the reader better understand your characters, and highlights why this version of the story was worth telling. So we want the reader to decipher enough about what was being hidden to gather new meaning from the story, BUT we don't want them to feel totally duped when the truth is revealed. A good novel should inspire a reread so that the purchaser can discover things they may have missed the first round. So it is imperative that you drop hints from the beginning that not only act as clues to the truth but also make us question the veracity of the source. They can be subtle, but they must be there.

Here are some other methods to help foreshadow the truth behind an unreliable narrator:

- Contradicting stories, mistakes, or inconsistencies
- Repetition, exaggerations, or overemphasis
- Incomplete or missing explanation of events
- Illogical information, time manipulation, or overlapping imagery
- A questioning of the narrator's health, sanity, or motives
- An authority, expert, or trusted character revealing the truth
- Flashbacks, diaries, news articles, et cetera
- Outright omission by narrator on first page (often overlooked by reader)

<u>Another Word of Caution:</u> Do not introduce a bunch of this stuff — or anything new that you have not mentioned before — at the end of the book. While this is a basic rule for all storytelling, it is twice as important when using unreliable narration. Make sure to plant your seeds early and play fair with the audience so that they can go back to the beginning and see evidence the points to how the end is totally justified.

What may help when writing is to consider the reasons why your character may choose to withhold or misrepresent information. Revenge? Self-preservation? Trauma? Naïveté? Think about her values and how she perceives the world. Give your narrator a compelling background, and ask yourself the following questions:

❖ What's unique about this person's experience?

❖ Why is the event they are recounting important to them?

❖ What knowledge or naivete does this character bring to the story?

❖ Why is the character conveying this story? What is their goal?

❖ What does this person hope to accomplish with her version of events (vindication, vilification, vengeance)?

❖ How does her overall characterization and personal agenda affect the narrative?

Strive to create reasons that are exceedingly personal, and avoid anything that is entirely plot based or for the sake of a hallow twist.

The final approach to using unreliable narrators successfully is to write the character so that they initially believe the story they are telling because the reader won't buy it if they don't. Gain reader trust by starting from a place of perceived honesty. If the narrator has no moments of truth or vulnerability, readers will not buy their story. However, if we see them working to put their best selves forward despite their faults, it will have more meaning and resonance when new truths are revealed. A successful unreliable narrator gains audience sympathy even as they fall prey to his deception. Like a powerful illusionist, a well-written unreliable narrator should make us want to believe.

Even if they are deliberately deceptive, give your narrator a sense of innocence or a logical personal stake because that will help put the audience on their side. But most importantly, it will allow for some sincerity. Every good lie is based on a kernel of truth, and that's usually how the narrator reconciles reality with the version of the story they are telling.

In short, tapping into your narrator's humanity is crucial.

The unreliable narrator is an effective technique mainly because we all have egos that play into our deceptions, and we all sometimes wish the truth were different. If the lies and idiosyncrasies you create appear genuine, the reader will bow to your technique. But remember, the unreliable narrator is more than a literary device, it's a fully realized portrait of humanity's flaws. So don't try to wedge this concept into a preexisting story. This isn't a place to "wing it" and hope for the best. Plan ahead.

Unreliable Narrators in Other Viewpoints

Can this technique be used in other viewpoints?

In Wayne C. Booth's book *The Rhetoric of Fiction* (1961), he states that for a narrator to be unreliable the story needs to be presented by a first-person narrator. And while I hesitate to give you too many hard and fast rules, I would tend to agree with Booth on this one. Remember, first person is given the premier distinction for unreliable narrators because the audience is immersed in the lead character's head and find themselves at the mercy of his interpretation — skewed or otherwise. That character's mind is the only way the reader can judge the events of the narrative; therefore, it is easy for the author to hide the truth, cast doubt, and create twists.

Writers are even welcome to use more than one first-person narrator as with the Rashomon Effect, a storytelling method named after Akira Kurosawa's 1950 film *Rashomon* wherein a murder is described in contradictory ways by four witnesses. The effect is meant to highlight the idea that our personal opinions and subjective perceptions make it impossible for someone to have an accurate interpretation of events. A pre-existing literary equivalent would be *As I Lay Dying* (1930) by William Faulkner, which uses multiple narrators to describe the circumstances around a character's pending death. For my money, the intricacies that come with plumbing the depths of someone's mind make first person the ideal viewpoint.

However, some contemporary artists have found clever ways to incorporate unreliable narration into the other viewpoints. For example, in *You* (2014) by Caroline Kepnes, the author uses second-person as a temporary extension of first-person to create the protagonist and unreliable narrator, Joe Goldberg. In the novel, the secondary viewpoint is a projection of what Joe believes his object of affection should and could be saying, doing, or thinking as opposed to the objective truth.

Incorporating unreliable narration in third-person limited is much harder because in this viewpoint, the speaker isn't consciously aware they're telling a story; therefore, the author's ability to disguise the narrator's unreliability is lost. In other words, the manipulation is much more obvious to the audience. So in third-person limited, what you get is an unreliable narrative rather than a narrator. This can still be beneficial if the goal is to have your character's untrustworthiness recognized early and you're content to have unreliability become his character trait as with *The Talented Mr. Ripley* (1955) by Patricia Highsmith. However, it is useless if the goal is a major third-act plot twist.

The best way to create unreliable narration in a third-person limited is to go deep with the characterization and indirect dialogue to blur the line between character and narrator. Take note of the two examples below.

Example #1: Normal third-person limited – Tonya *watched* as Marcus ignored her and smiled at her sister Nancy, shaking her hand. Tonya *heard* them exchange greetings and fumed with jealousy. If he slighted her again, he'd regret it, she *thought*.

Notice all of the distancing words that separate us from the point of view character's feelings — *watched, heard, thought*. By going deeper with the viewpoint, the narration becomes fused with Tonya's emotions, allowing her anger to color the situation and obscure the truth of the matter. Of course, Tonya's lack of objectivity makes our use of the technique obvious (no big plot twists here), but the determined author has succeeded in creating an unreliable narrative if so desired.

Now, consider this deep third-person limited version of the same text.

Example #2: Deep third-person limited – That asshat Marcus smirked at Nancy like a hound dog in heat. A microsecond later, he swooped in, snatched her hand, and clutched it against his cheek like he owned her. Then he whispered sweetly into her ear as if they were lovers. He wanted to kiss her. No doubt. But if he came near her again, he'd regret it. Tonya would make sure of it.

Lastly, let's consider third-person omniscient, which offers the most difficulty when incorporating unreliability because by definition the narrator should know and tell us everything. However, you can create an unreliable narrative if you give the narrator a distinct personality and motive — e.g. *Gossip Girl* by Cecily Von Ziegesar (2002) — then let the epistolary form (letters, diaries, news articles, social media posts, et cetera) do some of the narrative work, so the all-knowing but biased narrator is not our only source of information.

Based on these examples, you certainly do have various options when it comes to the point of view of your unreliable narrator, but it does get tricker along the way.

FAQ: Unreliable Narrators

What are some pitfalls of unreliable narration?

While this chapter has mostly focused on the benefits of unreliable narration, there is a downside. By creating a character the audience can't completely trust, you've limited their ability to empathize or even sympathize with him. Without that relatable element, it is difficult for the audience to connect with the story, which means your premise must be particularly captivating or speak to some universal emotion, like love, so the reader has something to cling to until the truth of the narrative is revealed.

Moreover, not every story needs an unreliable narrator. By adding such a technique to an already complex story, it could end up feeling like one gimmick too many. Sometimes it is better to give the audience the information they need to play along because that makes pulling the rug from underneath them more satisfying. They can then look back and say, *Even though the story has undergone a major plot twist, I completely understand how we got here. How cool!*

Does my unreliable narrator need to be a villain?

NO. This technique can be used for your protagonist or any point-of-view character in your story. This person or entity does not need to be inherently bad. In fact, the technique works just as well with children, innocents, or people who do not have intention to do harm. The term "unreliable" only refers to *how* they present the story, meaning they may inadvertently or purposefully misinterpret or omit the facts needed to fully understand the story.

Can unreliable narration be used in genres other than mystery?

YES! Since all narrators have the potential for some misrepresentation, this technique can be incorporated into any of the other fiction genres. Here are a few examples:

- *The Catcher in the Rye* (1951) by J.D. Salinger – Drama/Coming of Age
- *Life of Pi* (2001) by Yann Martel – Fantasy/Adventure
- *Lolita* (1955) – Drama/Romance

If unreliable narration is new to you, here are some other modern classics that have used this method to great success. And yes, all of these novels are movies too, but I encourage you to read the books first since the literary approach to this concept is quite different than the cinematic one.

- *American Psycho* (1991) by Bret Easton Ellis
- *The Girl on the Train* (2015) by Paula Hawkins
- *Fight Club* (1996) by Chuck Palahniuk
- *Gone Girl* (2012) by Gillian Flynn
- *The Murder of Roger Ackroyd* (1926) by Agatha Christie
- *The Perks of Being a Wallflower* (1999) by Stephen Chbosky
- *Rebecca* (1938) by Daphne du Maurier
- *We Need to Talk About Kevin* (2003) by Lionel Shriver

Characters

"Readers measure the good guys by the bad guys."
~Frank Robinson, author of *The Glass Inferno* (1974)

Characters are the lifeblood of your story. In order for the reader to care about your plot, he must care about the people in it. So once you've established a premise, develop your primary characters. For suspense, you may want to start by designing your villain. This may be different from the approach you would take when writing in other genres; however, in suspense stories, since the villain is known from the start or unmasked early in the narrative, his dastardly deeds are often what define the protagonist and her quest.

Which brings me to the quote that opens this chapter.

I chose this quote because it underscores an important maxim about characterization: No matter how well you construct the protagonist, her characterization means nothing if you've pitted her against a weak antagonist or an entity that fails to truly challenge her. In short, don't draft wishy-washy villains. Give serious thought to your bad guy's backstory and motivation. The audience should always feel that your novel's perceived threat is real and that your heroine will suffer grave (and lasting!) consequences as a result.

For this reason, it is often said that in suspense, the antagonist's actions propel the story in the early stages. He has a goal, and he's willing to break the rules to achieve it. The protagonist soon finds herself standing in the way of that success and that's how your story gains conflict.

Remember, no heroine can be dubbed courageous until she's forced to face her fears. Rising to the challenge will be what defines her, but how does a writer expose that heroine's weakness? Start with a worthy opponent who will act as the catalyst for her growth.

Villains

Why do we love villains like The Joker and Catwoman just as much as Batman? Because despite their evil ways, they are well-drawn characters with sympathetic backstories that legitimize their intent. We've all told lies or hurt someone for our own gain, but you wouldn't call yourself a villain, would you? Of course not. You undertook those minor misdeeds for a justifiable reason, a greater good. So if you want to create a villain who readers will remember, start by building a strong justification.

Villainous motives typically align with a universal idea that the reader can understand and somewhat commiserate with since we've all had painful or disturbing conundrums that have pushed us to the brink. That's why the motives most often used by the bad guy are variations on a desire for more money, power, love, or fear. Of course, these often get broken down further into things like hate, envy, rage, greed, or revenge. However, all of those things fall under the big four.

No matter what motivation you choose, start by identifying areas of vulnerability and redemptive qualities. A great example is Batman's Mr. Freeze aka Victor Fries. Now, bear with me on using a comic book example, but you will soon see how well this all applies.

Victor Fries becomes Mr. Freeze when the corporation he works for agrees to place his terminally ill wife in cryogenic stasis until he can find a cure for her illness. However, the company's CEO soon shuts down the project to cut costs, condemning his wife to death. Fries tries to reason with the CEO, but the CEO gets angry and knocks Fries into a batch of cryonic chemicals, turning Fries into a distorted figure of a man who can only survive in subzero temperatures. Everything that follows for Mr. Freeze — robbing, killing, et cetera — is an attempt to regain what he has lost. His *motivation* is not just anger or malice but also (and more importantly) *love* — the universal element that makes Mr. Freeze less monster and more human. As a result, *DC Comics* has built a more compelling confrontation (and a morally gray one) by making the bad guy's actions *seem* justified. And this is something you can do too, since suspense villains often embody the gray or dark side of an ethical argument.

Even if your manuscript doesn't give a detailed version of the villain's backstory, make sure to provide enough clues to help the reader understand the transition from man to maniac. Even if your villain is only a small part of the story, fully develop his characterization. Think about his life, not just in terms of the hero, but as a whole. What would he do if the hero didn't exist? How have his childhood dreams and goals shaped the person he is today? What was the life-changing event that turned him "evil"? What's your villain's greatest desire and why? How does he justify his crimes to himself? Give real thought to these questions so that you can view the story from the villain's perspective. This will allow you to write scenes with a villain who is properly motivated, rather than writing clichéd versions of evil.

You're also welcome to build your story so that there are two tiers to the villainy. Level one might include the sidekicks, henchmen, or entities that present a more immediate threat to the hero during the story's manhunt. These people could be less powerful precursors to the Big Bad or brainwashed followers that the hero eventually converts to aid in his quest. Of course, the second level is the villain himself whose cunning or strength will outmatch anything the hero has seen before.

In fact, a good villain is nothing without a level of intimidation. In our example, Mr. Freeze is not physically intimidating to Batman, but he is an intellectually intimidating. Victor Fries uses his knowledge of science to outwit our hero until the very end. Use this same leveling agent with your villain. Give your villain an area of expertise or specialized knowledge that makes him unique (or *better* than the hero). This will put your villain on an even playing field with your hero if you've created a superhuman protagonist OR ensure a suspenseful situation if your hero is an average person. Creating a villain who has goals and knows how to accomplish them builds tension in the reader. For a moment the audience will think, *is the hero going to fail?* You want to evoke that tension because it gets your audience emotionally involved. They won't want to put the book down. Create a villain who is too weak or too stupid to sufficiently challenge the hero, and the audience will get bored. The story's excitement dwindles because the hero's life hasn't really been threatened.

But with that said, a word of caution: Don't draft a villain who is substantially more powerful than the protagonist without giving the hero a way to "level up" (see *The Matrix*) or "even the playing field" (see Harry Potter and his horcruxes). As the story reaches its climax, you eventually want to work toward an "even match" to ensure a see-saw dynamic and guarantee that *each side* will need to make sacrifices and alter their strategy in order to gain advantage against their adversary.

Your villain should hold beliefs or ideals that not only oppose those of the protagonist but challenge or tempt the protagonist's entire belief system — remember, beliefs don't matter unless they are tested. Therefore, a well-written antagonist has their own clear goals and motivations for the events of the story, and takes specific action throughout the plot, that forces your protagonist to react. In addition, the conflict between the hero and villain needs to have impact on the overall story question. This means every time the two titans cross paths, one of them will lose something and be thrust into another disaster. There is a cost or sacrifice to their interactions and through these sacrifices the audience gets a view of how important their wants and beliefs are to themselves and the story world at large. Plus, your characters will be forced to change — a primary component to any character arc — as they grapple with the consequences of their moral and physical dilemma. These losses and the fallout that follows also act as one of the major factors for getting your audience invested in the book's conflict.

I know that's a ton, so let's wrap it all up in the simplest terms: A strong story thrives on conflict. When your villain's brilliance (initially) outshines your hero's moral strength, you create conflict. Even if we subconsciously know the hero wins in the end, we still expect the villain to have intricate plans and cunning schemes that actually work. Give your villain a goal that rivals the hero's and a logical plan toward achievement. Allow him to succeed until the very end — whereupon the hero digs deep and discovers something about himself that changes the tide.

Finally, a few logistical things:

If you start your first chapter or prologue with the main villain, keep it brief. The audience often creates a connection with the first character they encounter, so we want that to be the hero when possible. Also, when starting with the villain, try to keep his agenda hidden from the readers either by relaying the scene from the perspective of the victim or using the neutral voice of third-person objective. Why? Well, it adds a bit of menace and mystique if the villain lingers in the shadows for a moment. But more importantly, if readers know too much about your villain too soon, they may become frustrated with the hero for taking twice as long to obtain the same information. So, let the audience to learn about the antagonist along with hero. That way, they can experience the hero's cleverness and participate in his agenda.

Similarly, if you opt for an opener that showcases rape, torture, or mayhem, keep it short and don't linger. You may think you're setting a tone, but you could very well be alienating the reader. Audiences often shun the grotesque and fail to respond to intense brutality in the prologue or opening chapter, especially if that event isn't connected to a clear cause or identifiable character.

Bad Guy Behavior

Now that you have created a solid backstory for your villain and given her the grit to play dirty, start adding reprehensible traits that will have your readers screaming for your bad guy's death. I've created a short list of tension-building bad person behavior to get us started, but this is a small part of a larger character-building process. Don't arbitrarily adopt the list below. Avoid a villain who is bad for the sake of being bad. Brainstorm based on your character's backstory so that the dark traits you create heighten the action in a realistic manner and enhance the villain's personal stakes.

The Bruiser: This villain tortures and toys with our hero. She may already have a position of power over the hero, or she may create one using superior intellect and strength. This bad person has no problem inflicting pain and gets pleasure from the sight of seeing others suffer. This villain's motto: "Shoot first ask questions later," or "Hit them where it hurts."

The Pretender: This villain is hard to catch and confront because their reputation is pure. However, underneath this perfect exterior beats the heart of a vicious liar, cheat, killer, et cetera. This villain's motto: "Smile in their faces then do whatever the heck you want."

The Traitor: This villain starts out as the hero's friend or someone trustworthy. Information gained through her bond with the hero eventually destroys him. The villain is uplifted or vindicated through the betrayal of the hero. This villain's motto: "I'm just looking out for number one."

More often than not, a strong villain — one who is fueled by a justifiable motivation — can influence the tone of your story.

So get out there and make a great one.

Checklist: Villains

Give your villain a grand entrance. Because suspense has the villain on the page from the very beginning, his introduction should be memorable and impressive. Let the audience know how why and how this character is dangerous. Make the reader understand what horrific act or skewed belief has driven him to this morally corrupt behavior. You could even introduce your villain through an unusual feature or unique trait like a sixth finger or an odd scar. How did they get it? What's the story behind it, and how does he feel about discussing it?

· **Give your villain a realistic motivation.** What part of your villain's personal life or personality could provide believable motivations for his actions? Perhaps he is someone who does the wrong thing for the right reasons, or he goes too far in the wrong direction because he's lost sight of his true goal. Is he evil as a result of wound? Evil because he was raised to be evil? Evil out of obligation to another? Born evil? Evil due to a creature or entity from another realm? Look at the situation from all angles. What does he want and why? How does he believe the hero hinders his goal? How does he justify his actions to himself? Make sure to have a completely developed motivation — even if it is never fully shared in the story, it should be implied through his actions.

Give your villain a magnificent obsession. You bad guy's goal should be as essential to him as the air he breathes. He is willing to break moral codes and sacrifice everything to succeed. This is what makes him so dangerous, ruthless, and cunning but also what makes him vulnerable. His preoccupation blinds him to his other options.

Give your villain something to lose. The conflict between villain and hero should force them both to make sacrifices — in what they want and what they believe — and those sacrifices show the audience what's important to them as well as complicate the story so that the battle escalates moving forward.

Give your villain a persona. The best stories have uber-memorable villains, so don't be afraid to give yours a little personality. Hubris, hedonism, flamboyance, and self-righteousness are great places to start in order to make your hero grandiose. Also, consider whether your baddie is the private type who covertly executes her misdeed like Amy Dunne in Gillian Flynn's *Gone Girl* (2012) — or someone more grandiose, who puts his schemes out there for everyone to see like John Doe in the movie *Se7en* (1995).

Give your villain teeth. Don't you hate it when the villain in an old James Bond movie spends five minutes telling Bond how he is going to kill him and then doesn't do it? (If you don't know James Bond, then think Austin Powers because those movies spoof this concept well.) If so, then be sure to create a villain who can back up her threats. The story loses its stakes and its logic if the villain doesn't follow through with her plan to make things worse for the hero. Keep your villain dastardly and frightening by having her do things that physically or emotionally wound your hero. Every time your villain confronts the hero there should be a disastrous and permanent consequence — a consequence that the hero cannot immediately undo.

FAQ: Villains

Does a villain need to change? No. They can, but it it's not a story requirement. Because the narrative centers around your protagonist, that's the person who should change by the end of the novel. In fact, the protagonist often beats the antagonist by going through change or undergoing a transformation that would not have been possible if not for the push from the opposition. But with that said, if a villain does change, it is usually part of the cycle of redemption or triumph for the protagonist. Most of the time, the antagonist will not change.

Do all stories need an antagonist? Not every story needs a specific villain, but every great story must contain conflict. Whether that conflict is man against himself, man against nature, or man against technology, your protagonist should face a challenge that disrupts their belief system. However, it doesn't always need to take the physical form of a person. For example, in *Planes, Trains, and Automobiles* (1987), you may love or hate Del Griffith (John Candy), but he is not the antagonist of the story, rather he is the catalyst for Neal Page's (Steve Martin) realization about the true meaning of Thanksgiving. The central conflict, or antagonistic force, is Neal's inability to get home in time for the holiday. Or consider *Big* (1988) where there is no clear villain or even an antagonistic force, but the conflict is an internal one as Josh (Tom Hanks) learns to appreciate his childhood by seeing how difficult it is to be an adult.

Heroes

Think of the main character as the foundation for your story. Get the key elements of this person wrong, and you're building your novel on uneven, or potentially disastrous, ground.

Strive for a protagonist who's both ordinary and valiant. That is to say, rather than creating an unflappable or invincible type hero, it's usually more satisfying to the readers if you throw a normal person into increasingly harrowing situations. That way, he must summon all of his resources and inner strength to overcome the odds. Readers relate more personally to this type of main character and build a stronger bond. On the other hand, the hero may be an outcast or rulebreaker whose moral fiber or personal code leads him to risk his life for another. This sense of integrity is what separates the hero from the unscrupulous villain.

Either way, every main character has a vital goal based on their beliefs, and the story revolves around the actions they take to get said goal as well as the consequences that arise when they fail. Actions without consequences don't propel the story forward (and aren't memorable to the reader) because they have no outward or inward effect on the protagonist and fail to add to the story's conflict.

In addition, it helps to give your hero a flaw or blind spot that acts as his weakness and explains why he initially struggles to complete his mission. This can be a phobia, addiction, or bad habit. Or you can create a personal wound from the hero's past that the audience will find relatable such as a loss or failure. This will often be something that the villain exploits on his path to victory. You can tie this wound or flaw to the actions the hero takes as well as the internal and external conflicts the hero faces throughout the story to demonstrate how his personal problems have affected his past and foreshadow how they'll influence his future.

Either way, you'll also need to establish what's important to your hero and make it clear to the audience so that they can rally behind him when he succeeds and be crestfallen when he loses sight of his goal.

Finally, while your villain may occasionally succeed through luck, you can't allow your hero the same pleasure. Don't let him go through hardship unscathed. If your hero manages to succeed at a task on the first try, your story has a major tension problem. There must be a massive effort exerted at all times and a major consequence as a result. In the book *Scene & Structure* (1993) by Jack M. Bickham, he describes that the path to the hero's goal should always be blocked with a conflict that leads to a disaster that complicates the achievement of the goal. He suggests that, as a result, each scene should end in one of the following: "no" (goal blocked and protagonist forced to try new tactic); "no, and furthermore" (goal blocked and things get worse); or "yes, but" (goal seemingly achieved but a new problem emerges). This disaster then inspires a new goal or sets up a new scene. That's why your hero wins through hard work rather than dumb luck.

FAQ: Heroes

Does the protagonist need to change? Not necessarily. Fiction stories are meant to examine our morals and values through conflict. If your story doesn't have change, you've created a narrative with low stakes. However, this doesn't always mean the protagonist himself must change. In the end, either the protagonist's beliefs change (preferred) or the beliefs of the people around him change (acceptable). In other words, the protagonist must change his beliefs to succeed or the opposition must succumb to his beliefs as part of their defeat. For example, in *Ferris Bueller's Day Off* (1986), even though Ferris is clearly the protagonist his smug disdain for authority remains consistent throughout the film. However, his best friend Cameron (Alan Ruck) undergoes significant growth. He learns that life is too short to live in fear and that he should take risks, including standing up to his domineering father. Choosing to have the change occur in Cameron, allows the audience to revel in Ferris's rebelliousness while still delivering on the film's need to have an emotional catharsis in the finale.

Exercise: Villains and Heroes

Start working on your characterizations by developing a relationship between your protagonist and antagonist. Decide if they have a history and brainstorm where they may have first met. Or if their conflict is new, where will they meet? Is it in person or some other means? What triggers their opposition? What facets of your hero can be reflected in your villain or vice versa? Play with different scenarios until you discover something that excites you. Then write a short passage in the villain's voice describing his potential misdeeds. How will he execute? What traps can he spring on the hero? Next, write an entry in the voice of your hero. How does he respond to the villain's threats? Use both passages to start your outline.

Checklist: Heroes

❖ **Heroes are brave.** Those who start off self-conscious or cowardly eventually find their voice. In this instance, bravery is defined as being afraid but doing it any way.

❖ **Heroes are skilled.** Most have a special skill, talent, or profession. Some might not recognize its value at first, but as they work to overcome the obstacles of the story, they discover the importance of their abilities.

❖ **Heroes are resourceful.** Inevitably, a hero loses his resources or allies or becomes isolated from help and must dig deep to find a way out.

❖ **Heroes are flawed.** Most have a physical, psychological, or sociological flaw that initially keeps them from seeing the truth of their situation. This flaw may have formed from losing a loved one or being the victim of grave injustice. The villain may have a similar such flaw, but the difference is the hero is working to overcome his flaw by being heroic while the villain hopes to heal his wound through corruption.

❖ **Heroes are selfless.** This is what distinguishes him from the villain, who will only sacrifice for himself. Again, as with most of these, this may be a trait that the hero builds up over the course of the story.

❖ **Heroes are relatable.** Once again, "relatable," not likeable. Why? Likeable is much more difficult to pin down and implies that you need someone who is morally pristine. Since thrillers work in the gray area between black and white, you simply need a protagonist who is relatable or redeemable. Someone the audience can rally behind when situations get tough and the decision making gets squidgy.

❖ **Heroes are responsible.** While not every hero is paragon of righteousness, most have a moral code that rules their actions (think Batman).

Antiheroes

An antihero is a central character who is deeply flawed and has a twisted moral compass — e.g. he may do the wrong thing for the right reasons — but whose flaws become a potential source of redemption for himself and others. It is this redemptive quality that takes the antihero out of the villain category and puts them in a semi-heroic place where we want them to succeed despite their selfish motives and questionable behavior. Common examples include *Deadpool* (2016), *Logan* (2017), and Walter White from the television show *Breaking Bad* (2008-2013).

Antiheroes can be brilliant protagonists; however, their behavior may alienate some readers. So in this section, we will provide some tips on how to create these heavily flawed characters in a way that still elicits sympathy — or at least interest, which is really the key to getting the audience on your antihero's side.

Tips for Making Antiheros Work

Antiheros have struggles. We feel for those in jeopardy even if that jeopardy is the product of the character's own making. To want something so bad that you must fight to get it, often affords the character a little vulnerability in the audience's eyes because we are all familiar with the physical and emotional hardships of failure. And the more we can make those kinds of emotional connections to our antihero and their choices, the more human they will appear. We can also rationalize bad behavior when that character is struggling against a larger force or entity that's unflinchingly evil. We see this quite often in the crime genre where career criminals are striving to outwit a corrupt system. A prime example is the television series *Money Heist* (2017-2021), where we are introduced to a ruthless band of thieves who we eventually want to see succeed due to the way law enforcement changes the rules of the game. We root for the bad guys turned underdogs, even if they are employing horrific tactics, because sometimes being immoral is the only way to level the playing field (and we admire those who don't take shit lying down).

Antiheros are unpredictable. Nothing makes for a more compelling read than a character who consistently does the unexpected. We stayed glued to our seat to see what shocking, hilarious, vicious, or heartbreaking act they will engage in next. However, it is when this impulsiveness is used for good that the audience draws close to the antihero. This usually occurs at the moment when we least expect it, which is what makes it so satisfying. Consider the comic book character Harley Quinn who, madness aside, has transitioned from villain to antihero over the years, primarily thanks to the movie portrayals by Margot Robbie. She's a wildcard who is neither evil nor virtuous, rather a volatile blend of both, who also seems to have a soft spot for children and animals — which in the film *Birds of Prey* (2020) allows her to be a suitable protagonist via the bylaws of the antihero.

Antiheroes have a convoluted moral code. Their skewed way of looking at the world is what makes them so appealing. In one breath, they may want to act like the hero, shooting only if shot upon and rescuing the innocent. But as soon as things fail to work in their favor, they revert to their typical line of thinking: *Shoot first, ask questions never.* I selected that particular quote because it is a line from the television show *Ash v. Evil Dead* (2015-2018) where titular character Ash Williams (Bruce Campbell) learns early in the first season that he is forever destined to save the world, but throughout the series he struggles to stay (sober and) true to the mission, often failing to apply vengeance and forgiveness at the proper times. We see a similar illogical approach to heroism in *Deadpool 2* (2018) where Wade Wilson, who usually isn't a team player, joins forces with a small portion of the X-men to save a troubled youth.

Antiheroes are secretive. Personal confidences, riddles, or enigmas are not only interesting but addictive and memorable. By creating a character who hides his true feelings, you develop tension. The audience wonders *what is he thinking? Why is he doing what he is doing?* And by holding things close to the vest, your antihero is given room to surprise us. What they've hidden and why make speak to a grander moral purpose that will ultimately redeem them in the eyes of the reader or view. For instance, in the film *Suicide Squad* (2016) we are introduced to Will Smith's version of Deadshot, who is an expert marksman and assassin, but wants desperately to build a better life for his daughter. However, because of his dangerous lifestyle and poor choices, this is something that he initially keeps from the team that becomes his surrogate family.

Antiheroes have a sense of humor. For all of their dark behavior, the most memorable antiheroes are the ones that make us laugh. Not to mention, this is a great way to add a little sweet to their otherwise sour behavior and mitigate the bad taste in the audience's mouth. Similarly, it helps if your antihero is a hedonist in the manners of food, drink, or mischief as it will allow the audience to indulge in their own bad vices through your character.

Antiheroes are honest. Not in the traditional sense, but they are truthful with themselves about how dastardly or selfish they can be at times, which makes their behavior a little easier to swallow. Self-awareness is often something true villains lack, so this behavior definitely differentiates them from the crowd. But this approach becomes particularly interesting if writing in a close point of view like first person or deep third, where this battle of their good side versus their bad side becomes a central part of the story's internal conflict as seen in novels like *Darkly Dreaming Dexter* (2004) by Jeff Lindsay or its contemporary *You* (2014) by Caroline Kepnes. The close perspective creates an intimacy that bonds the character with the reader and makes it hard to break loose once we're inside their minds.

Antiheroes have a hidden heart. Even though most are egotistic and/or delusional, many antiheroes manage to soften their otherwise craggy façade by having a moment of selflessness. While this approach can take many forms, as noted in our previous examples, a highly nuanced example of this tip can be seen in the film *Kill Bill: Vol. 1* (2003). Early on, we learn of the horrific attempt on Beatrix Kiddo's life as well as her background as a highly trained assassin hellbent on executing a "roaring rampage of revenge." As she mercilessly slices through her enemies, she runs the risk of becoming as despicable as her adversaries, until we learn the main reason she is insistent upon getting to Bill isn't about herself but about her love for a daughter she thinks she's lost. This helps absolve some of her actions in the viewers' eyes because audiences feel for those who feel for others.

In a nutshell, these contradictions in the antihero's characterization are a sign that even a wayward protagonist can change. Readers will often forgive obnoxious or even heinous behavior if the character has the ability to learn from his mistakes and seeks to rectify the sins he's committed against himself and others. In short, his self-reflection leads to his redemption. And that redeemability goes a long way — which, combined with being captivating, is what makes antiheroes such fantastic leads for a suspense story.

Secondary Characters

Secondary characters should include people who enhance the hero's ability to get things done either by improving his skills, knowledge, or access. Examples of such characters are the sidekick, best friend, mentor, love interest, foil, and nemesis. Having these characters be at odds throughout via contrasting viewpoints, qualities, abilities, and beliefs ensures that their scenes will have plenty of tension and conflict. This will also help clarify the value system in the world where your story takes place. So take time to consider: What new perspective will this secondary character bring to the story? How is this different from the hero's point of view? And how can this person's outlook or skills augment or detract from the hero's own abilities?

Naturally, you want to avoid character cliches like the hooker with the heart of gold, the hard-boiled detective with the drinking problem, et cetera. Scratch the first idea that comes to mind, and work for a new angle. Try giving your secondary characters an unusual attribute, ability, or philosophy like a love interest who speaks five languages or a best friend who believes that everything he's learned about people can be summed up by the kids' series *Thomas the Tank Engine*. It also helps if some of the characters know each other or are connected in some way so that they can act as a support network for the hero. Start by establishing a history between characters or alluding to familial ties.

But in general, let your secondary characters evolve as your plot progresses. You don't need to do a character sketch of every character up front, just the main ones to get your story started and the rest will evolve as the needs for your story become clear. Let the plot decide who they have to be and what purpose they serve in the story before you solidify their existence. Have your characters interact with the world you've built, and give us their perspective on what it means to them. What do they think about what they are experiencing? This will give you the freedom to create tense motivated scenes with believable conflicts.

To keep the audience guessing, stop after each scene and consider what the reader would expect to happen next. List three directions the story might take, then scrap those and do the opposite. Work for the unexpected.

Conflict

In fiction writing, conflict is often created by an antagonist, but conflict doesn't need to come from a person. Conflict can be an oppositional force that stands between the protagonist and his goal. But either way, conflict must increase over the course of the story. This is an integral part of the narrative's rising action — the stronger the opposing force, the more room your character will have to grow as they fight against the opposition.

Therefore, you can also think of conflict as being based on action and interaction. It is a person's reaction to conflict that drives the plot. And over the course of the story, the protagonist's interaction with the conflict must move from reactive to proactive as part of his growth during the course of the narrative.

There are two types of conflict — internal and external — and they must work together to complicate plot and further characterization. Think of internal conflict as the struggle of opposing beliefs that occur within a character. These thoughts drive his or her development as a person and can encompass anything from mental illness to self-doubt to fearful emotions or unrequited desires. External conflict pits the character against a force outside themselves. These forces oppose the character's desires and create tensions, problems, and challenges that keep the hero from his goal. However, a story's external conflict should still contain a personal element that connects back to the lead character because if a conflict is personal, a character's reaction to the external obstacles will eventually reveal the emotional flaws and struggles that encompass his internal conflict. For example, the cop isn't just diffusing a bomb in an elementary school, he's doing it at one attended by his eight-year-old daughter. Or to put it plainly, every story should have both external and internal conflict — especially internal conflict because that's how the audience will relate to your character.

Moreover, make sure every scene has conflict and tension — even if it is as simple indecision, self-doubt, mistrust, paranoia, or a disagreement. Allowing the story to unfold without conflict makes for a dry narrative. Every scene needs that catalyst for disaster, so don't let your sequences end with an easy resolution. The conflict should result in a further complication that motivates your hero to take additional action. In other words, the conflict must lead to a setback — either an outward problem the viewpoint character must fix (e.g. a ticking timebomb) or an inward problem he must reflect upon (e.g. grappling with a choice) — before moving forward with renewed determination to try something new in the next set of scenes. This is how you drive your character's agenda and ensure his emotional growth.

Open your novel so that conflict and tension take the forefront as this is an excellent way to hook the reader. The mark of a great opening line is that it points to a problem or creates tension that draws the reader into the story. This doesn't need to be the book's overarching narrative conflict, but it should be significant enough that it leads the reader to the larger issues that will define the novel's main threat. Then as you approach the inciting incident escalate the conflict so that the story's primary challenge becomes clear. Each subsequent obstacle should build on the other so that audience begins to worry whether the hero has enough strength and resources to overcome the worst.

Lastly, make sure that the protagonist encounters true conflict, not inconveniences, minor accidents, or bad luck. Each problem should come with a long-standing consequence that forces the hero to suffer and evolve. Then put the emotion of that loss on the page so the audience can understand the difficulty and sacrifice involved. After all, the more severe the conflicts, the more compelling the story is to your audience. It is also important that the escalating conflicts are difficult enough that the solution isn't obvious. Easily overcome conflicts dilute the tension your story has worked to build. Conflicts shouldn't be predictable; they should deepen and grow along with the story as a whole.

Summary: Conflict

❖ Conflict is the struggle between two opposing forces.

❖ A character's goal + opposition = CONFLICT

❖ Conflict should appear in every scene; including sex scenes, chases, and celebrations

❖ Conflict provides tension and drives the story, and without these obstacles and opposition, the story is flat.

❖ Conflict is often used to reveal deeper meaning while highlighting character motivations, morals, and weakness.

❖ Conflict can be external or internal, and every story should have both (or at least the latter)

Tips for Creating Conflict

❖ Create a list of bad things to happen to your character

❖ Define your character's greatest fear then make it happen

❖ Demand that your characters sacrifice something of utmost important to them in order to reach their goal

❖ Find the drama in the mundane

❖ Make something irreversible happen in each scene (usually at the end), so the plot contains links of conflict

- Hold your character responsible for their actions

- Put your character's morals in direct conflict with what they must do to succeed in the story

- Put them in a fish out of water situation

Checklist for Writing Conflict

- What does your protagonist want? What are his internal and external goals? This will help you determine what's at stake and how strong the opposition must be to thwart, block, or overthrow their efforts.

- What does your protagonist stand to lose (consequences) if they fail? Think about the worst thing that could happen to your character to keep the high stakes.

- What does the protagonist stand to gain? This is the motivation that will keep your character fighting during the tough times.

- What things stand in the hero's way? How can he overcome or succumb? Conflicts that are easily beaten aren't interesting, so the opposition must be significant enough that the protagonist will struggle (try-fail) until he gains help or new insight.

Types of Conflict in Fiction

There are several types of conflict in fiction. Your story can straddle the line between several major dilemmas or focus on just one. But again, every story needs an overarching conflict, which are the types outlined here, as well as small personal conflicts for each scene.

Character vs. Self – an internal conflict or struggle from within; this can be a moral choice or a mental health struggle; notice that this is the only one on the list with a direct internal component even though the writer must work to infuse an internal conflict into each of these categories; e.g. *Fight Club* (1999)

Character vs. Character – most common conflict because it pits people against each other; one character's needs are in opposition to what the other wants; e.g. *Game of Thrones* (2011-2019)

Character vs. Nature – the protagonist is set in opposition to their surroundings—weather, wilderness, or a natural disaster; interesting because nature moves forward unchanged while man grapples with his internal and external reactions; key element is survival; e.g. *Castaway* (2009)

Character vs. Supernatural – the opposition is otherworldly—magic, demons, ghosts—which raises the stakes and creates tension by creating an unlevel playing field for your protagonist; e.g. *Ghostbusters* (1984)

Character vs. Technology – initially an external conflict, but often designed to raise a question about what it means to be human or what sets us apart from machines; e.g. *The Terminator* (1984) or *The Matrix* (1999)

Character vs. Society – external conflict with an opposition to government, culture, tradition, oppression, social norms; characters may be motivated to act by a moral code, freedom, justice, love, or a clear sense of right versus wrong; *Philadelphia* (1993)

Character vs. Fate – conflicts with gods or predestination; the protagonist tries to assert free will, a staple of Greek and Roman tragedies; *Oedipus the King* (429 B.C.) by Sophocles

Dialogue

Writing authentic dialogue requires having a clear picture of what information you'd like to convey in the scene as well as an understanding how the text will deepen your character's personality and propel the plot. In other words, what do you want the conversation (external and internal dialogue) to accomplish? Everything you write should move the narrative forward, resulting in a significant change in the characters and their situation. The audience should gain new insight with every dialogue exchange.

In short, each word should matter.

That's why fiction dialogue is a more heightened version of reality than natural conversation. We wouldn't want to portray how people actually talk with all the circumlocution, stutters, restarts, and pauses because it would be boring and difficult to read with any clarity. Real world dialogue relies on physicality, facial expressions, and context clues to solidify meaning. Therefore, fiction writers must be more efficient and direct in drafting their text. This is not to say that subtext, shade, attitude, or sarcasm cannot exist on the page. The point is that the construction of these conventions must be more deliberate so that the reader experiences the intended effect *and* gains a clear understanding of the goals and motivations of each person in the scene. In addition, we must share the scene information in an exciting and entertaining manner.

The key is to write dialogue where the characters are either in disagreement or discovery. Use subtext to highlight opposing agendas, hidden resentments, or subtle tensions bubbling under a typical exchange. That way, you're constantly sharing new data with the reader by setting up situations where your characters are able to express their desires, grievances, and motivations.

Eight D.I.A.L.O.G.U.E Tips

Dilute dialects: A little goes a long way when establishing dialects, accents, or speech affectations. There is no need for your Australian character to sound like Crocodile Dundee. Throwing in an *occasional* "mate," "no worries," or other such slang is enough to inspire a reader's imagination. Going overboard may offend your audience and distract from the story.

Identify your speakers: Make sure we know who is talking based on distinct speech patterns, proper dialogue tags, and the logical flow of conversation.

Activate the scene: Avoid a talking head scenario by keeping the story active. People rarely sit still and just talk — they pace, gesture, jump out of their seat when outraged. Place your characters in a location where they can do more than converse. Allow them to interact with each other and their surroundings. Doing so, will provide your readers with a clearer picture of the entire scene, inspire conflict (a must-have for every scene), and infuse your characters with some much-needed humanity.

Lose the lectures. Avoid passages where characters lecture each other. Realistic speech involves interruptions, starts and stops, silences, stares, disagreements, and the occasional yawn. Use nonverbal responses and other physical indicators (shrugged, laughed, coughed) to break up long blocks of speech so that the conversation occurs more naturally. Also, don't feel obligated to start conversations from the beginning or to end them with polite finality. Just like a good movie, a novel should cut to the chase and leave them wanting more.

Obliterate excess. As mentioned earlier, dialogue should never be a throwaway. Every word should have weight and purpose. If the dialogue doesn't fulfill some larger function within the narrative, those words must go.

Grasp grammar. This tip also refers word usage, capitalization, and punctuation—know the rules before you break them. This doesn't mean every sentence should reflect verbal perfection because people don't speak that way, yo! But knowing how to avoid things like passive voice, obsessive adverb usage, or poor comma placement can lead to a stronger manuscript. For example: *Let's eat grandma!* versus *Let's eat, Grandma.*

Utilize uniqueness. Create dialogue that reflects the specific time period, vocation, and location of your characters. Remember, a Navy seal and an interning doctor shouldn't share the same lingo or speech patterns. A character influences the language just as much as the language helps define the character. Take a hint from movies like *Pulp Fiction* (1994) where the laid back, quotable, badass dialogue is a direct reflection of Quentin Tarantino's seedy world of hit men. And yet, the speeches are realistic and relatable. Make sure your characters have an equally distinctive voice.

Extinguish exposition. Avoid jamming large amounts of exposition into dialogue. Instead, share some of that burden with the establishment of your setting or craft actions that indicate a reaction that exposes the exposition you wish to unveil. We'll expand on the do's and don'ts of this in the next section. Just remember, good background stays in the background and is weaved into the story without the reader realizing it.

Exposition in Dialogue

In the early stages of the book, when establishing the plot, you may be tempted to have the characters tell each other things they already know or speak about subjects they'd normally never discuss for the sake of informing the audience about backstory or some technical aspect of an upcoming event — be that a global crisis, the history of a case, or the hierarchy of the local judicial system. This act of two character re-informing each other of facts that are common knowledge in their world is known as maid-and-butler dialogue or the "as you know" trope.

The moniker comes from the stage — certainly during Shakespeare's Elizabethan Era but perhaps even as far back as the ancient Greeks of Euripides's day — where two characters (usually low status characters such as the maid and butler) would have a gossipy conversation to get the audience up to speed. This was meant to replace the convention of starting with a chorus or a narrator/character who addresses the audience. Such conversations usually go something like this:

> "Hey, Mike. Do you remember how we met in graduate school during Dr. Anderson's quantum mechanics class?"
>
> "Absolutely, Bob. As you know, it was during that course that I came up with my initial theory for teleportation ..."

Putting quotes around backstory isn't dialogue.
To be clear, maid-and-butler dialogue isn't the same as two characters mulling over clues and deciphering what they could potentially mean. That is an essential part of any fact-finding mission and will need to happen whenever your main character discovers something that changes her view the case. Maid-and-butler dialogue is a telling technique rather than showing technique, and it almost always reads as clunky, dull language.

So if the point of the above scene is to inform the audience about Mike's superior brainpower and hint at the possibility of seeing a teleportation device later in the text, show us those ideas through behavior and interaction, not reminiscence or gossip.

Fortunately, the audience's tolerance for this technique in literature is very low. Unfortunately, this problem is so prevalent in television and film that writers still think it is an acceptable way to deliver exposition. A word of warning: Film is a visual medium so even if the characters are clearly providing super boring backstory to clarify things to come, the viewer can gain stimulus from their environment, their accents, or the way they are dressed. We do not have this luxury in literature, so we must be cleverer about how we convey data or background information.

One way to do this is to bring in a neophyte character who acts as a stand in for the audience and looks at the situation with new eyes so that his or her questions about what's to come do not feel so contrived. This person's naiveté may lend a bit of comedy to the unfolding of the information, which will keep the audience engaged and turning pages. Not to keep bringing up Harry Potter, but his arrival into the wizarding world as depicted in the first and second books of the series (as well as the movies) are great examples of how incorporating a novice or fish-out-of-water character can make the inclusion of backstory, the establishment of a world, or the explanation of a new concept appear more seamless.

Another method is to incorporate news broadcasts or newspaper clippings that give the reader a quick overview of the problem and how it effects the larger world. And of course, if all else fails, the purest method is to sprinkle information evenly over the course of several scenes like breadcrumbs. Basically, save each specific piece of backstory for the moment when it is most relevant rather than dumping everything onto the page in one spot, giving away too much too fast. Good fiction sours when it fails to progress forward, so don't interrupt the reader with something from the past until they are clear about the present — and even then, do it briefly in a couple lines, not a couple chapters!

We must also ensure our dialogue remains as present and active as possible. An exchange that describes an off-stage event (even one in the adjacent present) doesn't have as much impact on the audience as a showing that sequence in real time. Where possible, show don't tell. However, actions or physical feats that are discussed rather than shown may be necessary if writing in a perspective where the audience is confined to one viewpoint; so in those instances, infuse your dialogue with more tension by creating a reason for the information exchange and ensuring the characters fall into disagreement about its veracity or importance or interpretation or what to do, et cetera. Allowing the news to cause conflict guarantees that both characters are active participants in the exchange and opens the door for additional characterization.

For example, a college gal named Lisa goes on the perfect date and returns to tell her roommate Jan that she's found "the one." Unimpressed, Jan wants nothing more than to return to the video game that has occupied most of her night. Lisa insists she listen and steps in front of the television to finish her point, causing her roommate to wipeout before reaching the game's top score. Jan, of course, blames Lisa and responds in a rage that exposes her friend's abysmal dating history. This leads Lisa to take a second, less idealistic look at her date, whereupon some suspicions are raised about her "perfect man," which act as a catalyst for the next step in the plot.

In fiction, the narrative should be balanced between dialogue, descriptive elements, and exposition — and in this case, exposition means establishing a novel's setting or building a character's background so that the reader understands story's intention and the characters' motivation, not an information dump.

Within this narrative trio, dialogue should reflect a character's beliefs, background, interests, and desires. This allows them to confess their fears, feelings, and attitudes in their own words. Consider each character's goals and what motivates them when crafting dialogue. Will their agenda cause them to be curt or courteous? Anxious or eloquent? Maybe someone has an accent based on where they grew up. Maybe they had rough upbringing that makes them mistrustful, so they treat every interaction as a confrontation. How characters talk to each other should reveal a ton about who they are —

sweet, controlling, smart, or dumb — and what they want out of the events that are set to unfold.

Whatever the case may be, conversations prove more interesting when the language for each person has its own rhythm and sense of expression. Use these differences in dialogue to shape the conflict between your characters. Start by figuring out why each person is talking and what they want — or rather, how are they using their dialogue to persuade and resist?

Often, we think of dialogue as a static thing. But language, like music, has movement. We can imply a lot about both the tension between characters and the speed of the interaction by crafting dialogue that plays with word choice and sentence length. Consider this scenario.

> "The defendant persuaded you to bring testimony today, correct?"
> "Yes, sir."
> "You've known him for nearly a decade?"
> "Yes."
> "Roomed with him in college?"
> "Ye—"
> "Officiated his wedding?"

Here we have a prosecutor grilling a witness on cross-examination. Note how the dialogue helps to shape the setting and the relationship of the characters without delving into a long explanation of where they are and why. In this instance, we removed the dialogue tags and physical beats and added increasingly short sentences to drive home the idea that the attorney is applying pressure. Of course, this is a brief example, but you can go much further in this regard, pushing and slowing the pace by varying syntax and being selective with diction.

Once you've completed the dialogue for your scene, read it aloud. Listen to the rhythm. Check to see if it sounds like language your characters you would use. Does it flow naturally, or do you find yourself tripping over unnecessary or complicated words?

Checklist: Dialogue

❖ Incorporate backstory only when and where it is needed.

❖ Avoid maid-and-butler dialogue.

❖ Keep the narrative moving forward with as few backward glances as possible.

❖ Ensure each dialogue exchange has conflict and builds character. Dialogue should never be a throwaway. Every word should have weight and purpose.

❖ Cut extraneous material like greetings, departures, and other space wasters such as having characters constantly address each other by name when talking one on one. The 1987 film *Fatal Beauty*, starring Whoopi Goldberg, is a hilarious display of this dialogue faux pas. *Mike Harper? What the hell are you doing here? Didn't I tell you never to come here, Mike Harper? Dammit, Mike, you're going to get us both killed.*

❖ Study the proper use of dialogue for any character meant to use jargon or specialized knowledge from a scientific or technical field. Integrate the language in a manner that allows the audience to derive meaning from context clues, but don't sacrifice authenticity. Do your research.

Setting

You can't create suspense without invoking the power of a good setting. Nothing hooks an audience better than giving them the feeling that they too have crept down the eerily dark hall, climbed the treacherous mountain, or outrun the enemy. And for that reason, writers should think of setting as much more than the physical location for a novel. Yes, setting provides the "when" and "where" of a story, but smart artists know it can also influence the "why" of your tale — or rather, the reason things are happening. Remember, actions arise out of conflict, and conflict is often the product of our environment.

Consider the Overlook Hotel in *The Shining* (1977) by Stephen King. The remote location and its supernatural activity literally and figuratively cause discord between the occupants. This is not to say that you need to personify or bring your otherwise inanimate setting to life, but the locations you choose shouldn't be arbitrary. They should contribute to the narrative by establishing a mood, providing an obstacle, or mirroring a theme. For example, *Sex and the City* would take on quite a different flavor if set in Spokane, Washington, or Salt Lake City, Utah, so use your setting to reflect on how your characters feel about their surroundings.

In fact, we should approach the development of setting with the same seriousness that we do characterization by asking ourselves how the atmosphere will complicate or facilitate our story question. What obstacles does the setting help create? How does this location affect how my characters speak, dress, behave, et cetera? What makes this setting unique, and how do those elements advance my plot?

Use your locations as a metaphor that builds additional meaning into the narrative. Regardless of whether you're writing a disaster thriller or a romantic comedy, the setting should enhance the story's authenticity and drive the action. In this regard, perhaps it is easier to think of setting as the canvas upon which the story's hardships unfold. I think this is an interesting approach to the definition since setting often acts as the unifying element between environment, character, and conflict.

So, use your initial setting to hook the reader into the story. For instance, if you're writing a fantasy that encompasses a whole world of magic or an international thriller that spans several continents, start small and only expand once you've acclimated your audience. Give each scene its own unique setting — and hence, its own set of attributes and problems apart from the story's overall backdrop — that will further anchor the reader to your specific place and time. While you don't ever want to leave the audience in limbo about "where" and "when," you also don't need drown them with a tsunami of information. Setting is something that you will work on beat by beat. Take your time and do your best to pique the senses of your reader. What does your world sound like? Smell like? Does it have futuristically smooth lines or the rough edges of a desert landscape? Immerse the audience bit by bit rather than relying on a single, static visual representation.

Description

Imagine you are describing a new love interest to your best friend. Would you start by describing his eye color and height, or would you talk about the way he jumps up to take a shower the minute you finish making love? Most people start with the pillow talk because it gives your bestie so much more information about your boyfriend and the dynamics of the relationship than a simple run down of his vital statistics.

Focusing on behaviors and habits is also the preferred method when creating character descriptions for fiction because such details help build a memorable personality and attitude. In other words, make sure your descriptions are more than just a laundry list of physical attributes. Instead, work to include actions, reactions, and quirks that will have a significant impression on the reader. For example, which is better?

> *Marc sat at the conference table in a rumpled blue blazer.*
>
> *Marc sat at the conference table with the disheveled look of a homeless man freshly roused from sleep.*

In my opinion, the second gives us a clearer picture of Marc and is far more memorable. Sure, the first sentence clearly tells us what he's wearing. But in the second sentence, not only do we get the impression that he is inappropriately dressed, but there is also an indication that he's also probably ill-prepared for whatever comes next — which creates an instant impression about Marc and his level of responsibility.

Bottomline, we want our details to do more than create an empty snapshot of our world. They should also speak to a character's behavior or attitude in a manner that will trigger an empathetic response from our audience. Work to create descriptions that serve multiple purposes. This may mean going deeper into your point of view and describing objects the way your character would see and experience them. Use active verbs to show how your character feels and mix sensory information with the internal and external action of the scene to develop a description that is truly unforgettable.

However, this is not to say that you should never tell us what a character is wearing. After all, physical details or clothing descriptions can help to clarify the reader's understanding about certain aspects of setting or character — e.g. a coat hints at seasonal setting, a uniform suggests a specific profession. But if those physical details have no bearing on the story or could be changed without affecting the outcome or if they fail to aid character development, why bother? Obviously, the information is not needed.

Besides, readers appreciate when the action isn't brought to a halt by a fashion rundown, so don't introduce each new character with an immediate description dump. This tactic is detrimental to a story's momentum because the potency of the action is diluted while everything is placed on hold. It also invites predictability and drains tension if all the characters are introduced the same way. A stronger approach is to spread description throughout the scene by incorporating some details into the dialogue and aligning one's physical attributes with the behavior in the scene.

For example, your meddlesome neighbor may have a big nose, but rather than simply saying that, indicate that she often leads with her snout like a bloodhound on the trail of a good bone. Remember, readers like to see characters in motion, so devise descriptions that aren't static. Also, use the dialogue between characters or the way someone speaks to shape an image of how that person behaves — and by extension, what they are like. A person who uses broken English and lacks social graces conjures a different picture than someone who calls everyone "sugar" in a lyrical southern accent. In addition, don't be afraid to have characters talk about each other, which helps shape relationships and demonstrate behaviors. Finding ways to incorporate your descriptions more seamlessly into the text will help your story maintain a faster pace, which is essential for suspense tales.

Concrete Language

We cannot have a discussion about description and setting without mentioning concrete language. This refers to the tangible or sensory elements of your description. In essence, it is the practice of being precise rather than generic. This concept is often taught in conjunction with diction because it involves selecting words that have a specific rather than a general meaning.

Concrete language is preferred because it conveys more information and makes your message clearer. And luckily, it is very easy to do. When writers say, "show, don't tell," they are often referring to the concept of concrete language. Showing is the act of giving concrete details, which adds texture to one's writing. But as with anything, be selective. We want to inform the reader, not overwhelm them.

- **General:** store
- **Less General:** department store
- **More Specific:** Sears
- **Concrete:** Sears at the Galleria Mall

***

- **General:** music
- **Less General:** electronic music
- **More Specific:** dubstep
- **Concrete:** Skrillex's "Bangarang"

***

Notice how each iteration provides more information and greater detail to hook the reader. This technique may be important if you're receiving revision notes about a lack of specificity.

General: Our vacation was great fun.

Concrete: Our rafting trip was filled with adventure.

General: The red and white flowers were blooming in our yard.

Concrete: Crimson and white petunias bloomed around our backyard patio.

This is not to say that abstract ideas like the gut feeling that comes when a character discovers they are being watched by a strange entity in the woods doesn't have its place. Just make sure that when you take that approach, you are doing so consciously and that you are not relying on a generic concept to convey what should be a very personal moment for your character. You will still need to dig deep to be descriptive and be mindful that storytelling is a combination of symbols, actions, sensory details, and emotions.

Checklist: Setting and Description

❖ Are the descriptions full of sensory imagery and concrete language?

❖ Does each description serve a larger purpose in the story by aiding in characterization or setting?

❖ Do the descriptions align with the character's behavior to help make them more memorable?

❖ Are the descriptive elements spread throughout the scene rather than being dumped in one paragraph immediately upon the character's initial introduction?

❖ Does the dialogue tell us anything about the characters? And is the dialogue distinct enough that we can differentiate between the speakers based on their attitude, diction, and point of view?

❖ How does the environment help enrich the characterization and action?

❖ Are the characters interacting with their environment and each other in a manner that reveals more about the situation and possible conflict?

Stakes

Every story must have **high stakes**. Why? Because low stakes, or no stakes, implies there are no repercussions for failure and no rewards for victory. Under such circumstances, readers wouldn't know what outcome to root for or why they should care. Every aspect of the story would appear easy or inconsequential for the hero, which makes it difficult to create conflict and suspense — key ingredients for a successful story.

But what are stakes? And how do we create them?

Stakes are defined as what the protagonist stands to gain for his success or lose for his failure to reach the desired goal — this includes both the external and emotional consequences for his actions. Stakes are an essential story element because they force characters to stay vigilant despite the rising odds and insurmountable obstacles. And for our readers to care about our characters' goals, we must show there is something important at stake. Basically, the larger the consequences of success or failure, the more important the goal appears.

Writing a story with stakes means giving your characters choices with lasting consequences, so don't make your protagonist infallible. Allow her to make bad decisions that get her hurt or cause her to lose a loved one — or have her make good decisions that lead to further complications. In essence, every choice must have repercussions that affect the story in a significant manner. These will become the narrative stakes and will play a role in motivating the character to act. They will also help the reader become invested. To put it in literary terms, high stakes move the plot forward, engage the reader, and keep the characters growing and changing by fueling the motivations that drive them toward their goals. Stakes also aid in creating tension and suspense because when the audience realizes that the heroine faces legitimate danger, their concern and uncertainty about her success rises.

How to Add Stakes

The overall stakes in your story need to be high enough to sustain tension and reader interest throughout the narrative. I think the best advice on how to do this comes from James Scott Bell's *Super Structure: The Key to Unleashing the Power of Story*. He notes that stakes should always involve some form of death — whether that's an actual physical death as with a murder, a professional one such as with the loss of one's career, or a psychological one where the hero is battling some inner turmoil. Just like the novel's action, the stakes will increase as the story progresses.

If you're new to the idea of rising stakes, please realize that whether a consequence is harsh or mild will depend on both the genre of story and where the story begins. But in general, the audience will gauge whether your story stakes are successfully escalating by how much the loss or sacrifice affects the character. The plot's increasing stakes should force the protagonist to make riskier choices so that by the final act, some aspect of his personality, physicality, or spirituality has grown and matured. He's doing things he never would have thought possible, and the audience admires his determination in the face of uncertainty.

This also means that you as the writer must stop to show how the events of the narrative have taken a toll on the protagonist. You must also have a clear understanding of the character's breaking point — how much failure will erode his self-worth and/or his ability to focus on completing the mission. The reader gets to see the hero at his most vulnerable and becomes more invested in his plight as he figures out how to move himself out of loss into victory.

To define a story's stakes, ponder the following:

❖ What does the protagonist want to happen? What's her primary goal?

- What stands in the way of her goal?

- What does the protagonist hope to gain from the win?

- What will it cost her to get what she wants?

- How invested is the protagonist in the outcome? How much and in what way does achieving their goal matter? Is she willing to do almost anything to get what she wants? (This must be a "yes" answer!)

- What's at risk? What does the protagonist stand to lose if she fails? What are the internal and external consequences or repercussions?

- Does the goal — whether won or lost — constitute a defining moment in the main character's life?

To escalate the stakes, think about increasing the value of the goal, the need for the goal, or the penalty for failure. Alternatively, you could stack the odds against the protagonist by hindering his ability to act via decreased abilities, increased obstacles, lack of intel or influence, loss of allies or resources, missed opportunities, a phobia, et cetera.

Keep the audience guessing by avoiding stakes that remain constant or ramp upward in a predictable manner. The development of a successful story has a rising progression the undulates like a roller coaster delivering thrilling moments of action and suspense tempered by moments of reflection or levity before ascending to the next level where the penalties are even greater. Monotony of any sort will bore the reader and pull them out of your story. We must find innovative ways to constantly add new complications and make things worse for the characters — then follow through on the threats those dangers pose. Don't hold back. Bad things like loss, sickness, and death must happen to prove the stakes are real and lasting. The audience expects the protagonist to endure some suffering on the road to her goal and will root for her as she struggles through the process.

Another great way to elevate the stakes in your story is to incorporate a ticking clock to put the reader on the edge of their seat. This technique works because the time constraint makes success seem less certain as the deadline draws near and the heroine's options dwindle. It is also an extremely flexible method since a ticking clock can be incorporated into the frame of the overarching story or as a limited time period attached to a specific event. For example, ticking clocks can act as the grand countdown to some impending doom that begins in the first act — like 1998's *Run Lola Run* — or initiate a race against time that's triggered in the final act — like Ferris dashing through obstacles to beat his family back to the house in 1986's *Ferris Bueller's Day Off*. In both films, the consequences for failure are dire, but they are defined by their genres of thriller and comedy, respectively — Lola's (Franka Potente) boyfriend will die and Ferris (Matthew Broderick) will be forced to repeat his senior year of high school.

Another ticking clock option is to implement a time limit that the reader learns about but the protagonist doesn't. This amplifies the suspense via the use of dramatic irony, which triggers the nail-biting audience response: *How will our hero succeed with the odds staked against him?* Mix in a near miss, or a moment when it seems like the hero has won but things just get worse, and you have the ingredients for suspenseful sequence full of tension and stakes. Just remember, regardless of the technique used, make sure the ticking clock — and a way to measure its progress — are clear to the *audience* as a way to help reinforce the stakes.

Lastly, one of the biggest tips for building stakes is to connect your character's internal and external stakes to the larger conflict. That is to say, large-scale problems are often the backbone of conflict for a story. *The bus will blow once it hits fifty-five miles per hour. The terrorists will kill all the hostages. The asteroid is set to hit earth.* These disasters include massive stakes that affect more people than your protagonist. However, you should always try to tie some of your heroine's personal stakes into those major conflicts so that your story has a more relatable level of immediacy. Personal stakes involve the individual and can include physical, emotional, and/or mental threats.

For example, in the film *Die Hard* (1988), based on the novel *Nothing Lasts Forever* by Roderick Thorp, we have Officer John McClane fighting to not only save himself but an entire floor of office workers held hostage by a group of international terrorists. Those are external stakes on a large scale. However, the story is also wrapped in personal stakes since the reason McClane is there in the first place is due to his wife's position in the office. This combines his personal stakes with the task at hand — particularly when we consider that in the wake of the terrorists' first kill, John's wife becomes the de facto hostage leader, which puts her in further danger.

Of course, the amount of personal stakes you can add to those large-scale problems will often hinge on the type of story being told. Comedies, romances, domestic or psychological thrillers tend to already have stakes aligned with relationships or personal obstacles. *If I don't quit cheating, my wife will leave me.* On the other hand, stories with a larger scope, like spy stories, action adventures, or fantasies, usually have bigger stakes, so you'll need to work hard to include a personal element. *Failure to defeat the Dark Lord will result in an upheaval of the wizarding world, the enslavement of Muggles, and the loss of the friends who have become my surrogate family at Hogwarts.* Regardless, it's best to combine personal and grandiose stakes where possible to ensure adequate internal and external tension for your character.

In addition to large-scale and personal story stakes, each *scene* should have something significant on the line. Naturally, these stakes don't need to be nearly as dire, but it is a necessary part of keeping a scene interesting and will add layers of complexity to your protagonist's quest. A fantastic way to determine the stakes for each scene is to consider your protagonist's goal, motivation, and conflict as it pertains to each interaction. Then consider: What will she lose if she fails to achieve her goal?

But with the said, stakes don't need to increase every scene. Some scenes may reinforce stakes or remind readers what's at risk while other scenes can deepen stakes by having the character become more heavily invested in the wrong solution.

Furthermore, it is worth noting that subplots have their own stakes — and because of their limited narrative space, they may feel smaller than ones within the main story. Therefore, the stakes may appear to shift or decrease when the novel moves from mainline to subplot. However, the stakes within each subplot should rise respectively.

As an alternative, you can also use subplots as a place where characters completely fail with no opportunity to redeem themselves or the situation. Dealing with the fallout of that one wholesale failure could then motivate the protagonist to act when he would otherwise falter. The failure also has the benefit of making all the other potential pitfalls in the main storyline seem more horrific (and more likely to occur!) by providing a small glimpse of what an ultimate disaster might look like — and of course, the hero's fear and the audience's apprehension about that dreaded misstep creates additional story tension.

Before adding stakes to a scene, ask yourself these questions:

❖ What does the viewpoint character want? (**goal**)

❖ What is at stake? In other words, what does the POV character fear will happen? (**motivation** – the thing compels her to act and avoid disaster)

❖ What will it cost her to get what she wants? (**conflict**)

Conflict reveals character, and to some extent creates it, based on how a character reacts to adversity. Conflict should align with the scene goal and should not rely on a linear attack. Make the conflict multifaceted by having the viewpoint character and the antagonist altering their tactics, shifting their approach, revising their logic, and escalating their efforts. The struggle to overcome conflict ultimately leads to disaster so that the point-of-view character must realign his approach for the next scene. This disaster should be a consequence of fighting for the goal she has yet to attain. Warning: The writer should not fix or undo the disaster in the subsequent scene because **true stakes have long-standing repercussions** and because the reader develops sympathy for the viewpoint character as she tries and fails. This struggle leads the audience to wonder how the character will possibly answer the overall story question as each disaster brings "newly threatening" circumstances that keep the character in flux and the audience guessing.

If your unfamiliar with these concepts, an in-depth explanation of this approach can be found in Debra Dixon's *GMC: Goal, Motivation, and Conflict: The Building Blocks of Good Fiction*. But in the meantime, here are some rookie GMC mistakes to avoid:

❖ If there is no sacrifice involved, you haven't created a strong enough goal. So you must ask yourself, what's the worst thing that could happen if this character fails? Or what's the worst thing your hero could lose? Then follow through on those ideas at some point in the narrative.

MASTERING THE ART OF SUSPENSE

❖ *Because they are evil* is not adequate motivation. A character's motivation should be personal and specific. *I am fighting for revenge because the evil pharmaceutical corporation killed the only man I ever loved then destroyed his cancer cure and now they are after me to shut me up* is better motivation. This is crucial because evil is subjective, so you must define the moral playing field for your audience.

❖ Mere bickering is not conflict.

❖ A misunderstanding is not conflict.

❖ Conflict, like action and stakes, must escalate as the story progresses.

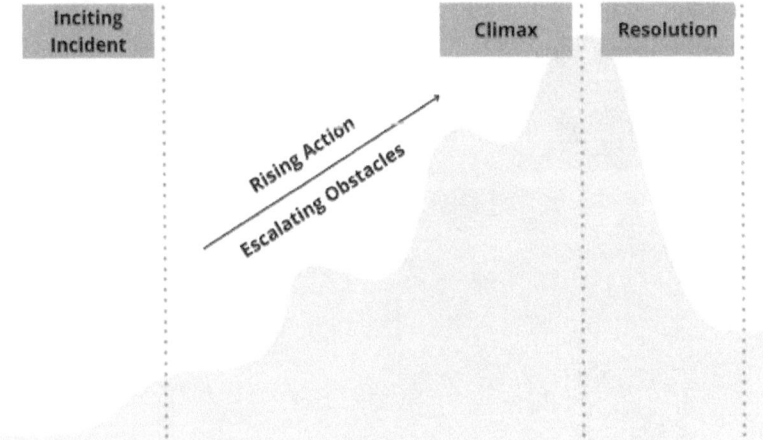

A Word on Suffering

Earlier in this chapter, we defined suffering as the hardships our characters must endure — often through failure. We also noted that in order for the audience to care, a character's suffering should be attached to falling short of an important or worthy goal. What I neglected to mention is that if suffering is taken too far, for too long, it becomes torture — both for the character and the reader — and you are likely to lose your audience. **There should always be the slightest twinge of hope to keep the reader invested.**

Similarly, avoid suffering that is repetitive in nature. If you create a character who keeps blacking out, the audience may have sympathy for him initially, but they'll eventually wonder why he isn't doing something about this persistent problem. Don't allow your hero to succumb to a setback. Of course, he may do so temporarily to gain his bearings, discover a new truth, reflect on what he's taken for granted and/or failed to learn. But in the end, suffering is meant to be a catalyst for change — an opportunity for your hero to rise from the ashes of the underdog position and become better (or at least more effective). It's also worth noting that the audience feels most fervently for a protagonist who suffers because they've given up something important to help another (i.e. sacrifice) or because they have something important taken away from them in battle or when their suffering comes occurs due to the maliciousness of others.

Pacing

Pace is defined as the rate of a narrative's forward progression — how swiftly or slowly the story moves for the reader. This is often based on things like sentence length, scene length, and how the scene is structured. But two of the most substantial elements of pace stem from what's happening in your story and what mood you hope to convey through the narrative.

For example, use a standard or **steady pace** to advance the story when nothing extraordinary has occurred other than the typical aspects of character development, setting, clue development, et cetera. To establish the standard pace, use an equal blend of description, dialogue, narration, and backstory. This uniformity will create a smooth reading experience where no one element draws attention, rather the prose moves forward at a fluid yet steady pace. Consider this the "ordinary world" or the "all is well...for now" or the "calm before the storm" pacing.

Employ a more **brooding pace** when you want to set a new tone, create a mood, or foreshadow an event. To create this pacing, work to highlight the sensory and emotional descriptions of the viewpoint character. The goal is to make the imagery feel real so that the audience has a visceral reaction via the five senses. Like the character in the scene, the reader becomes alert to the heightened atmosphere and lingering pace.

Consider this example from my mystery novel, *Poetic Justice*. This is a moment during the protagonist's initial confrontation with her nemesis.

> As the last word slipped from her lips, she twisted her body, grabbed the water pitcher from the table, and flung the contents at me.

Everything slowed to the tempo of a dirge as the fat wave of frosty liquid crashed against my face. Darkness enveloped me. I was fifteen again and back in that pool.

Water thrust its way past my nostrils. Droplets seared the back of my throat. Panic-stricken heartbeats hammered so loud it muted all other sound. Pressure threatened to collapse my lungs until I recognized I was holding my breath in anticipation of a more treacherous onslaught.

Gasping for air, I groped at my bowtie blouse — the soggy clumps of fabric an unnerving reminder of my watery tomb. Voices clamored from all directions.

"Not so high and mighty now, eh, Sooty?"

Notice how the heightened descriptions of the setting and the character's emotional fallout are juxtaposed with her personal impressions and past experiences to create a vivid atmospheric effect. I wanted to paint a picture where disaster and decision, inaction and action, life and death are balanced in such a way that we get a powerful dose of who this character is and what this story will be about. As is required with every scene, this pacing propels the story forward, but the mashup of sensory and emotional input gently strings the audience along with the promise to eventually delve deeper into the viewpoint character's physicality and mindset as she prepares for trouble on the horizon.

Incorporate a **quick pace** when the story's action begins. Of course, this includes chase scenes, arguments, big scares, or anything that gets the protagonist's blood pumping. Faster pacing helps to highlight conflict and ensures those encounters feel more intense.

Develop a quick pace by creating shorter, tighter scenes. Reduce the language to focus on a single event or topic. This leaves your audience with fewer elements to decipher. They can move more swiftly through the text. Their eyes race across the page. They turn pages faster. Their pulse speeds up.

To do this, you may revert solely to dialogue, i.e. keeping verbal tags and action beats to a minimum. Or this could simply mean reducing descriptions to short sentences full of strong verbs and action — just enough to provide a mental cue that the narrative has gained momentum and a significant moment is in progress.

> Crack! A branch snaps to Gina's left. Another to her right. Soon, the forest is alive with sound. Surrounded, she lifts her bow. Point. Aim. Shoot. Point. Aim. Shoot. A rapid succession of recoil, reload, repeat...until the trees are quiet again.

However, keep in mind that what goes up must come down, so don't plan to maintain this higher pace forever. Even during non-stop action thrillers like *The Terminator* (1984) or *Speed* (1994), there are moments when the narrative slows to shift the story more toward world building or suspense.

Speaking of suspense, we typically use a different approach to pacing when we want to create anxiousness in the reader. A suspenseful or **tense pace** is like a striptease designed to slowly pull back the layers of one grand moment to build anticipation. Therefore, avoid confusing this with the portentous or quick pace. In our suspenseful moments, we want to drive action and build details but in an intriguing manner that gradually unveils the outcome.

Picture the scene from *Scream 2* (1997) when Sidney Prescott and her roommate Hallie are trapped in the back of a police cruiser while the blood thirsty Ghostface killer sits unconscious in the driver's seat. Both women must crawl over the madman to escape through the driver's side window because the back doors are jammed and attempts to break the rear glass might wake their captor. The audience bites their nails and perches on the edge of their seats as the two women decide what to do. We know it is only a matter of seconds before the killer awakes, so time is of the essence. A scene like this is a perfect example of tense pacing because it's run time is only three and a half minutes, as our heroines twist and bend their way out of the deadly trap, yet it feels twice as long because we don't dare tear our gaze away from the screen. We cross our fingers hoping for their success while at the same time assuming the worse.

Create a similarly tense pace in with your prose by adding the threat of danger to an already stressful or unusual situation. This can be done by amplifying the small but menacing details through sensory description to elevate the tension and signify impending doom — the hiss of heavy breathing that might wake the madman, the shadow that appears to shift into the shape of a stranger, the echo along a darkened corridor, or the broken window of an apartment where nothing has been taken. By making your character (and hence, the reader) hyperaware of sensations and sounds, you are toying with our emotions and the speed of the story's forward progression. Of course, you must follow through on the foreshadowed threat — in an unexpected way! — for this pacing to be successful and to maintain the trust of the audience who may abandon your story if every use results in a thrill-less fake out.

As an example of how the foreshadowed threat must play out, let's go back to our example from *Scream 2*. While Sidney and Hallie are attempting to escape from the car, there is a moment when Sidney contemplates unmasking the killer, but must retreat when an accidental honk of the horn threatens to wake him. The fake out reminds us of the danger and doubles the stakes for Hallie who has yet to make her exit from the back seat. And wouldn't you know it, even though both women successfully escape from the car, Ghostface pops up behind them as they make their escape, delivering on the promise of bloodshed set up at the start of the scene.

Now, even though the techniques used to build this tense pace are typically indicative of a slower narrative — heightened imagery, sensory description, longer sentences, point-by-point details, richer adjectives, internal dialogue, reference to stillness and silence, et cetera — the approach itself might still *seem* fast to your readers. Why? Because this pacing format is primarily used when the stakes, consequences, plot twists, or reveals are at their highest and most tantalizing. In such instances, even though you as the author may be painstakingly teasing your way through the text, the reader's curiosity will quickly drive them through the narrative as they frantically scramble to discover how events unfold.

To be clear, these four approaches to pace can be used to create highs and lows within a single section, switching as you move from one scene to another. Or they can form the basis for an entire chapter — this is particularly true of thrillers since most of them are formatted to have one scene per unit. Either way, the key is to switch between the different techniques throughout to keep the audience on an emotional roller coaster that strikes the right chord for your genre. Fast-paced scenes with action or high suspense are tempered with slower-paced scenes involving reflection and detection.

Genre and plot structure can also play a role in a story's *overall* pace. For example, in terms of genre, a traditional mystery, which typically focuses on the mental or puzzle aspect of the crime, is going to move more slowly than adventure fiction or a thriller. The latter are action based, so the faster pace comes from the need to solve the dilemma or capture the culprit within a specific time frame — e.g. before the next execution, bomb, natural disaster, et cetera. Also, in terms of structure, a story told in chronological order may have a steadier pace than one told primarily in flashback or as a frame story.

But at the end of the day, you ultimately have control, so make decisions that will enhance your narrative while keeping the reader invested.

Violence and Action

If your novel qualifies as a mystery or a thriller, it will surely have some action. This could be as simple as getting knocked over the head or as complicated as a seven-page foot chase through a Mississippi swap. To make it convincing, you will need to depict some violent action. This often manifests itself as a physical call and response between two or more characters where one makes a move and the other reacts then counters.

To begin, decide what purpose you want the sequence to serve within your manuscript. Is this an escape plan, rescue, or attack? Are you hoping to show your heroine's strength or vulnerability? Will this character emerge battered and defeated or unscathed but with nowhere to turn? Does she expect the attack, or is she exhausted and caught off-guard? You don't need to answer all of these questions verbatim, but you do want a clear idea of how the event should play out before it starts. This will ensure the action serves the narrative as opposed to being a gratuitous moment serving no one but the writer.

Next, make the violence believable. Nothing destroys the world you're creating than a lack of realism. So if you're writing a military thriller with bombs, armored vehicles, automatic weapons, and hand-to-hand combat, you should have a clear, researched understanding of those elements. Make it real, but don't overdo it with extraneous details. You can order a set of firearm maintenance handbooks through your local bookstore, speak with a veteran, or enroll in a self-defense. As mentioned during the thriller subgenres section, it's best if you have experience in the area you've chosen. This is not the time to wing it. Your audience will know.

In fact, scenes depicting violence may prove difficult for some writers because our artistic medium lacks a visual component. By that I mean, the act of describing a horrific event is often anticlimactic because the audience is already light years ahead of your scene in terms of meaning. We must work doubly hard to keep the audience invested by utilizing vivid descriptions and sharp pacing. For example, spend too much time describing a knife to the gut and you run the risk of boring your audience who are well-versed in bloody mayhem thanks to the media. And yet, in a film where action is depicted visually, the audience stays tuned because they can absorb many things at once — where the victim is stabbed, how he reacts, where he falls, how he falls, whether the attack is gruesome enough to be fatal, et cetera. In fiction, we don't have the luxury of doling out those details as efficiently, but we also don't want to lose our readers as we attempt to do so.

Smart authors aim for techniques that are less focused on description and more focused on channeling tension, building character, and eliciting emotion. Fortunately, there are several methods for depicting violence that will not only reinvigorate audience interest but also add a ton of suspense. In this chapter, we'll outline those techniques so that you can create a scene that will leave the reader breathless.

Reveal Character and Advance Plot

Violent scenes should propel the plot forward through strong characterizations. How a person deals with adversity says volumes about their morals and values. Consider the duel in *Harry Potter and the Chamber of Secrets* (1999) by J.K. Rowling. The event solidifies the long-standing grudge between Malfoy and Harry, and helps with world building by introducing specialized weapons and tactics unique to the story's milieu. In other words, the violence must tie into the story's plot. Use violent scenes to resolve pending problems or create new ones. In essence, you shouldn't be able to remove the action sequence and still have a cohesive narrative.

Show Vulnerability

Even though we want our hero to succeed, there will come a point in the action where he'll need to falter. No one is invincible.

Besides, invincibility is boring. Even Superman has his weaknesses, and the best violent scenes allude to those weaknesses even when the hero wins. This can come in the form of taunts from the villain that reveal the hero's physical limitations or through the hero's thoughts. A brief moment of reflection can show the audience how the events are affecting the hero internally.

Danger should also be at the backbone of every suspense story. Even if it is only the momentary threat of peril, the consequences of a misstep must be real. We should never threaten the protagonist with something false simply to shock the audience. *It was all just a dream* is the deathblow of the modern novel. Everything must serve a purpose. So be clear about what the protagonist stands to lose if they fail and what they will gain if they succeed. This is how we set the novel's stakes for the audience, and every good conflict has high ones.

Take a brief look into the hero's mind to establish stakes. What's on the line? What motivated your hero into action? Betrayal? Survival? Dishonor? A short reflection gives the audience time to catch their breath and discover how the action scene fits into the overall story.

Consider the Crazy 88's fight scene from *Kill Bill: Vol. 1* (2003). The number of foes is insurmountable. The Bride can't possibly leave unscathed, but revenge and love for her lost child drive her forward. Meanwhile, the vicissitudes of her fate — the will she or won't she succeed — keep the audience engaged.

Also, make sure the scene's resolution leads to a transformation or revelation for the protagonist, and show your characters dealing with the aftermath of a fight. Give the sequence long-range consequences that aren't easily reversible. Remember, healing from any violent situation takes time. Memories from the event will trigger reactions for days, months, or even years to come. Highlight the physical and emotional pain, and make sure to utilize that information to shape each characters' behavior moving forward.

Use Vivid Verbs

Use strong verbs to truncate complex concepts. A violent fight scene is not the moment to wax poetic with flowery sentences. Commit to short phrases. Action verbs and tight phrasing will increase the pace, highlight danger, and promote urgency. The audience will notice this subconsciously as they read and become less likely to skip over the passage for fear of missing something vital. Reduce character dialogue and thought. Focus on movement, reflexes, and reaction. Use all five senses. This leaves the reader breathless and adds tension as their eyes fly across the page.

Shift the Focus

A writer can use point of view to highlight important events through shifts in focus. Consider this the literary equivalent of camera work — panning wide to establish danger or zooming in close on a character's reaction. Here's an example:

> The intruder bursts through the front door of the mansion. His muscular body fills the door frame with menace. He holds a Glock in front of him, but shots ring out from the darkness before he can fire. The man staggers. Blood trickles from his chest. His face twists with agony.

Notice how the scene moves from a wide shot of the doorway to a half-shot on the intruder's chest to a close-up on the man's face. All of the action remains in third-person, but the passage shifts to where the action unfolds, adding nuance without losing concision.

Control the pace

Give the audience a chance to catch their breath between action sequences and to process what they've learned with scenes that reflect on the consequence of the action or recap what the hero has learned. Staying in high gear for too long can wear out the audience and can start to feel monotonous. Plus, it isn't believable. Even the most interesting man in the world slows down long enough to simply sit and have a beer. Give the audience highs and lows so they never know what to expect.

Unnerve the audience by reducing the pace. Think of this as the fictional equivalent of slow motion. Since it adds a profound gravity to the moment and forces the audience to think about the consequences, this is best used when describing a major injury or fatal wound for a primary character. Here are some ways to incorporate this method:

- Keep the focus wide
- Inundate the reader with details and descriptions
- Use longer sentences
- Include internal dialogue to provide reactions to the action

Get pulses racing by speeding up events. Playing with time, especially with chase or fight scenes, will place the audience on the edge of their seats. Practice this approach using these elements:

- Keep the focus tight
- Keep details to a minimum
- Keep sentences short and direct
- Reduce internal and external dialogue
- Use powerful verbs and maintain the active voice

Create worry by omitting the violent act. Carnage doesn't always create tension or even fear. When depicting violence, less is more. In fact, readers' imaginations will create horrors more gruesome and terrifying than anything found on the page.

Consider those Halloween parties as a kid when you put on a blindfold and stuck your hand in the bowl of peeled grapes. Unaware of the truth, your imagination runs wild, and you envision a squishy vat of eyeballs and start to build a story about how they got there.

When describing gore or depicting violence in fiction, why not implement the same strategy? Let the part imply the whole. Our imaginations will do the rest. Give the reader just enough to terrify — the severed finger, the dangling eyeball, the sound of a chainsaw in the distance as the lights go black. Because when given the chance to fill in the blank, the audience will conjure up something far worse than you probably intended.

Omitting the violent act, returning for the painful aftermath, and not knowing exactly what happened in between is unsettling and may be best suited for scenes that are too emotionally or physically graphic to share like rape or a mass shooting. Use these tips to incorporate this technique:

- ❖ Show the POV character's vulnerability
- ❖ Provide a strong precursory image leading into the violence
- ❖ Cut away and avoid describing the violent act itself
- ❖ Provide a vivid depiction of the aftermath
- ❖ Include a long-term consequence

As you work through these techniques, think about the message your scene will convey. After all, an action sequence isn't solely about violence. It's about the emotional growth of the protagonist as she encounters new obstacles. Remember, violence only serves the narrative if it somehow affects the characters. So use strong verbs, perspective, and pacing to distill that vulnerability into a killer scene that advances the plot and leaves the audience dying for more.

Although to be fair, the choice between this subtler approach to violence versus outright grisly gore heavily depends on the context within a scene, genre expectations, and the intended audience. This caveat has not been stated to negate the previous section, rather simply to note that not every ideology on fiction is one size fits all.

So with that in mind, there may come a moment when a gruesome description will be unavoidable — whether that's to punctuate a disastrous encounter, to confirm the end of a threat, or illustrate the viciousness of the villain. In those instances, you can still inject your manuscript with the unexpected by underplaying the grotesqueness of the situation. A scene deliberately scrubbed of figurative or overly descriptive language is a powerful way to draw the audience into a violent scene and get them to pay closer attention. This type of understated approach is especially useful in police procedurals where you may want to just provide facts, but it can work with any suspense story. The key is to avoid being vulgar by making those violent scenes more about the characters and their *response* — or the elements driving the scene such as the problems and conflicts that *result* from the mayhem — rather than leaning into the pure revulsion that materializes when a grotesque moment is designed merely to disgust.

Moreover, a savagely violent scene runs the risk of taking the reader out of the story, not only because of its gratuitous nature, but also because of the lack of nuance being exercised. All of sudden, the writing is crude, boorish, and heavy, lacking the lighter and more delicate dance that comes with intellectual striptease of suspense. Work to keep your prose nimble, flexible, and forward-moving so as to captivate rather than nauseate.

Cause Problems

In action sequences, you will need paint your hero into a corner where their back is against the wall and it feels like they will never overcome the odds. In such situations, you don't want to employ a far-fetched or unrealistic solution. One way to make sure their eventual escape or success seems plausible is to eventually have the tables turn so that their impossible predicament is actually the best position to be under the given circumstances. The 2022 Netflix film version of Mark Greaney's 2009 novel, *The Gray Man,* is an excellent example of this. Early in the second act, Sierra Six appears doomed when he finds himself in police custody, handcuffed to a cement park bench with an army of villains gunning for him. He appears to be a sitting duck, but as the square fills with baddies, it becomes clear that he is actually in a pretty good position because with a few quick kicks, he seizes the police officers' guns and uses the bench as a trench/shield to fend off the hooligans. What was once a death trap is now an asset.

Lastly, it sometimes helps to set some of the groundwork for your sequence in an earlier part of the story so that you don't need to stop to explain extraneous details once your action sequence has begun. For instance, if you know your novel will contain a foot chase that takes place in a certain part of your fictional city, drop tidbits of information about landmarks and street traffic early on. That way, when your hero is off and running, you can keep the focus on the action without getting bogged down by setting.

For more information on depicting fist fights, duels, and riot battles in fiction, I highly recommend *Writing Fight Scenes: Professional Techniques for Fiction Authors* by Rayne Hall and *Fight Write: How to Write Believable Fight Scenes* by Carla Hoch.

Checklist: Violence and Action

Action sequences are an essential part of any thriller because they ramp up excitement and spell conflict for your protagonist. They also help with pacing because they increase momentum and stakes as the events unfold. Action can also drive character because the reaction your hero has while under pressure speaks to his morals, motivations, and goals. However, action scenes are difficult because readers are counting on you to tell them exactly what they need to see.

To make these scenes feel real, you must have a credible understanding of real-life movement and the consequences of being hurt or hit then fill those cause-and-effect moments with sensory detail. In other words, reaction is just as important as the action in sequences involving fights, chases, et cetera. We'll need to see characters under pressure, characters in pain, characters emotionally distraught and even physically destroyed. Don't shy away from the rough stuff. Do your research. Know what happens to the body when a person is shot or how it feels to get the wind knocked out of you when jumping from a speeding train. Then be sure to add the sensory details of what it sounds like when a bone breaks or how the smell of blood turns sour when a person tries to cauterize their own wound.

❖ What purpose will the action serve in propelling the plot?

❖ What is at stake?

❖ What will this scene reveal about the characters? How will you show your hero's strengths or vulnerabilities?

❖ Are there any elements — settings, landmarks, personal history, weaponry, et cetera — that need to be established ahead of time to streamline the scene?

❖ Are you highlighting the hero's emotion in conjunction with the action?

Chase Scene

The words "chase scene" mean different things to different people. Some immediately think about car chases like *Bullitt* (1968), *Vanishing Point* (1971), or *The French Connection* (1971). Others may think of the outrageous boat chases that seem to pop up in every James Bond movie from *Quantum of Solace* (2008) to *From Russia With Love* (1963). However, the one thing all of these famous chase scenes have in common is that they aren't simply gratuitous action. They all work to develop character and advance the plot. Eliminate or rewrite any chase scene that fails to meet these basic criteria.

One of my favorites is the heart-pounding foot chase that occurs during the twelfth chapter of William Golding's *Lord of the Flies* (1954), a novel about a group of boys stranded on a deserted island. At this point of the story, Ralph has lost his role as leader and has escaped into the jungle to fend for himself when he discovers the other boys have decided to hunt him. What's magical about this chase scene is the language, which is full of sensory imagery and powerful emotions: "The ululation rose behind him and spread along, a series of short sharp cries, the sighting call. A brown figure showed up at his right and fell away. They were all running, all crying out madly. He could hear them crashing in the undergrowth and on the left was the hot, bright thunder of the fire."

The other beautiful thing about Ralph's desperate situation is that it causes him to reflect on the what's happened, illuminates the story's themes of power and identity, and spurs some emotional growth in his character as he realizes how far they've all sunk. And when the chase comes to its climactic conclusion, with Ralph crashing onto the beach thinking he's reached the end of his life only to find rescue, he breaks down:

"The tears began to flow and sobs shook him. He gave himself up to them now for the first time on the island; great, shuddering spasms of grief that seemed to wrench his whole body. His voice rose under the black smoke before the burning wreckage of the island; and infected by that emotion, the other little boys began to shake and sob too. And in the middle of them, with filthy body, matted hair, and unwiped nose, Ralph wept for the end of innocence, the darkness of man's heart..."

This just goes to show that there is so much that can be done with a chase scene and that there are a myriad of successful approaches. While I can't claim to give you the perfect formula for every scenario, I am confident these basics will help fortify the foundation of your scene whether you choose to have your chase take place via land, air, or sea.

Plan Your Chase

To ensure that your scene has realistic action as well as tension, plan ahead. This means determining the purpose for your scene, what's at stake, and how the hero's world will change when the chase comes to an end. It also requires determining how the setting can be used to both the hero's advantage and detriment as well as what actually happens during the chase and in what order.

In addition, you'll need to know the layout and logistics for your locale. You don't want to claim your car chase takes place in Central Park only to discover that the route you've chosen is only open to pedestrian traffic. Visit your locations to get a better idea of what's possible or use resources like YouTube and Google Maps to gain clear visuals when travel isn't possible. If you're creating your own settings, then draw a map to keep in your story bible so that the chase scene descriptions remain consistent.

In addition, you'll need to determine, and make clear to the audience, what's the final destination for the pursued as well as what method they'll use to track their progress toward that goal.

Scout Your Setting

Choosing and establishing your location is an essential part of creating a chase because different locales offer different environments depending on the season, time of day, weather, et cetera. For instance, a daytime chase could mean a plethora of pedestrians and the potential for property damage while a night chase may make it difficult for the characters to navigate. A winter chase brings the treachery of snow while a summer chase in a tropical jungle poses additional external dangers such as poisonous snakes and frogs.

Consider these elements when planning your location along with things like what can the hunter do to slow down his prey (and vice versa)? Decide what you'd like to happen and consider how your locale could complicate fight scenes or offer hiding places. Use familiar objects in unexpected ways. Look for strong visuals, smells, and sounds that you can amplify to make the setting seem more real.

Be Mindful of Pace

The pulse-pounding urgency of your chase should be reflected in the scene's pace. Make every second count. Don't bog down the scene with superfluous description. Be concise. Focus primarily on sensory information and movement. What is it like to take a punch? Fall from a fence? Dive into an icy lake? Use short sentences, brief dialogue, and vivid verbs to convey the action and keep the scene moving swiftly. This may mean using allusions and analogies to get the point across faster. Keep it simple, and allow the audience to fill in the gaps using their imagination.

Tap Into Proximity

Look for clever ways to keep the audience informed about the progress of the hunter and the hunted. Remember, tension is usually at its highest when capture appears imminent, so it is difficult to build tension if the audience cannot determine whether the hero is on the verge of success or failure.

Also, don't allow the hunted to completely outrun the hunter. Keep them close, and use proximity to play with audience anticipation. A near miss around a sharp corner or a last-second evasion thanks to an oncoming vehicle can create quite an adrenaline rush. Better yet, chases that take place in confined spaces, like the finale of *The Terminator* (1984), are particularly suspenseful since both the audience and the character grow increasingly anxious about being trapped in a location that seemingly has no escape.

Use Viewpoints to Your Advantage

In general, it is best to choose a point of view that gives the reader a front row seat to what the hunter or the hunted might be feeling and sensing during the pursuit. To achieve this effect, opt for the first-person viewpoint or third-person limited. Both points of view allow the reader to feel the sharp snap of a broken bone or smell the smoky stench of a rifle blast, and they both help limit the reader's experience to the viewpoint character's sphere of influence.

Of the two POVs, third-person limited may offer more flexibility since it opens the door for creating a series of scenes where the narrative cuts between the pursuer and his prey — or you could even add a third person, such as a handler who may be aiding the hero in same way. The point is that for a chase scene, writers should work to align the action with a character because this leaves room for the incorporation of suspense. That is to say, if the audience is locked into experiencing things beat by beat just like our hero, we can use this as an opportunity to add a surprise or a twist about what lies ahead. This is much more difficult to do with third-person omniscient where the all-knowing narration has a distancing effect and is downright impossible with third-person objective where we never get inside the characters' heads to learn how the action affects them.

The bottom line is that a chase should be packed with emotion and adrenaline. If we don't choose a viewpoint that allows us to experience that, we are diluting the effectiveness of our prose.

To help build your chase scene, consider the following:

❖ How does the chase begin?

❖ Who is being chased and why? What does this event tell us about them?

❖ Who is in pursuit and why? What does their presence mean to the overall plot, and how does this event relate to their story goals?

❖ What's at stake? What do each of your characters — the hunter and the hunted — stand to gain or lose?

❖ What role does the chase serve in the overall narrative? How does this event advance the plot?

❖ What location or scenario would put the *protagonist* in the most danger?

❖ Will this scene involve real weapons or makeshift defense apparatus made in route? What skills do the hero and his adversary have? How will those skills help evasion or aid detection — will they clash or overpower each other?

❖ What brings the chase to an end?

❖ What is the aftermath? How does everyone react to the event? What is the physical and emotional fallout? What result will this event, and people's reaction to it, have on the scenes that follow?

Regardless of whether your hero is the hunter or the prey, you should always aim to saddle him with as much trouble as possible. Chase scenes are a prime opportunity to amplify that stress. So make the setting and situation as difficult as possible while simultaneously decreasing the hero's preparedness by removing resources or allies. The more vulnerable your character is during the scene, the more the reader will feel for him. Moreover, since these scenes are designed to illustrate characters' strengths and weaknesses in the face adversity, we are also creating signposts for the reader that indicate how and in what ways these people will need to grow over the course of the narrative.

In general, a chase scene should have a beginning, midpoint, climax, and ending. Both sides will have their respective goals and obstacles while the main conflict between the two will provide the action and lead to the climactic event that concludes the chase. As the scene develops, the traits and talents of the participants will shape the tempo of the chase. For instance, if both are spies adept at gunplay or hand-to-hand combat that will create a streamlined, fast-paced scene, and the reader will expect to see those skills at play. On the other hand, if the scene contains a trained assassin chasing a civilian, the sequence should feel more frenetic with the person being pursued using the elements in their environment in unusual ways to avoid capture.

If your chase scene is long, use the midpoint to make it clear why your hero isn't having success — whether that's because he's outnumbered, outgunned, outsmarted — and have him endeavor to change his approach as a result. This may involve him bending his core values or taking action he's never attempted before. Also, as we move toward the scene's climax, make sure the hero's adversary pulls out her most dastardly trick. This will reinforce that your hero is in grave danger. It will also reinforce the scene's high stakes and sustain audience interest.

The chase should end due to either a brilliant maneuver or an unfortunate miscalculation by one of the characters, not dumb luck or coincidence. And to aid that conclusion, we can certainly use foreshadowed elements (think "Q" giving Bond a laser watch) or even supernatural powers if it's part of the genre and established in advance, but we never want random hocus pocus or deus ex machinas to rule our fiction because it ruins the work's credibility and pulls the audience out of the story. So whether the chase ends in capture, surrender, evasion, or death, show the event and the characters' reactions to illustrate the seriousness of the situation. The hero, in particular, may have an emotional or physical fallout that the audience needs to experience. Or if there is an epiphany or a task he must undertake as a result, make it clear to the audience how the chase led to that decision.

Checklist: Chase Scenes

Like all other depictions of violence, keep descriptions straight-forward and simplistic to avoid complicating the image or having the audience predict your next move. And since chase scenes are often longer than the typical action sequence, they must advance the plot and/or teach us something new about the core characters in the process. Also, endeavor to not only put action but reaction and emotion on the page so that we understand how these events affect the characters and those around them.

When crafting a chase scene, treat it as if it has its own narrative arc by including the following elements:

Purpose and stakes. What initiates the chase? Devise a way to show the audience why the chase matters. Give each character a goal, determine what success looks like, and define the consequences for failure. The decisions and actions made during the chase should reverberate throughout the plot and affect the scenes that follow.

Inventiveness. Brainstorm a unique locale, route, or mode of transportation for this event. Avoid cliches and work toward an unexpected twist to overcome. Develop innovative ways to keep your reader informed of where everyone is in the chase — who is ahead, who is behind, and how close or far apart they are as the conflict unfolds.

Rising action. Set a time frame or create time pressure for the chase. Establish increasingly detrimental obstacles by saddling the viewpoint character with difficulties like an injury or forcing him to help someone along the way or destroying an object he could use to end the chase (like a gun, car, or map). It also helps if the action is presented from the point of view of the character whose fate we care about most so that we can experience their frustration.

Midpoint. Allow the hero a brief reprieve where he is able to regroup. This is typically the point where he becomes more proactive — e.g. he stands his ground to fight or turns the tables so that the hunted becomes the hunter.

Climax. Amplify the emotional and physical pressure by adding one major moment where the hero must fight for his life — a real do-or-die scenario where his ability to escape is genuinely called into question. This should encompass or lead to the event or situation that will show how the chase ends and what result it ultimately has on the hero's current situation.

Ending. If you're hoping to end your chase with a twist, plant a red herring earlier in the story that tricks the audience into thinking they know how things will end, then use it in a completely opposite way or have it backfire, forcing the character into an alternative. Let the audience think they are going to see a routine evasion or capture, then turn the tables so that they are faced with something unexpected like a surrender...or even a death.

Exposition

Imagine you've written a story about a man on trial for waterboarding his daughter. In the opener, you introduce the trial's prosecuting attorney. You do this with a three-page run down that reveals several things: She put herself through law school. She once ran for mayor of her hometown. She teaches at the local university. She can't swim due to a fear of large bodies of water, and she grew up in a foster home where she was bullied and nearly drowned by her adopted siblings. You include all of that information in the opening scene because you want to make the correlation that by trying the case and winning, she is overcoming her past.

Although common, this approach is faulty. An abundance of backstory at the start of a novel, can have the adverse effect of grinding the narrative to a halt and boring your readers. You're essentially providing information before it's relevant. In the beginning, your goal should be increasing your reader's curiosity, not squelching it with too many details.

The only thing necessary in this opening scene is that your protagonist is a successful lawyer. It is not until the story gains momentum and the other elements of the plot unfold, that the rest of the information becomes relevant. In fact, waiting until the audience knows more about your character and her plight will give those additional details greater resonance. For example, during a major setback in the trial, perhaps you include a flashback to her own horrific water torture event as motivation.

Remedy this problem by starting your story in the right place, i.e. a few moments before the ordinary world falls into chaos. Focus on the early signs that something's amiss so that you can open with action or movement. Then gradually add exposition as needed using multiple techniques such as action, dialogue, documents, memories, and flashbacks.

Action – Writing is the medium of "show, don't tell," so use body language and behavior to help illuminate some of the history between characters.

Dialogue – The best way to convey backstory through dialogue is to have a character talking to a novice or someone new to the situation so that they can act as a stand-in for the audience. You can also have the character engage in an inner monologue warning themselves to avoid repeating whatever mistake or past event you hope to insert as backstory.

Documents – Fictional documents such as texts, news articles, letters, and literature can convey background information about characters. You can deliver the document in full to the audience through the text of your novel and/or have a character summarize its value. Just be mindful to keep such works short to maintain momentum (and so that readers aren't tempted to skip the passage).

Memories – A recollection of a past event can be triggered to help build backstory. Things that typically unlock memories include a familiar saying, a familiar face, an object, a song, et cetera. Memories are brief and can be conveyed in a few sentences or paragraphs. For that reason, they are often the best way to convey background information because unlike full flashbacks they don't break or bend the pace of the story by moving backward for an extended period of time.

Flashbacks – When a character must recall events that took place before the current narrative, you have two ways to effectively convey those ideas. If the recollections are short, the character can simply describe the event either in dialogue with another character or as brief internal dialogue triggered by an object or emotion related to the memory. If a longer recollection is needed, you may consider doing a flashback where you replay the event for the reader.

Flashbacks

Flashbacks can be a fun way to establish a small story question. For example, if we open a chapter with a traumatic event then revert to a blissful situation that occurred two days prior, the reader looks forward to finding out what happened to change things so drastically — but this only works if your true intent it to place a spotlight on something that will ultimately move the story forward. If not, this may come off as a cheap ploy or a distraction, causing the audience to wonder: *Why not just start things in the right place to begin with?*

As alluded to in the previous section, a flashback is backstory that is being dramatized for the audience, and they are often used to enhance characterization. For instance, an extended flashback can dredge up old trauma and demonstrate how a character's previous good or bad behavior informs their present actions as well as explain why things exist as they do in the present. So in many ways, a flashback can be used to illustrate a character's motivations or even to stimulate conflict since the person experiencing the flashback must deal with those past emotions. And in some cases, seeing a character under the soft glow of a newly ignited flashback, helps the audience to sympathize and better engage with him — even if that person is villainous.

Flashbacks can also be a source of tension if those motivations, secret sources of conflict, or pivotal events, echo or foreshadow a dastardly deed. Just be sure that your deep dive down memory lane focuses on information that's pertinent to the main storyline. Avoid including extraneous or irrelevant material, and return to the present as quickly as possible because audiences prefer immediacy. Unfortunately, a flashback negates that agenda because it sets itself up as a scene from the past...more on that in a moment.

Logistically, the main difficulty writers face when creating flashbacks is remembering to include shifts in tense and time. When using this technique, it's crucial that you have language to help delineate the beginning and end of the flashback. This can be a transition based on an action like the protagonist sitting down at her desk and shaking her head at the tragic memory or it can be a change in tense.

If your novel is written in present tense (*she <u>arrives</u> at the mortuary*), the flashbacks must be written in the past tense (*she <u>poisoned</u> her husband*). And if your work is written in the past tense (*she <u>arrived</u> at the mortuary*), create each flashback using the past perfect tense (*she <u>had poisoned</u> her husband*).

Past perfect is also called the pluperfect and can be formulated as follows:

had + [past participle]

Past perfect is helpful for when you reference some point in the past but want to discuss an event that happened even further back in time. That's why we use it when moving into a flashback but not in other areas of the text. Let me repeat: You should not use past perfect throughout your manuscript. Most commercial fiction is written in the simple past tense. You can also experiment with present tense, but this may prove difficult for suspense where several events and activities take place simultaneously or during a short span of time.

Once you've transitioned into your flashback and made the shift in time clear using the past perfect, you can revert to the regular past tense during the unfolding of the events to avoid the cumbersome usage of "had." At the end of the flashback, you will again need to show a shift in time either through a statement or transition. A couple uses of the past perfect should be included as well until you've returned to the main story thread where you can again resume past tense. Also, add a reminder of the setting, mindset, or timeframe that you're returning to as a way to reacclimate the reader to the present.

As you can see from the description of this technique, transitioning into a full flashback can be quite cumbersome and can diminish momentum, so use them sparingly to keep your pacing tight. In fact, avoid flashbacks in the first three chapters of the story. Early usage is rarely effective because we don't know enough about any character's current situation to care about their past or determine the value the recollection will serve within the main narrative. Let readers use those early chapters to embrace your key characters. Numerous flashbacks can pull them out of the reality you're trying to build. Plus, this desire to dwell on the past at such an early point in the narrative would suggest that maybe your story should have started in a different place or that your inciting incident may have taken place much earlier than originally thought.

However, as easy as it is to advise you to avoid them, the truth is that suspense stories — particularly those like psychological thrillers, spy thrillers, and action adventures — fluctuate through time and space in a manner where flashbacks are often necessary. So if you've chosen a genre where that's the case, I'd like to give you the best advice possible. But first, let's review the drawbacks of flashback use:

❖ The shifts in time inherent to flashbacks are confusing to the reader and troublesome for the writer.

❖ They often destroy the forward momentum of the story by stopping to look backward.

❖ Some writers are under the false impression that the technique gives them permission to include irrelevant information and fail to realize audiences don't need massive amounts of history to understand the present.

❖ They are difficult to enter and exit without the reader seeing the contrivance of the story element. In other words, when flashbacks are poorly executed, they point to the fact that the reader is reading and that very fact takes the audience out of the story.

❖ They often fail to provide new insight to the present situation.

❖ Readers sometimes skip over them.

Remember, there are other, less intrusive ways, to convey information about the past as discussed in the previous chapter. Again, this is not to say that flashbacks should never be used, just that they should be approached with a certain level of skill and forethought. Consider these techniques for a proper flashback before attempting them in your work:

❖ If you must use a flashback, keep it concise. Work to avoid whole chapters full of flashback. This is not about creating filler text; it is about tapping into an emotional resonance that could not be achieved in the present.

❖ The thematic underpinnings of the present and the past should connect. For example, if your current scene's emotional resonance deals with loss than the flashback should echo the element of loss in some manner that helps to propel the real-time storyline, which is the primary function of the technique.

❖ The flashback should be mostly dialogue and action, rather than narrative description, to maintain reader interest and to avoid the story become stagnant.

❖ The shifts in time must be seamless so the audience understands when they've moved backward and when they've returned to the main timeline. Avoid cliched setups like, "I couldn't help but think back" or "The memory of his smile hit me like a ton of bricks."

❖ After the flashback, return to the same setting and situation to avoid reader confusion.

Frame Story

Another type of flashback is the frame story. This is an advanced form of flashback where the entire narrative plays a role since it essentially a story within a story, where an introductory or main narrative establishes the groundwork for a more important storyline or for a set of shorter narratives. The frame establishes the present timeline and leads readers from that first story into one or more new narratives embedded within.

Frame stories are usually used help readers understand aspects about the embedded narrative(s) that may otherwise go misinterpreted or prove difficult to understand. Since this literary device involves going backward from the main narrative timeline, one can consider the meat of the frame story (i.e. the embedded secondary storyline) one big major flashback. The benefit of this format is that the reader gets two or more perspectives on the event — the hindsight viewpoint of the frame narrator and the candid viewpoint of the embedded narrator — which enriches the meaning of the story by opening up several levels of interpretation. For a quick reference, note that *The Princess Bride* — whether you're familiar with the 1973 fantasy romance novel by William Goldman or the 1987 movie starring Fred Savage and Peter Falk — utilizes the frame narrative.

What's interesting about the frame story, creating one as well as reading one, is that the frame can't be an afterthought. The two stories must have a layered purpose, so review these questions before considering this technique: Why is the secondary being told (and why now)? What demands does the secondary story make on those who are listening? How do the secondary story's themes relate to the scenario established in the frame?

But the big question with a frame story is how to create suspense if the person reciting the story has played a role in its unfolding or gives away part of the outcome in preparation for the telling the tale.

Although the secondary story within the frame may lose some immediacy by nature of being a flashback, it gains the opportunity for one of the key players to look back on those events and interpret them. This means the audience receives two possibly contradictory perspectives — the protagonist within the frame and the wiser person outside the frame who can comment on what it all really means. In other words, the frame offers the audience the added fun of figuring out which interpretation holds more value. Also, by using the frame to interrupt the embedded story at crucial intervals, we add suspense as the reader waits with anticipation to see how the internal events affect the frame and how those things within the frame will change while on hold.

Checklist: Exposition

❖ Have I avoided the habit of inserting a huge paragraph a background the moment a new character is introduced and instead weaved the information in through dialogue and action?

❖ Have I picked the most efficient method of delivering backstory for this scene (action, narration, documentation, dialogue, memory, or flashback)?

❖ Have I activated a memory for this backstory with a trigger from the environment, or have I given a good reason why the narrative should stop to include this information?

MASTERING THE ART OF SUSPENSE

❖ Is the background information serving more than one purpose (e.g. providing a clue to the mystery *and* add characterization)?

❖ If I am using a full flashback, have I made the time shift clear through transitions and the change in tense? And have I used that same technique to return to the main timeline at the end of the sequence?

❖ Have I done my best to ensure, that despite the insertion of backstory, the flow of the scene moves forward with the least disruption to the pace?

Cliffhangers

A cliffhanger is a gripping situation — such as a dangerous dilemma or a shocking revelation — left temporarily unresolved. But by delaying the outcome, the writer creates suspense. The audience's interest is piqued, and they continue turning pages to determine what will happen next.

In her 2012 article for *The New Yorker*, "The Curious Staying Power of the Cliffhanger," Emily Nussbaum describes the phenomenon in more poetic terms:

> "Narrowly defined, a cliffhanger is a climax cracked in half: the bomb ticks, the screen goes black. A lady wriggles on train tracks — will anyone save her? Italics on a black screen: 'To be continued . . .' More broadly, it's any strong dose of 'What happens next?' — the question that hovers in the black space between episodes. In the digital age, that gap is an accordion: it might be a week or eight months; it may arrive at the end of an episode or as a season finale or in the second before a click on 'next.' Cliffhangers are the point when the audience decides to keep buying..."

Bottomline, the cliffhanger is a promise to the reader that all of their questions will be answered if they're willing to wade through the dark void of ignorance. But most importantly, to be successful, the technique must be highly effective at keeping the reader engaged.

According to online edition of *New World Encyclopedia*, cliffhangers are said to have their roots in the medieval Middle Eastern literary epic *The Book of One Thousand and One Nights*, whose stories were passed down orally until the ninth century and the compiled in various forms. The element that nearly all versions share is the frame story of the Sassanid Queen, Scheherazade, who is forced to wed a tyrant king who marries and kills a new wife each day. To delay her death, she tells him a story each night that ends on what we would today call a cliffhanger, allowing her to live another day to finish the story and start the process anew.

However, it is Charles Dickens, the great nineteenth-century novelist, who is often credited for popularizing the cliffhanger concept. Many of his early novels, such as *The Pickwick Papers* (1836), were serialized and printed episodically to tremendous success. "The instalments would typically culminate at a point in the plot that created reader anticipation and thus reader demand, generating a plot and sub-plot motif that would come to typify the novel structure," explains Leslie Howsam in *The Cambridge Companion to the History of the Book* (2015). While a definitive term had yet to be coined, Dickens had definitely found a formula that generated a rabid readership. Nussbaum's *New Yorker* article confirms as she notes, "In 1841, Dickens fanboys rioted on the dock of New York Harbor, as they waited for a British ship carrying the next installment [of *The Old Curiosity Shop*], screaming, 'Is little Nell dead?'"

Despite the fervor for Dickens work, the term is thought to have originated during the serialized run of Thomas Hardy's *A Pair of Blue Eyes* in *Tinsley's Magazine* (September 1872 to July 1873). At the end of one installment, the novel's heroine, Elfride Swancourt, is walking with her love interest, Henry Knight, when he slips and falls off a cliff. By literally leaving the hero in a lurch, the author puts the audience on a razor's edge, dying to know how things unfold. The story then resumes next issue with Henry questioning the nature of his existence and Elfride rescuing him with a rope fashioned from her Victorian outer garments. Of course, it turns out that this literal cliffhanger doesn't have quite the pulse-pounding twist readers expect today, but it does standardize the idea that these horrific or stressful moments should still be grounded in a universal human experience in order to achieve the desired effect. In fact, as you work to build your cliffhanger, be sure to let the audience experience the urgent moment of dilemma or disaster alongside the character, so stay in their viewpoint.

The most common way to execute a cliffhanger is to pause the action just before something significant is revealed or an anticipated action takes place. Cliffhangers usually appear at the end of a chapter, but that does not mean the next scene needs to pick up with the answer to the cliffhanger. It may be appropriate to stretch reader anticipation by briefly switching to a new point of view or location — perhaps one with a different pace, emotion, or tone. You can further set the reader off balance by returning to the original scene before the newly introduced issue resolves itself, thus creating another cliffhanger. But don't do this too many times. Develop a sense for the breaking point where the audience may start to feel manipulated, and being willing to admit that sometimes it pays to have the scene reach its climax without inserting a cliffhanger. After all, they must do more than simply pose the question, *What's next?* A successful cliffhanger must have enough on the page to lure readers from one section of the narrative to another with ongoing interest.

Plot Twists

Daniel Kahneman, Nobel Prize winner in behavioral economics, posed the idea in his 2010 TED Talk[1] that the mind can be divided into halves known as the experiencing self and the narrating self. The experiencing side handles emotions such as fear, sadness, excitement, et cetera, while the narrating half weaves those sensations into a story to make sense of it all. Kahneman notes that once we have a story that seemingly makes sense, our minds often consider that information reality even though it was formed as justification rather than experienced as fact.

This process can become problematic for the reader (but helpful to the writer) in the area of fiction because this indicates that the audience is susceptible to fallacies, emotions, and prejudices that an author can exploit to help hide duplicity and foreshadow twists to come. These misinterpretations of cause and effect unfold in the same manner as the misdirection employed by an illusionist when he does a trick. We know it's sleight of hand, but it still mystifies as if it were actual magic.

Writers committed to puzzling their fans with plot twists should take advantage of what Kahneman and magicians already know: Our perceptions are faulty. We all have blind spots and see patterns that don't exist. But because our misconceptions are innate, they manifest in ways that we can anticipate...and exploit.

In essence, why not use the reader's inherent biases and blind spots against them to build a better plot twist? I stumbled upon this concept while listening to an NPR segment with cognitive scientist Vera Tobin[2]. Follow the link to a copy of the transcript if you'd like to review that interview. You can also purchase a copy of Tobin's book *Elements of Surprise: Our Mental Limits and The Satisfactions of Plot*

---

1. https://www.ted.com/talks/daniel_kahneman_the_riddle_of_experience_vs_memory
2. https://www.npr.org/transcripts/661878959

(2018) for a more detailed dive into the subject. In her work, Tobin argues that even though a plot twist takes advantage of our mental limits, it's still a sophisticated artform that requires a clear understanding of man's mental capacity. I concur, so let's briefly examine a few cognitive elements that you may want to exploit to help trick your audience.

❖ The **curse of knowledge** is when a person assumes that others know what they know.

❖ **Confirmation bias** is when we seek information that confirms our beliefs.

❖ **Anchoring** involves relying on the first story you hear, never correcting your assessment once new knowledge is introduced.

❖ **Availability bias** is the act of believing that the most readily available idea holds more validity than ideas or concepts that are less accessible.

❖ **Hindsight bias** is our tendency to state that something is predictable once it has already unfolded. Consider this the *I could have told you that was going to happen phenomenon*.

❖ The **inactive viewpoint** is when a person immerses themselves in the narrative and does not challenge the story being told even if part of it is illogical.

❖ **Apophenia** is the act of creating connections between things when there isn't one.

MASTERING THE ART OF SUSPENSE

We can always misdirect the reader using the usual tools of red herrings, MacGuffins, or misinterpretations of intent, but imagine how much easier your task as a writer would be if you could misguide the reader without doing anything at all...because their brains have tricked them into misleading themselves. That's the perception gap that we've alluded to in the opening paragraphs. A perception gap occurs when a novelist communicates ideas, but the intended interpretation is misinterpreted by the audience.

In order to use this gap in your favor, examine your narrative, is there a place where you can exploit one of the cognitive elements above? What things will the audience assume to be true that upon closer examination could actually be false? What dual interpretation could this event contain? What could this event mean that might not be immediately obvious?

Audiences tend to trust their personal experiences over new input, so when you begin laying the groundwork for a plot twist try to mirror the characteristics of a common or universal belief, but include one major difference that has the capacity to change the true interpretation of the situation. Readers will often reject or overlook that rouge element because their minds are trained to trust their instincts, and it would take too much mental effort to reconfigure things or install new beliefs. Like water, the human mind prefers the path of least resistance.

Plus, people are often slower to change their beliefs about things if the suggestion comes from an outside source (e.g. a novelist dropping seemingly incongruous clues). Change most effectively occurs when we initiate the idea ourselves, based on our own data collection. Similarly, audiences are also inclined to ignore things they don't understand and substitute them with alternatives based on their own biases and beliefs. So it is essentially the reader's unwillingness to change and consider the alternative that helps make plot twists possible.

This phenomenon is further aided by the fact that your story will have numerous situations and characters who will provide varying opinions and clues to keep your audience occupied so that they pay more attention to one thing than another, essentially muddying the waters of thought. This leaves room for the reader to lose sight of certain possibilities or forget about the inconsistencies between characters' perspectives. And since most people fail to realize that their subconscious minds are constantly making micro-decisions and engaging in leaps of logic to fill in the gaps of their awareness, they miss obvious clues and fall prey to misdirection without even realizing that it is happening.

You can further facilitate this entire process by drafting a narrative that's well-constructed and emotionally charged. After all, the more relatable and compelling the story, the less likely the audience will remain on guard to see the slight changes you're making in the matrix to justify that twist.

Don't believe me? Reexamine *The Sixth Sense* (1999). During one of Dr. Crowe's (Bruce Willis) first meetings with Cole (Haley Joel Osment), the reality behind the film's plot twist is revealed in plain English. In fact, the infamous line in question is even in the movie's original theatrical trailer, essentially spoiling the movie for anyone who's never seen it. Yet, we initially ignore this obvious truth. Why?

> **Cole:** *I see dead people.*
>
> **Dr. Crowe:** *In your dreams? While you're awake? Dead people, like in graves, in coffins?*
>
> **Cole:** *Walking around like regular people. They don't see each other. They only see what they want to see. They don't know they're dead.*

The twist works because the story seems to establish Dr. Crowe as the main character — introducing his wife, his problems, and his former troubled patient in the movie's opening scene. So the reader gets used to the idea of seeing things from the doctor's perspective despite clearly witnessing him get shot ten minutes into the movie. *Then* the narrative refocuses the story on Cole, who takes the role as the story's new protagonist even though most people don't acknowledge the shift or the fact that he is the only person who ever directly addresses Dr. Crowe; however, these are the first of many signs that something is amiss. Cole also becomes the narrative's catalyst for a new interpretation, yet the audience's failure to acknowledge this leads to two false assumptions: Cole is in therapy, and Dr. Crowe is alive. Together these misinterpretations act as one powerful misdirection that leads to a memorable plot twist (and a powerful meditation on redemption) that we're still talking about and analyzing nearly twenty-five years later.

Defining Plot Twists

In the first volume of my Writer Productivity series, *How to Craft a Killer Cozy Mystery*, I define a plot twist as a significant shift in the audience's perception of the story's conflict, specifically how the reader understands the external, internal, and philosophical conflicts that work together to form the narrative. To put it plainly, **a good plot twist subverts audience expectations on all levels — physically, emotionally, and thematically —** *and* **the main character's entire worldview changes.** Two often cited but incredibly pertinent examples are the Keyser Söze twist at the end of *The Usual Suspects* (1995) and the end of the 1968 *Planet of the Apes* film (loosely based on the 1963 novel by Pierre Boulle) when Charlton Heston discovers he's actually on Earth.

Plot twists often appear at the midpoint or end of a story and must make sense within the narrative; therefore, the event or element should be adequately foreshadowed or should hide in plain sight. This will keep the audience from feeling completely cheated or duped. Providing an element of foreshadowing, allows the reader to take a retrospective look at the story and understand where the plot twist started. Just remember, the bigger the twist, the harder you must work to justify it (and hopefully, the better the payoff).

According to *Mastering Plot Twists* (2018) by Jane K. Cleland, a true plot twist should also heighten your story's pace, move the action forward, and encompass three parts: an element that sets your story off balance, a reversal that takes the plot in a new direction, and a moment of danger that adds "urgency and dread." This is great advice for making sure a plot twist doesn't fall flat.

In addition, you must also give the twist a significant series of consequences that alter the physical, emotional, and intellectual, and thematic stakes for the protagonist, all of which will help the audience know how to react to this change. After all, if the audience is confused, they cannot have a clear emotional reaction, which means your plot twist — no matter how earth-shattering — will have no real effect on the reader.

To start developing a plot twist, consider a high-impact life event that could cause your protagonist to question her beliefs about her current reality. For example, the death of a loved one could cause your heroine to start digging into her past where she unearths a life-shattering family secret. So perhaps another simple way to develop a plot twist is to consider how the twist will alter the protagonist's belief system, behaviors, and emotions. You can also create a plot twist by providing new evidence that will cause the audience to shift their assumptions about where the plot is heading for the duration.

When first creating a twist, you may find that your brain fails to leap past the most obvious solution or event, so give yourself plenty of time to explore the world of possibilities before moving forward. Again, we want to give our readers the unexpected while at the same time enriching our characters and adding new dimension to the story.

Now, you may be asking yourself how a plot twist differs from a turning point. Well, they're not all that different except that a plot twist is designed to shock and disrupt the audience's belief system as much as the protagonist's — thus, twisting what we thought we understood into something new. Whereas, a plot turn is simply a revelatory moment for the main character and may even be foreshadowed heavily enough that an observant reader will see the turn coming even if the protagonist doesn't. Turning points are less about stunning the audience and more about character development, i.e. putting the protagonist in a new situation or forcing them to face a new problem.

Checklist: Plot Twists

Use these questions to guide your thinking about the creation of a plot twist:

- ❖ What does my reader expect to happen?

- ❖ How can I realistically subvert that expectation?

- ❖ What can I do to subtly foreshadow my twist?

- ❖ Based on this new moment, how will the story's meaning change? What new beliefs will the characters adopt?

- ❖ What makes this situation physically or emotionally harmful to the main characters?

- ❖ Does this moment propel the plot forward in a believable manner?

Make sure your twist gathers together as many narrative threads as possible. Consider how various plot twists have fooled you in the past. Yes, the shock was certainly memorable; however, wasn't the most satisfying part of the twist your new ability to look back at the story and discover something completely new? Or better yet, to look back and find significance in a previously trivial detail? That's because the twist should be the magnet that brings together seemingly disparate elements. It should answer a question that we didn't know we should have been asking. To achieve those effects, you should not only use foreshadowing but also develop a clear idea of what the thematic, physical, and emotional goals are for your narrative and how they'll logically shift by story's end.

Once you've written your full manuscript, double check the effectiveness of each plot twist with this questionnaire:

- ❖ What new information was revealed?

- ❖ Does it complicate the conflict or introduce new dilemmas?

- ❖ Does it intensify previous goals and characterizations?

- ❖ What unexpected motivation was revealed, and did it put a new spin on the narrative?

- ❖ With the twist in place, what new lesson or theme is being imparted about life or the story at hand?

- ❖ Will this plot twist surprise both the reader and the characters?

- ❖ Will it provide suspense?

❖ Is the moment believable, and has some aspect of it been foreshadowed?

Work to create a scene that relies primarily on character interaction and dialogue to reveal the twist. Avoid unveiling such moments solely through exposition or internal monologue because it dilutes the moment's power and slows the narrative pace. In addition, keep in mind that **this is not about altering the story you've told thus far. It's about forcing the audience to change their perception about what was included.** Therefore, it is important to develop a twist that is logically plausible within the world you've built and in conjunction with the characters you've created. Avoid having a character do or say things that are incongruous to their previous behavior just to make a plot twist work.

FAQ: Plot Twist

Can I have more than one plot twist?

Of course, a story can have more than one plot twist. Just remember that each twist should enrich the overall narrative by adding new information, deepening characterization, heightening the tension, and increasing the stakes. To disguise your twist while simultaneously keeping it in plain sight, you can incorporate misdirection in the form of red herrings, unreliable narrators, MacGuffins, and so forth. To pull this off seamlessly, involves a lot of thought and planning. That's why many authors limit the number of twists to two major ones — at the midpoint and at the end — and I suggest you do the same to avoid confusing your audience or overtaxing yourself.

Are there any pitfalls to creating a plot twist?

Yes! Most hinge on the fact that audiences are so hip to the phenomenon that it has become harder to fool them and doubly harder to impress them. Now, while it is worth noting that psychologists Jonathan Leavitt and Nicholas Christenfeld did a study in 2011[3] indicating that audiences still get just as much enjoyment (if not more) out of plot twists even if they've been spoiled in advance, you don't want to take that risk. Most agents and editors aren't kind to poorly done or easily unraveled twists, so do yourself a favor and avoid the following mistake:

Don't confuse a deus ex machina with a twist. Having someone or something heretofore unseen swoop in out of nowhere to save the day in the final chapter is not a twist. I don't care how much backstory you give that character in the moment of their introduction, it is just going to feel like a cheap trick. The same admonishment applies for final chapter scenes where the hero or villain gain strength (or weakness) based on some random talisman we haven't previously seen. The egregiousness of just tacking things onto the end and calling it a twist cannot be overstated. Do not do this because it is lazy writing that will only enrage your audience. Strong plot twists are weaved into the story from the beginning through character, behavior, setting, circumstance, exposition, and foreshadowing. Do the work!

Types of Plot Twists

Below, you will find examples of some common plot twists gleaned from pop culture. Writers are brainstorming new ones and redefining old ones every day, and I encourage you to do the same. Please note that I have mostly provided film examples since those more often allow for a common point of reference.

❖ **Family Secrets:** *Star Wars* (1977) – This plot twist involves a reveal about the main character's lineage.

❖ **Role Reversal:** *The Harder They Fall* (2021) – This plot twist uses gender stereotypes or the reader's own in-

---

3.   https://journals.sagepub.com/doi/abs/10.1177/0956797611417007

herent bias to sway audience belief in one direction only to shift that belief later in the story.

❖ **Double Trouble:** *The Prestige* (1995 book, 2006 film) – A plot twist where two characters originally perceived as different people turn out to be the same person (or in the case of our example, one person is revealed as being two).

❖ **Evil From Within:** *Raising Cain* (1992) – This plot twist exposes the main character as the narrative's antagonistic element or reveals that the protagonist has concealed the ugly truth surrounding his or her involvement.

❖ **Unreliable Narrator:** *Memento* (2001) – Similar to the above, this plot twist reveals the main character's distortion of the facts in their telling of the tale. These omissions can be an intentionally malicious deception or an unintentional one — such as an impaired or suppressed memory due to ailment, age, or psychological trauma. The misdirect here is that the person's altered version of the story distorts the audience's perception.

❖ **Good Guy in Disguise:** *Harry Potter and the Deathly Hallows* (2007 book, film 2010 & 2011) – A plot twist where the assumed bad guy turns out to be an ally or temporary savior. Tread carefully with this one and use adequate foreshadowing. The key is to balance the character's dark and the light elements as this itself is the true quality of humanity. Otherwise, if you set up the character as evil incarnate then later claim he's harmless, the extreme whiplash will alienate your audience.

❖ **Big Bad Goes Undercover:** *The Dark Knight Rises* (2012) – This plot twist reveals the villain as someone unexpected or proves someone is the exact opposite of what they appear on the surface.

❖ **Bigger Big Bad:** *The Avengers* (2012) – This plot twist reveals that the person or entity the hero thinks is the big threat is just a precursor to something or someone even more menacing.

❖ **From Bad to Worse:** *The Butterfly Effect* (2004) – In this plot twist, the protagonist's perfect solution to the conflict makes matters worse, delaying resolution and introducing a new climax.

❖ **It Was All a Dream:** *Vanilla Sky* (2001) – This plot twist exposes the story as a dream, fantasy, alternate reality, computer program, or hallucination of one or more characters. Unless cleverly executed with foreshadowing and a strong theme, writers should avoid this plot twist as it typically annuls the efforts of the story and results in reader disappointment instead of delight.

❖ **Trouble in Paradise:** *Planet of the Apes* (1963 book, 1968 film) – This plot twist challenges where and when the story is really taking place — hell is really heaven, Earth is really Mars, reality is really simulated, et cetera.

❖ **Dead Again:** *The Sixth Sense* (1999) – In this plot twist, a character thought to be alive is revealed as dead.

❖ **Dead Alive:** *Godzilla* (1998) – A plot twist where a character presumed dead resurfaces later in the story either as himself or in some other form to provide aid or conflict to the protagonist.

Notice from the examples that a plot twist has more impact on the story than something like a surprise, whose affects are fleeting — much like the highly maligned jump scare.

Plot Reveals

Be advised, a plot reveal is different from a twist.

A plot reveal is new piece of information or an answer to a question that affects the direction of the plot moving forward. In contrast, a twist makes us look differently at the past and the narrative has to be reinterpreted because both the reader and the characters overlooked some aspect of the truth.

A reveal can be any number of things such as a family history, an object, a suspect's motive, or a location. Whatever it is, the reveal is a moment of truth that infuses the story with another round of suspense. Now, the audience has a fresh set of questions to ponder: How will this new information be used, and what will unfold as a result?

So as you plan your story, you'll need to plant some evidence, ideas, or objects along the path that will play a significant role in advancing your hero's agenda. Don't feel compelled to provide every answer immediately because catering too closely to the audience's curiosity kills suspense. Instead, think about how you can stretch out the discovery of that information so there is a slow reveal simmering underneath the story's main action. This may involve a few near misses or following a steady breadcrumb trail of clues to build anticipation. The result is that the audience eagerly awaits for the pieces to coalesce into a comprehensive whole. They are emotionally invested in learning the truth, so they tear through the pages seeking answers.

However, be advised that a slow reveal isn't the same as withholding, which is something we want to avoid. Withholding is about omitting information with little to no intention of filling in the gaps while reveals tease the reader with bits of information so that the revelation unfolds at the most opportune moment for conflict (e.g. revealing the truth of the bride's affair just as she's about to walk down the aisle).

Foreshadowing

Regardless of whether you're using unreliable narration or some other literary form, writers of suspense fiction should establish a clear sequence of events that leave the audience ready to exclaim, *Even though I didn't see the ending coming, the story could not have ended any other way!* You can ensure this reaction through the use of foreshadowing — either blatant or subtle — so that the audience can recognize (in retrospect!) the breadcrumbs laid along the path to your resolution.

Foreshadowing occurs when a seemingly unimportant event or object is mentioned to lay the groundwork for future reveals. These hints about what's to come are significant because they work to either increase the reader's empathy for the character or increase the audience's anticipation about the outcome. Moreover, foreshadowing can emerge through the use of almost any literary element — setting, plot, dialogue, characterization, action, et cetera.

We are highlighting the importance of foreshadowing in this book because it is a precursor to suspense. It is the element that gets readers worried, curious, or eager to know more about the dangers, secrets, and complications lurking ahead. For example, early indicators of the protagonist's fear of the dark will make us wonder how they will deal with that problem when things become bleak. Or if we want to use foreshadowing to reveal character and build motivations for later actions, we can drop hints about their latent strengths, intentions, dreams, or talents. For example, in *Back to the Future III* (1990) there are several hints throughout regarding Marty's love of the cowboy classic, *A Fistful of Dollars* (1967), which becomes the inspiration for how he outsmarts Mad Dog Tannen during the gunfight in the movie's finale.

Foreshadowing also can help justify plot twists or any other inexplicable events that fail to align with the cause-and-effect trajectory of your narrative. In other words, this technique can help a situation seem less random and more plausible, potent, and impactful. Without proper foreshadowing, you may find that readers describe your ending as unsatisfying, contrived, or farfetched.

If you're unfamiliar with this literary device, consider "The Lottery" (1948) by Shirley Jackson. Her short story is set in a quiet farming community and opens on the day designated for the lottery drawing. The characters never state the purpose of the event, but the truth is foreshadowed through the actions and reactions of the characters as well as the objects used during the ritual. Jackson's story is quite powerful, so I hesitate to reveal the ending. But I will say that the villagers keep their distance from the big black drawing box, mothers worry for their sons, children gather stones while the adults huddle in tight circles, and the reader gets the eerie feeling that this lottery isn't about a million dollar jackpot.

Foreshadowing should appear at the start of a story but can also surface in the middle or the early part of the last act as a reminder of things previously mentioned. In order to use the technique properly, place clues, hints, or details about an event as early in your narrative as possible. This means if you have a 3,800-word short story like Shirley Jackson's "The Lottery" (1948), you need to follow her example and foreshadow the truth of the ritual from the first paragraph. You can even use things like the title, chapter headers, the cover, or the illustrations if applicable.

Just don't wait until the last hundred words, and make sure that the references are subtle, varied, and spread throughout the earliest parts of the text. Place the clues in a manner that seem ordinary or join them in combinations that lead in the opposite direction. Think of foreshadowing as a delicate balance between teasing and telegraphing . The audience should walk away with a small hunch, not a full-blown belief. Anything too obvious dilutes the story's suspense and the audience's pleasure of piecing things together themselves.

Also, don't editorialize or have the protagonist make a statement that is actually an aside to the audience indicating the true outcome. For instance, avoid the following: *If I'd known that would be the last time I'd see Julie alive, I would have told her to stay out of the ocean that day.* This takes nearly all of the mystery out of Julie's trip to the beach because it gives away her death. It is equally egregious when the author steps forward to address the audience: *When she walked into the office, she had no idea this would be the day she'd get fired.* If the reader is inside a character's head, we as writers can't insert ourselves to make comments about the result — that pulls everyone out of the story and it's not foreshadowing! But the worse offense is when such statements blatantly remind the audience that the narrator survived to tell the tale: *Had I known I'd be staring down the gun barrels of three drug dealers, I never would have accepted that invitation to Mike's bachelor party.* Don't step outside the story to create suspense, the key is to stay in the moment and build emotion. Remember, it isn't until all of the foreshadowed clues coalesce that the unsettling outcome should be revealed.

What's fun about foreshadowing is that you can add these inferences at whatever point best suits your writing process. If you're a plotter, add clues as you brainstorm. If you're a pantser, go back through your completed manuscript and decide which events need foreshadowing, then backtrack a couple chapters to insert your hints. But keep in mind, the darker and more complex the story, the more foreshadowing you'll need to implement to justify each event, particularly the shocking conclusion. Be smart about the size and frequency of your foreshadowing — doing so, will not only increase the suspense but also improve the overall credibility and unity of your writing.

Checklist: Foreshadowing

❖ **Hint at memories or secrets** your main character harbors and that will later be revealed to disempower, embarrass, or hurt the protagonist. Similarly, you can drop early clues about talents or phobias to suggest how the hero will succeed or fail at future challenges.

❖ **Use as symbolism.** For example, in Shirley Jackson's "The Lottery" (1948), the black collection box and the black dots on the tickets are symbols of death but also help to foreshadow how the story will end.

❖ **Create an event, situation, or anecdote** (i.e. a short tale told by another character) as a precursor or example of what may happen later on a larger or more disastrous scale. In other words, creating a sequence that ends harmlessly is a good way to foreshadow something more sinister. For example, in your opening scene, a little girl plays near the edge of a pool and drops her favorite doll inside. A lifeguard sees and quickly retrieves it for her. Later in the fifth chapter, a man dressed in overalls, who happens to be the same lifeguard, comes along and kidnaps the girl. Although the child had been warned about strangers, it now makes sense that she would leave with an authority figure who had helped her earlier.

❖ **Be subtle.** Avoid telegraphing or forecasting the truth by being blatant or obvious.

Chekhov's Gun

While many may simply describe Chekhov's Gun as another element of foreshadowing, it is better defined as a dramatic principle writers must grasp in order to understand the process effective plot development. At its heart, the term suggests that every event or detail within a narrative must play some meaningful role. This concept is meant to dissuade writers from including superfluous information that does not pay off in the final act.

The term derives from the work of Anton Pavlovich Chekhov (1860-1904), a Russian playwright best known for *The Seagull* (1896), *Uncle Vanya* (1898), *Three Sisters* (1901), and *The Cherry Orchard* (1904) as well as his collaborations with Konstantin Stanislavski, founder of the Moscow Arts Theatre. Chekhov is often quoted as being one of the greatest playwrights of all time and for that reason his work is often cited amidst examinations of literary history and criticism.

The term "Chekhov's Gun" derives from the ways Chekhov characterized dramatic writing as discussed in a November 1889 letter to Aleksandr Semenovich Lazarev, according to *Russian Literature in the Nineteenth Century: Essays* (1976) edited by Leah Goldberg and Hillel Halkin. The quote attributed to him is as follows:

> "Remove everything that has no relevance to the story. If you say in the first chapter that there is a rifle hanging on the wall, in the second or third chapter it absolutely must go off. If it's not going to be fired, it shouldn't be hanging there."

Admittedly, you may find variations of this quote in your travels as this has since become a well-worn piece of literary advice in the writing community. But wording aside, the lesson remains the same: Any detail that is foreshadowed or prominently featured must serve a narrative purpose and provide a significant payoff by story's end. Otherwise, you are wasting the reader's time by hinting at possibilities that will never come to pass. So Chekhov's Gun isn't an adage that applies solely to firearms, it is guiding principle for keeping our manuscripts focused and unclutter.

A great example of this concept at work can be found in Chekhov's *The Seagull*, wherein Konstantin Treplev kills one of the birds with a rifle and later brings the gun (and the carcass!) onto the stage — eventually, he uses the same rifle to commit suicide offstage. Can you see how the presence of the firearm would feel extraneous if it did not eventually play a role in the culmination of the plot?

Of course, with your own work, you can always put a deeper spin on the situation to create a twist so that the gun is used but not in the way the audience expects. For example, rather than a suicide or a literal death, the gun is stolen and used to frame a character for a crime — thereby creating an emotional or professional death. In such a case, you would still be following through on the promise made by the presence of the object while delivering a narrative that leaves no element unused or unexplained.

Misdirection

Writers are like magicians in that we must distract the audience away from the real ending to help maintain the element of surprise or to invoke a twist. We send readers' attention spiraling in the opposite direction so they won't see the truth coming. Our goal is to have them expecting one thing while on the cusp of receiving something entirely different.

We keep the reader guessing by doing the unexpected while foreshadowing the truth about what's to come; that way, the audience remains invested. However, in those instances when these hints deliberately lead the reader down the wrong path, we're exercising a technique known as misdirection. This is the act of placing the audience's attention on something other than the truth. When writers employ misdirection, they aim to place the reader off balance. Common methods of misdirection include red herrings and MacGuffins.

You will find that these techniques are invaluable because they can help alter the pace of the narrative, change the direction of the plot, and obscure clues until the most opportune moment.

However, it is important to remember that this is the art of misdirection, not misinformation. Writers should never lie to the reader. Instead, aim to cleverly mislead so that the reader lies to himself. In other words, these techniques require a careful assessment of how much or how little to offer the reader while remembering that we don't want to be unfair and we don't want to complicate matters.

In addition, the use of misdirection must serve the plot. Avoid misleading without a specific payoff. Make sure that your use ties into one of the technique's two main implementation methods:

❖ To obscure or conceal something important so that it can be revealed at a later time

❖ To deliberately change the course of the story in an unexpected way so that the reader eventually realizes that it's been destined for that path all along

These techniques can be used outwardly via the author's attempt to mislead the reader and within the text where one character works to misdirect the others in the story — or both, the choice is yours!

But why bother with misdirection? And what role does it play in building suspense? Misdirection helps to draw out the anticipation and uncertainty that comes with waiting for the narrative question to be answered. *Will he or won't she find the killer?* The more we keep our audience guessing, the more attention they'll give to our story and the more they care about the outcome. In essence, that's the cycle of suspense.

Red Herrings

Although most often talked about in terms of crime fiction, red herrings are used in nearly every genre. According to the online edition of *Merriam-Webster*, the term's first known use was in the 15th century, simply referring to fish "cured by salting and slow smoking to a dark brown color." The entry also notes that many attribute the term to the 18th century practice of dragging smoked fish across the trail of hunting dogs to test if they would stay on task or become distracted. Thus, the secondary meaning listed is "something that distracts attention from the real issue."

Other sources, such as the *Oxford English Dictionary*, note the term rose to popularity in 1807 when an English journalist named William Cobbett wrote an opinion piece for the *Political Register*, a weekly London newspaper he founded in 1802. In the article, he facetiously mentioned that as a boy, he'd used the smoked fish to train his hounds as previously described. The fictional story was meant as an analogy for the "political red herring" being perpetrated by his fellow members of the press, who seemed intent on distracting their readership with England's victory over Napoleon rather than revealing the truth of the country's domestic problems. This has caused some people to call into question the truthfulness of the hunting dog attribution. However, regardless of the origin, the term is now considered a prominent literary device and a rhetorical strategy.

In fiction, a red herring is meant to have the same effect: misdirect the reader and lead them down an alternate path. These false leads are either planted by the writer to misdirect readers or by the villain to cover his trail and misguide the protagonist. But unlike standard clues, which are usually cleverly hidden, red herrings work hard to get the reader's attention — i.e. they are meant to be seen and followed. Basically, this is a type of unreliable clue that provides a *temporary* diversion from the truth thereby allowing for a more unpredictable conclusion. Note, the word "temporary." You must eventually course correct and tell the audience what purpose the information, event, or interloper was meant to serve. We don't want a red herring to feel like a total lie so also incorporate clues into the story that foreshadow the true meaning.

When it comes to forming a red herring, the rules are the same as they are for any form of misdirection. Don't cheat the reader by intentionally omitting key information or attempting to mislead with no payoff. Your red herring should be linked to some element of plausibility within the story so that it, again, doesn't feel like an outright lie. Your goal is to use the events of the narrative, the protagonist's own naiveté or false assumptions, and the audience's cognitive biases or previous experiences to send the readers or the characters off in a new direction.

If we think back to our example from Agatha Christie's *The Murder of Roger Ackroyd* (1926), Dr. Sheppard's position in the story as the "Watson" type character is a red herring because it makes the audience *assume* things about him, like his innocence, even though his actions and conversations made tiny indications to the contrary. Admittedly, this approach boarders very closely to a lie of omission, but notice how Christie narrowly sidesteps that pitfall by using Hercule Poirot as the real detective, Dr. Sheppard's memoir as a framing device, and the physician's insincerity as breadcrumbs leading to the real outcome. By allowing the reader to fall for cliches or make assumptions, you aren't cheating them — subverting tropes is a sign of strong fiction. In fact, reinventing stock characters or developing ways to use what the audience already knows about these elements to create something unexpected, may be the easiest way to enter this technique if you're new to the concept.

However, red herrings can take many other forms — some may be tangible (a blood-stained rug) or intangible (observations and opinions). Red herrings can also be faulty reasoning on the part of your protagonist or someone downplaying information that may later prove vital or even an essential character whose appearance causes confusion, confrontation, or distraction. An excellent example of this last one is Sirius Black's appearance in *Harry Potter and the Prisoner of Azkaban* (1999) by J.K. Rowling. Throughout the novel, Harry and the audience are lead to believe that Black is a vengeful Voldemort supporter hoping to kill "the boy who lived," but by story's end, we discover Black is actually Harry's godfather working to protect Hogwarts from a hidden traitor.

Red herrings can also help complicate a story's mystery and prolong its suspense by making the audience question aspects of the narrative such as a character's background or motive, the plausibility of an alibi, the importance of a location, et cetera. And like the other forms of misdirection discussed in this chapter, they are designed to sustain audience interest by falsely suggesting how a clue or situation is connected to the possible solution without revealing the truth behind the final conclusion.

The key to a well-balanced diversion is to disclose information that *seems* to obscure all roads to success and make victory impossible. This glimpse of the unwanted outcome should create worry in the audience, causing them to overlook the truth because they fear the worst.

Once a reader falls prey to a red herring, they are often hesitant to trust their instincts and may find it difficult to decide what direction the narrative is really meant to take. This uncertainty is highly effective for creating and sustaining suspense. However, red herrings should be used sparingly to avoid discouraging or confusing the audience and to maintain the overall integrity of the narrative.

A red herring comes to an end once those questions or false assumptions are resolved and the truth is revealed. This can occur mere chapters after the red herring is put into place or be part of the final act twist. Just be sure that the true meaning of your red herring or the real reason for the false connection is logical and satisfying (funny, heartwarming, or shocking) in terms of the story being told. It also helps if the result or reveal attached to the truth of the red herring further complicates matters by raising additional questions or leads to what appears to be a dead end until the truth is revealed. For example, in *The Da Vinci Code* (2003) by Dan Brown, it *appears* that Bishop Manuel Aringarosa is part of the conspiracy at the core of the plot. Later, the reader discovers the bishop is merely a pawn to the real villain (see what I did there). We know the author was intentional with this red herring because of the Italian to English translation of the character's name: "aringa" means "herring" and "rosa" means "red").

So whether you're using a red herring to disguise a killer's identity or to establish a plot twist for your fantasy or Western, the red herring must connect with your storyline and characters in a way that has a larger payoff when the reader eventually learns the truth.

MacGuffin

Another classic form of misdirection in mysteries and thrillers is the MacGuffin, which is an object, event, or character that helps jump start the plot but often doesn't have the same impact on the conclusion. To put it plainly, a MacGuffin usually occurs in the first act but declines in prominence as the story advances. More often than not, the item's perceived value comes from what it represents to each character as opposed to what it does or what it is actually worth. Even still, it's the glittery appeal of the MacGuffin's initial appearance that draws the hero into the adventure or motivates the protagonist to act, yet **its true purpose is distraction**. Therefore, this technique is often preceded or followed by red herrings that carry the protagonist and reader further away from their investigative goals.

According to William Harmon, author of *A Handbook to Literature* (2012), English screenwriter and script doctor Angus MacPhail is believed to have originated the term during the filming of Alfred Hitchcock's *The 39 Steps* (1935) — even though Hitchcock was the one who would eventually become synonymous with MacGuffins and suspense in the 1940s. While it is unclear exactly how MacPhail developed the concept, it is suggested by the online version of *Merriam-Webster* that the aforementioned duo — who also worked together on *Spellbound* (1945) and *The Man Who Knew Too Much* (1956) — may have borrowed the term from an old comedic story:

> "...in which some passengers on a train interrogate a fellow passenger carrying a large, strange-looking package. The fellow says the package contains a 'MacGuffin,' which, he explains, is used to catch tigers in the Scottish Highlands. When the group protests that there are no tigers in the Highlands, the passenger replies, 'Well, then, this must not be a MacGuffin.'"

Origin aside, this taps into the powerful idea that an audience who anticipates an ending or solution will remain invested in the narrative even if the original element of attraction proves immaterial or invalid. That's the power of the MacGuffin.

In fact, a MacGuffin can be as simple as an object — microfilm, flash drive, disk, or code — or it can be as complicated as a line of evidence that identifies or incriminates the culprit. MacGuffins can also be a person such as a rogue agent, a scientist who has invented a once-in-a-lifetime-cure, or a besieged diplomat.

Interestingly, use of the plot device now known as a "MacGuffin" is said to far predate the term. In "Medieval McGuffins: The Arthurian Model" — a 2005 article published in *Arthuriana*, a quarterly journal published by Perdue University — the author Norris J. Lacy asserts that the Holy Grail mentioned in the bibliographic works about King Arthur could be cited as an early example of a MacGuffin. Since the Holy Grail is defined as a coveted object that is crucial to initiate and advance the plot but whose final disposition is never revealed, it fits the definition as an early narrative example.

Perhaps, a modern and more familiar example of the MacGuffin can be found in *The Maltese Falcon* (1929) by Dashiell Hammett. The title refers to a priceless statuette that is sought by many and that becomes the root of trouble for our protagonist, private investigator Sam Spade. However, our hero's quest for and eventual possession of the falcon isn't the point of the story. In fact, the statuette only appears in two scenes of the novel. Despite its perceived significance, the Maltese Falcon is actually a MacGuffin. Why? Its presence sets the plot in motion, brings together all the characters within its web of influence, and reveals that they are all willing to do anything, including murder, to possess it. And yet, even though the statuette is also a big part of Sam Spade's call to action, his goal (and the novel's true narrative question) is to figure out who murdered his partner and subsequent others. Not only that, we soon discover that the Maltese Falcon is worthless.

But why include such an item if that's the upshot? Well, MacGuffins are not only helpful for driving the plot, they are also excellent ways to reinforce a story's theme. In Hammett's novel, the Maltese Falcon can be viewed as a thematic manifestation of corruption and greed. By illustrating everyone's desire to obtain a priceless gem, at the cost of life and death, it highlights man's destructive nature.

So when crafting your MacGuffin, the item doesn't necessarily need to have a detailed history, but you as the author do need to have a clear idea of how your item will distract from the real issue while still having a logical connection to the world being built by playing an emotional or thematic role in the narrative.

Checklist: Misdirection

As you begin creating elements of misdirection for your fiction, keep in mind that the approach you use shouldn't come out of nowhere. I've stated this several times, but it is imperative that your misdirection — whether it's a red herring or a MacGuffin — plants its roots in the logistical backbone of the current story. In other words, we always want the audience to be able to finish the book and say, *That wasn't what I was expecting, but it makes sense.* Then they should also able to immediately retrace their steps to discover where and how they got tricked.

❖ Have I created a character, object, or event that propels the plot while at the same time taking the readers' attention away from the real solution?

❖ Does the moment or element of misdirection also provide a hint that foreshadows the truth?

❖ Does the misdirection I've created connect to the story's overall theme?

❖ Has the truth behind the misdirect been explained prior to the conclusion? Is there a payoff?

Analyzing Evidence

As you're writing, make sure to provide for moments, especially after interrogations or action sequences, where your characters can slow down, digest what's happening to them, and puzzle through any clues they may have picked up along the way. This will not only help with pacing, but give your audience an opportunity to acclimate themselves as well. This downtime also provides space for an epiphany or a moment of reflection that will help move the story forward. Such flashes of inspiration may be as simple as realizing the importance of a seemingly insignificant detail or it could be as complex as finding the villain's weakness. Either way, the moment should fuel the plot and create turning points in your narrative.

To incorporate this concept, create special scenes where characters can think aloud about what happened, clear their emotions, brainstorm, make a decision, and formulate a plan. Develop interaction between the hero and his allies (i.e. mentor, sidekick, or colleagues) to draw on their collective powers and better analyze the problem at hand. We see this all the time in traditional mysteries, most notably with Dr. Watson and Sherlock Holmes. But for the sake of speaking in broad examples that will help everyone, consider the modern James Bond films where Bond confers with "M." Or think about the modern *Mission Impossible* films when Ethan Hunt calls on Luther and Benji to supply technical and administrative expertise to his dilemma.

Basically, you want to give your hero a sounding board so that he can prepare his mind for the next task. Ideally, this interaction would take place with someone who has specialty knowledge in an area your hero lacks. That way, the secondary character complements the main character, allowing the two parts to come together to make a greater whole. However, if you have a protagonist who is a lone wolf, these moments of contemplation can also be employed using indirect dialogue, often referred to as internal monologue.

Regardless, the techniques for analyzing clues in a group or reflecting on them as an individual are the same. Have your character review the harrowing event in question and highlight all the pertinent information. In doing so, you also want to impart all of the sensory elements so that, as the character analyzes or reflects, he can have a strong emotional response (inward and outward!) to the things being brought to the audience's attention. That emotion should spark the realization of the clue or event's significance, allowing the hero to put together what really happened or define what the clue should mean. From there, the hero (and his team if he has one) should brainstorm through a series of questions or *what if* scenarios about the situation until he has a new theory or plan that moves the story forward in a new direction.

Checklist: Analyzing Evidence

Don't forget that moments of contemplation are just like any other scene and should contain some conflict. If you're building a group scene, this can manifest itself as an argument between characters with differing viewpoints on the evidence or debate over what should be done next. Or if this is a moment of introspection, self-doubt or indecision may act as the conflict holding the hero back. The key is to incorporate this required element while remaining focused on the evidence.

❖ Where are some logical places in your story where the protagonist can take a moment to reflect? Hint: This usually works best after a tense confrontation or action-packed event like a chase scene.

❖ Will this be a team effort using lots of external dialogue or will the hero reflect alone using an internal monologue? What element of conflict or self-doubt can be infused into the exchange?

❖ How will the clues be explained, and how does the main character react to this information? What is his emotional train of thought and the outward manifestation?

❖ What conclusion will be drawn? What's the epiphany?

❖ What problems, theories, questions, or actions will move the story forward?

The Climax

At the end of your final act, you will need to develop a major showdown, confrontation, or battle that resolves the major story question you've been working toward throughout the narrative. This direct confrontation between protagonist and antagonist is known as the climax.

This is typically the point in the story when the villain is at the height of her power and the most vicious applications of her strength on display. And while our hero may be weakened, he isn't powerless. He has a new improved theory or plan, and it's time to execute. Everything he's learned throughout the novel comes into play, and the weaknesses he initially brought to the table have been turned into strengths. And yet, when confronted with this do-or-die moment, the hero initially struggles. His best laid plans crumble — and even if he does appear to succeed, he is confronted by an even stronger stratagem or an unforeseen adversary. But just when things reach their darkest — defenses depleted and on the brink the death — the hero learns another lesson, turns a corner, or digs deeper to find the fortitude that leads to victory.

Your climax includes the story's toughest challenges and highest stakes. This is where protagonist faces his greatest fears, so it is crucial that the series of scenes that encompass your climax contain the highest levels of action and suspense. Make sure that you have escalated your conflict and tension so that it reaches the pinnacle in this moment. If it does so earlier, your climax will feel impotent and readers will walk away dissatisfied.

One way to ensure suspense is to move back and forth between the climax and other seemingly unrelated but crucial scenes that are playing out along the same timeline. For example, while your police detective turned hero is on the roof having a knife fight with the big bad, we cut to his partner rifling through the precinct's files only to discover a clue to where the villain hid a bomb. The audience rushes through the scene anxious to get back to the protagonist, but they have now been given an additional item to worry about. Suspense mounts. Things are getting hectic, and we don't know how our hero will accomplish it all.

If you choose to go this route, let the audience's anticipation drive the pace. Don't skimp on details or cut logical moments to achieve the desired effect of additional tension. The climax should be long enough to fulfill the reader's desire for justice (retribution, et cetera), and it must unfold based on the cleverness, strengths, or talents of the protagonist, not dumb luck or coincidence. Remember, this is the moment the book has been building toward and the sequence the audience has been waiting for — and they expect details! And if you can include an emotional element into those scenes — e.g. think Indy working to save his father at the end of *Indiana Jones and the Last Crusade* (1989) — you'll make the entire event more memorable. After all, the more the victory means to the hero, the more it resonates with the reader.

In addition, the reader will need to see the bad guy suffer, die, or in some way receive his comeuppance in order to feel satisfied with the ending. I was once told by a writing professor that the antagonist needs to suffer a fate equal to or worse than his victims — although that doesn't mean the hero should dole out the punishment. Often, for the sake of keeping the protagonist morally pure, novels are configured so that the villain's hubris or cowardice has him fall on his own sword or miscalculate his ability to escape death.

Regardless of whether you follow that specific philosophy, it must be stated that the villain should not escape completely unscathed unless the story was centered on him from the very beginning. Basically, good should triumph over evil — or at least gets the upper hand. Unlike traditional mysteries, suspense stories tend to muddy the lines between good and evil, so there is a gray area where stories don't end on the side of "good" as much as they land on the "acceptable" side of two evils. So even if your story doesn't end happily, the narrative should at least end in a manner that suggests the conflict has been sufficiently resolved.

And of course, contemporary fiction readers love a good twist, so try to incorporate an unexpected situation that in retrospect seems logical but remains obscured until the very end.

But with those elements in mind, remember that a truly successfully climax must be emotionally satisfying. The reader expects a catharsis when the story's tension and suspense have finally dissipated. They also assume the hero will walk away having learned something about himself or the world around him.

And finally, leave the reader with something that will resonate with them long after they've finished the book like a powerful closing line or a correlation to some universal truth that they can ponder and share with others.

Now that you've been given some insight into what makes a climax successful, consider this list of pitfalls:

❖ Avoid anticlimactic endings where the payoff isn't as significant as promised or the big reveal turns out to be something that was obvious from the start.

❖ Avoid altering your character's personality in the final act to accommodate a happy ending.

❖ Avoid endings where the main action takes place off stage. Readers of suspense expect to be in the heart of things, so devise a closer that shows your villain at his most ferocious.

❖ Avoid killing off the bad guy if he is just going to resurface again moments later in a totally unbelievable way.

❖ Avoid endings that offer a tidy solution to complex conflicts. The climax isn't something that should wrap up quickly. The audience expects, nay, desires a messy and complicated ending. They want to luxuriate in the struggle that should come with solution, so give each story question the attention they deserve and make sure the resolution makes logical sense. Of course, this doesn't mean drag things out unnecessarily. Instead, work to find the balance between chaos and closure.

❖ Avoid killing off the hero without some significant payoff. Usually, when a hero dies at the end of a commercial fiction novel, it serves a larger purpose that creates a satisfying ending in the narrative such as sacrificing himself for a secondary character who will continue to thwart evil for the overall greater good. Watch the James Bond film *No Time to Die* (2021) to see this done right.

❖ Avoid endings that unfold without sufficient depth or detail.

❖ Avoid heroes who succeed by luck, coincidence, or some modern deus ex machina. Remember, we want the protagonist to triumph via his wits, courage, and determination.

Deus Ex Machina

Deus ex machina refers to any plot device used to resolve an unsolvable conflict or point of tension through the unexpected appearance of a heretofore unseen character, object, action, or ability. It is a Latin phrase that means "god from the machine" and refers to the crane that carried a god over the stage at the end of many Greek and Roman plays. This god often appeared suddenly and unexpectedly to provide a solution or decision to a difficult or impossible problem.

According to the online version of *Merriam-Webster*, this concept dates back to at least 5th century B.C. They also note that Euripides was a notable Greek playwright who made early use of this technique in his tragedies. We can see this most notably in his play *Medea* (431 B.C.) where the titular character takes bloody revenge on her unfaithful husband by killing their children and his new fiancée, but she escapes reprimand when she is rescued by a chariot sent by her grandfather Helios, better known as god of the sun.

Today, stories rarely use a deus ex machina because they are typically considered unearned endings. Since they introduce a new element or new rules at the end of the novel, many writers believe this betrays the narrative by defying the story's logic and undoing all the layers of earned characterization.

Denouement

The portion of the story following the climax is known in literary terms as the denouement, which is French for "an untying." During the denouement, order is restored — i.e. the good are rewarded and the bad are punished. All conflicts should be resolved. Every major question answered. Each loose end squared off. All secrets revealed and entanglements unraveled. This may be a scene or series of scenes and can be as simple as your hero reporting to his superior everything that happened and clarifying details not explained during the showdown. Or it may be as complicated as your hero having a series of recovery scenes at the hospital while the police question her about her involvement. Whatever form these scenes take, the idea is that the content provides a clear resolution and sense of finality for the audience. This is also your opportunity to leave the reader wanting more either by alluding to a new mystery to come or hinting that the resolved threat might resurface in a new way. This will help make your ending memorable and, assuming your text is a series, create interest in the next book.

Checklist: Denouement

❖ Have I tied up all loose ends and subplots?

❖ Have I provided meaning to the reader about what happened during the showdown or climax?

❖ Have I summarized the showdown or climax and/or made the protagonist's feelings about that resolution clear?

❖ Have I implied how the protagonist's life has or will change as a result of the story's events?

❖ If applicable, have I planted seeds for the next book?

❖ Have a provided a memorable closing line?

Epilogue

The epilogue is an **optional** follow-up section to the end of the book that briefly covers personal events that occur some significant period of time after the story's main question has been resolved and concluded. Epilogues are typically marked within the text to indicate its separation from the main story. This means a novel should make narrative sense even if the audience fails to read the epilogue.

To be clear, the story's denouement — i.e. the resolution as defined in the previous section — should be strong enough to conclude the story. In other words, the main plot will have been resolved, so your epilogue should only be there if you plan to include additional information to create character depth or add thematic resonance.

What's included in an epilogue often depends on genre, but may be things like weddings, funerals, adoptions, rehabilitation, or recovery. However, if it doesn't enhance reader understanding or simply adds icing to an already frosted cake, cut the material.

Like the prologue, the purpose of the epilogue has been so hotly debated that some writers now refer to this section using the musical term "coda." Why? Well, the tendency in contemporary fiction is to place epilogue-like material into the section of the novel where the denouement normally lives. Once again, I must stress that the denouement is the resolution to the conflict while the epilogue is how the denouement has affected the characters over an extended period of time moving forward into the future. Modern writers have mashed those two concepts together to form a hybrid entity often referred to as the "coda." This is really just a final chapter that builds on the resolution by providing greater insight into the characters' personal life and how that's changed since the conclusion. This part of the story may have a slightly different tone or mood than the primary narrative — hence the term "coda," whose definition is "a concluding musical section distinct from the main structure," according to *Merriam-Webster* online.

However, it is important to note that unlike the epilogue, the coda is not marked intext to indicate its separation from the main story. Also, please be advised that the epilogue should not to be confused with the afterword, which is a final statement about the novel's topic made by the author or his contemporaries. See the glossary for more information.

Whether you include a clearly marked epilogue or the more nebulous coda is up to you. I have simply introduced these terms for your enlightenment. My recommendation is that you concentrate on building a strong climax and denouement because those are the key ingredients to a strong ending...and a vital part of what audiences expect.

Research

Research is the foundation of writing. When we draft a novel, part of our worldbuilding may involve the collection and examination of information on Ancient Rome, modern-day Russia, or the effects of global warming on hummingbirds. Regardless of the subject, research plays a role in our prose by helping us make better decisions about where to take the narrative. Think of research as the grand assistant to imagination where one ensures the other thrives.

Unfortunately, some writers are so intimidated by the idea of research that they forgo the process altogether even though research should be as satisfying as writing. As the old saying goes, "If you're not enjoying your research, you're writing the wrong book." Remember, if you're invested in what you're writing, you have a much stronger chance of impressing the audience. That's why research is an important step for writers of all levels and genres. So, here are a few tips to make the research process quick, painless, and positive.

Be Organized. Create a plan of attack before pounding the pavement for relevant sources. Pinpoint the specific topic for research to avoid wasting time. For example, narrow things down to the aftermath of the Third Punic War rather than the broad topic of the Roman Republic. Use folders to organize relevant findings, giving each subject its own file.

Be nosey. The best way to fill your novel with accurate and realistic information is to do an expert interview. Seek out attorneys, cops, doctors, military officers, et cetera, and ask them what makes their job tough or rewarding. Inquire about specialized tools, training, or jargon. This insider look into their world will legitimize your topic and provide a sense of humanity and passion to the profession. To secure the best shot for accurate and innovative information, aim for people who are at the top of their fields. Local universities, professional organizations, and clubs are all great places to start. Prepare for these interviews by drafting your questions in advance and requesting a predesignated interview time. Study the topic so you can use your time wisely and ask intelligent follow up questions.

When interviewing experts, ask high-value, open-ended questions that prompt conversation and involve more than a "yes" or "no" answer. This approach gives your interviewee the best opportunity to share their expertise in their own words and increases the chance they'll reveal compelling information you may not have known to ask. But as you probe into their world, be respectful of their time. If they cut your hour-long interview in half because they have a meeting, don't get upset. Find ways to maximize the session by leading with your most pressing concerns and leaving a questionnaire if they're open to it. Always ask if you can contact them for follow-up information, and confirm the best method.

Strive to foster a connection between their world and the world of your novel. Be kind, not combative, and thank them for their expertise. Utilizing their knowledge will make for a powerful audience experience and ensure your novel includes nuances that make it stand out from the competition.

Be Collegiate. Using your town's college or university library is often more effective than going to the public library. You'll gain access to electronic databases that offer scientific studies, research reports, polls, statistics, government surveys, and expert opinions not available on the internet or in your average bookstore. Of course, you'll still need to authenticate the material by cross-referencing the author's qualifications with other noted experts, verifying that the work is current, and pinpointing the purpose of the materials (i.e. making sure they are not a company's promotional advertisements disguised as a research study). The librarian will be happy to assist you, and most universities offer free library cards to local residents.

Be Joe Friday. The 1949 radio police procedural known as *Dragnet* (later turned into several shows and a feature film) centered on a detective named Joe Friday, whose catchphrase was "Just the facts." Joe rebuked gossip, extraneous details, personal bias, and speculation. This is the same mindset we should use when conducting research for a project. Track down the source and settle for nothing less than verifiable facts, data, eyewitness testimony, science, et cetera. If finding the source material proves impossible, verify the information through three reputable secondary outlets before incorporating those findings into your work. And in those instances where no solid answer seems apparent, concede that sometimes failing to uncover an answer is the answer. Instead, devise a fair and balanced way to have characters discuss what you've found, lay out the facts side by side so that the reader can draw their own conclusions, or fill in the gaps with your imagination — after all, we are writing fiction.

Be Attentive. Istanbul was Constantinople. Things change. What we were sure of yesterday, may be false today. You are the head of your research department, so keep abreast of changes by double-checking even those things you think you already know.

Be Meticulous. Although similar to the advice above, this tip is especially important if you're using a real location for a chase scene (like the streets of Time Square) or if you're describing a specific process (like dismantling an AK-47). Readers are notorious for finding the smallest thread of illogic and asking WHY, WHY, WHY until the whole story unravels. One false statement or inconsistency like claiming the "G" train runs through Times Square, can put the credibility of your book in jeopardy, so be thorough.

Be sensible. Once your coffers are overflowing with information, the knee-jerk reaction is to stuff everything into the manuscript to show how productive you've been. The problem is that you're writing a novel, not a textbook. Your primary goal is to entertain. So when considering how much research to add, focus on things that will advance the story, aid characterization, or enhance setting. Ask yourself: Is it relevant information? Is it accurate information? And is it new information? If you come up with a negative answer for any of these, reconsider whether the information is worth adding. Also, remember that some of your research will be direct in its application while some will be indirect, i.e. merely informing how the idea shapes the story. Either way, make sure these additions meld seamlessly with the voice and style of your work.

In general, dialogue is an easier medium for incorporating research than the narrative text, but genre will also dictate how deep you'll need or want to go. For example, because of the jargon used in hospitals and the complexity of certain health procedures, medical thrillers often have quite a bit of research on the page. However, a military romantic thriller that requires just as much research, due to its setting on a naval battleship, may not utilize its research verbatim because the material speaks more to protocol, locale, and plot than the literal words on the page.

Bluffing your way through the research or ignoring it altogether will only result in a book that's unbelievable. Enough people have been inside operating rooms, joined the military, dealt with attorneys, or been on trial themselves to have a clear idea of what is and is not possible within a particular field. Avoid reader backlash. Study your novel's main concepts before you begin. Doing so, might be a springboard to larger ideas.

And finally...

Be proactive and continue to work on research techniques throughout your career. Here are some books that will help in that regard:

❖ *The Modern Researcher* (1992) by Jacques Barzun and Henry F. Graff

❖ *The Craft of Research* (2016) by Wayne C. Booth, Gregory G. Colomb, et al.

❖ *Researching Online for Dummies* (2000) by Reva Basch and Mary Ellen Bates

FAQ: Research

How much research is too much?

If you've spent so much time on descriptions and explanations that you've lost sight of characterization or advancing the story, it is too much research. If reading it aloud sounds like gobbledygook, it is too much research. We don't ever want to do anything to confuse the reader — and that includes adding too much information. Novels with suspense must move quickly, so don't add anything that doesn't serve a purpose.

How should I organize my research?

By subject. You can use files and index cards to then put each topic in alphabetical order. If you prefer to do this on your computer or a website like Trello, that's even better. Most writer's software, like *Scrivener*, have a specialized research folder where you can collate materials. So even if you don't use everything, save you work — including how you found each source and where you found them — because you never know what will come in handy for a future book.

Should I travel to the locations that I plan to depict in my work?

When researching locations, go to the real locale if you can. This will help you experience what's unique about the place and spark ideas about how to best utilize the locales in conjunction with characterization and action. Explore with your five senses unencumbered by the technological distractions of everyday life. Put down your camera phone. What sounds do you hear? What odors attract or repel you? Is the temperature what you expected? What adjectives would you use to describe the taste of the place if there is one? How does being there make you feel? Does the space appear bigger or smaller than you imagined? What are the dimensions? What does the location remind you of? How would your characters act in this environment?

Once you've recorded everything you can into one big mental picture, grab your cellphone and take video. Record a voice memo with your impressions. Take notes so that you remember the experience for your next writing session. Collect any brochures, guidebooks, or online accounts you can find to supplement your experience. The more mediums in which you can capture your experience, the better you will be able to convey the setting or activity when the time comes.

If you can't visit, read books, talk to people who have visited, or contact a native. Interact with as many people as possible. Or if all else fails, find a YouTube video that provides a site-seeing tour or fact-filled overview. Locations and settings are an essential part of storytelling. If vivid enough and vital enough to the narrative, they can become their own character rife with dangers, pitfalls, and history (consider the luxury ocean liner in the 1969 novel *The Poseidon Adventure* by Paul Gallico).

The more work you put into your research, the more it will pay off. And the more you know about the world you're trying to build, the easier it will be to foreshadow clues and create connections between seemingly disparate elements.

However, this shouldn't be an excuse to procrastinate on your writing. After all, you don't need to have mastery on a subject to start a novel. Not every piece of research needs to go into your story. In fact, most of it will probably be distilled into a few brief paragraphs of background to motivate a character's actions or help you state the facts with confidence. The rest can be set aside for future use or to spawn new stories. Just remember, that whatever research information you choose to include must move the narrative forward or aid in characterization. If the material can't accomplish those aims, it shouldn't be in the manuscript. Trust the voice that says, *Enough is enough.*

If my outline is light, is it okay to turn to my research for inspiration?

Absolutely! When you run into the wall that is writer's block or you're experiencing a downturn of energy for the project, reread your research. New facts often spark new ideas and delving back into that material may help remind you why undertaking the project was so important.

Generating Ideas

If you are short on ideas, start by thinking about what world your story will encompass — the federal government, Hollywood, private education — and what themes or moral questions your novel will cover in its exploration of that social space. What conflicts or tensions can your protagonists face?

If this proves too daunting, look for inspiration in the news headlines. Allow the text and images to inspire you. From there, create a list of twenty topics that you will examine for use as potential plotlines. The seed for a story can be large or small, simple or complex. Ask yourself, what is the big social or political threat, or the common worry, that plagues the world today? Every decade has a defining feature. The sixties had free love, the eighties had the war on drugs. Think about what dangers arose as a result? What monsters or villains can you create to reflect today's or yesterday's problems both literally and thematically? Keep in mind, the only thing that distinguishes a grand idea from a dud is the excitement that manifests as that seed takes root. Do outlines, free association, or further research until you find something noteworthy.

Never discount an idea. Even your own disparate interests (skateboarding combined with Tai chi) have the potential to spawn something great. Read everything — in your genre, out of your genre, poetry, nonfiction — you never know what will spawn a new idea. Determine what's interesting to you or what you want to learn more about and engage in some research to inspire new ideas for the story you want to tell.

If research isn't your thing, consider writing about something that angers, agitates, or scares you on a deep emotional level. If it evokes a visceral reaction, it is possible that your readers may act similarly. To start, create an alternate world revolving around that disturbing person, place, or thing. Then greatly amplify or exaggerate the problem so that it becomes something that others cannot ignore or they may be adversely affected by as well. Finally, create a character or situation where that angering issue has to be thwarted, resolved, or eliminated... OR ELSE someone meets their demise, the fate of the world hangs in the balance, or some other high-stakes scenario.

Another way to develop ideas is to combine two pre-existing concepts to create something new. For example, Gretchen McNeil once described her novel *#MurderTrending* as a mashup of *The Running Man* (1987) and *The Breakfast Club* (1985). The trick for making something like this work is to focus on one major image or one key aspect from each part of the mashup and use the "what if" portion of the premise building technique — which we will outline in a moment — to create new characters, new technology, and new scenes that will make the new idea uniquely yours.

Of course, it goes without saying that using mashups to brainstorm is never an invitation to steal verbatim text. That's plagiarism. Anyone directly using another person's work without giving them proper credit is committing a crime. The purpose here is simply to give your thoughts direction and narrow your vision to a manageable timeframe or genre.

Once your brainstorming session has produced a compelling problem, setting, or character, work to build a story concept that puts the protagonist's success and well-being in jeopardy. In suspense stories, the premise often involves a social question that has a morally gray area where you can provide a valid justification for both sides of the argument via a battle of wills. *Are we too dependent on computers? Are law enforcement cameras an invasion of privacy? What is acceptable behavior within a war?* Consider invoking an ethically ambiguous concept to help heighten your conflict, intensify the protagonist's stakes, and create impossible dilemmas.

How to Write a Premise

Once you've generated a clear idea to write about, the next step is to write a premise. A premise is a short but enticing two- to four-line statement that outlines the plot. The premise is the cornerstone for all your ideas, and the beacon that will guide you as you work. If you can pinpoint your premise prior to outlining or writing, the narrative will be easier to draft because you will have already identified the goals and motivations that will drive your main characters.

But first, since the theme is arguably the most important aspect of devising a premise, let's take a few moments to define the term before we delve into the technique of putting everything together.

Theme is defined as the story's main idea or the statement a piece makes about a given topic. An effective theme in fiction also points to what the main character and the reader will learn about themselves over the course of the story. Even though commercial genre fiction (mystery, sci fi, romance, horror, et cetera) is mainly meant to entertain, it should still center around a theme, philosophy, or moral concept that will challenge the main character and provide an answer to the story's overall question. This can be as basic as "crime doesn't pay," "what goes around comes around," or "love conquers all," but bestselling authors go deeper than this. Be mindful that a story can most certainly have more than one theme and that themes should be universal, meaning they apply to everyone regardless of a person's status or station in life.

When looking to devise a theme, consider what stance or attitude you have about the topics your story will cover. This is considered the tone your work will take and is conveyed through your diction (word choice) and style (manner of expression).

Be advised that the theme does not need to be overt and isn't necessarily something the characters are consciously sharing through dialogue and action as much as it is the author's careful use of characterization and setting to convey an overall subtextual message to the audience. Consider the theme something that the author helps initiate but that the reader will ultimately find between the lines as characters encounter obstacles along their tumultuous journey to the conclusion.

Premise Formula

Step 1: Consider your theme. What social problems or issues will your novel explore? How is your story familiar yet intriguingly different than others in the genre? What point will your story ultimately make? What emotional experience will it deliver? And how do all of those answers play into the theme? Respond to each question and keep writing until you have several captivating answers. Only then, should you undertake the endeavor of crafting your premise. Establishing that theme early will add context to the dilemma your character must overcome.

Step 2: Brainstorm your character's internal/external goals and motivations in relation to the novel's theme. Outline these desires and drives using strong verbs. Also, develop a brief description of your protagonist using vivid adjectives. Use the chapters on conflict, character, and setting to assist you.

Step 3: Summarize the specific crisis, obstacle, or conflict your protagonist will tackle during the tale. To do this, imagine a scenario involving your protagonist, then consider what would happen if things went horribly awry. Use vibrant detail. This will be your "what if" sentence. The section on stakes will assist in this area.

Step 4: Draft your premise using two sentences. To being, start your first sentence with "imagine." That will help you brainstorm, but basically, this first sentence will set up the ordinary world of your story along with the theme and protagonist that you brainstormed in the earlier steps. The second sentence should be the "what if" question outlined in the third step that poses the major problem that will act as the primary narrative question for your tale. Again, make this an impossible situation so that your story is teeming with high stakes. Your goal with this last step is to put everything together into one (present tense) compound sentence that will become the premise that guides you through the writing process.

Here's an example using *Minority Report* (2002), starring Tom Cruise:

❖ **Theme:** The future isn't set.

❖ *Imagine* a world where crimes can be predicted before they happen.

❖ *What if* the strait-laced cop in charge of predicting those crimes is accused of murder and has to go on the run?

❖ **Premise:** Chief John Anderton is the face of the Pre-Crime Program, where violent acts can be predicted before they happen, but when the tables are turned and he's accused of a future murder, he's forced to go on the run to clear his name.

Here's an example using *The Wizard of Oz* (1939), starring Judy Garland:

❖ **Theme:** There's no place like home.

❖ *Imagine* a lonely, young girl runs away from her farm in search of respect and a more colorful life.

❖ *What if* the girl becomes trapped in a strange land where an accidental run-in with a wicked stranger puts her and her friends lives in such danger that she fears she may never see her family again?

❖ **Premise:** When Dorothy runs away from home, she finds herself stranded in the strange land of Oz where she must protect herself, and the friends she creates along the way, from the tyranny of the Wicked Witch of the West, whose hold over the land stands between Dorothy's home and Oz's happiness.

A strong premise should spark a myriad of ideas that you can write down as potential parts of your story. Once you have all of that information, develop an outline that defines each scene in your novel. If you're a pantser and the idea of outlining or plotting ahead sounds miserable, consider at least brainstorming your beginning, ending, and the overarching story question in advance. When you finally sit down to write, start with the conclusion then craft the opening. By knowing where you're going — or as personal development author Stephen Covey would say, "beginning with the end in mind"— you give yourself a roadmap to the finish line that will help you stay on track.

Checklist: Premise

Even if you don't use my process, make sure your premise encapsulates the following:

❖ What is the inciting incident?
❖ What motivates the protagonist to act?
❖ What worst-case obstacle will she face?
❖ What w*ill she or won't she question* does this story endeavor to answer?
❖ What is the main setting?
❖ What is the overarching theme?

Your premise will act as the foundation on which you will build your story. Come back to these answers whenever you are unclear what direction to take with your narrative.

Subplots

Subplots are a fantastic way to add more depth and complexity to your work. However, crafting a subplot is tricky because they must help drive the main plot and develop characterization while also telling their own story. Therefore, your subplot should not be an afterthought or something that you plug in last minute because you need to fortify a mushy middle. Like every other aspect of your story, subplots should have a definitive purpose and play a pivotal role in the overall narrative.

Every good novel-length narrative should have one or two subplots. Avoid incorporating more than this because you create more work for yourself and run the risk of confusing the reader by pulling too much focus from the primary narrative. In the mystery genre, one of your two subplots often involves the personal life of the main character or sleuth. The other may involve a family member, friend, or one of the story's secondary characters. Regardless of who the subplot centers around, this information eventually braids itself into the main story and aids in clarifying the conclusion.

Create meaningful subplots by considering the personal problems of the protagonist. You could also place a secondary character in an unexpected situation or role, develop a seemingly unrelated story problem for them, and correlate the emotional root of that problem to some aspect of the protagonist's struggle. If it's easier, reflect on these questions:

❖ What personal problem could your main character deal with that could initially appear unrelated to the overall plot?

❖ Is there a secondary character who may help or hinder the protagonist? And if so, how and why? Is it possible to mirror some aspect of the principal storyline through a character who acts as a **foil**[1]?

❖ What seemingly unrelated problem can the secondary or main character grapple with that will eventually lend to the primary story question?

❖ What unexpected correlations (emotional and physical) can be made toward the main conflict and eventual resolution?

Again, strive to create two separate subplots for your story — one related to protagonist, the other to a secondary character — that will converge into the main storyline as the plot progresses.

Successful subplots have an engaging conflict, progress the story, develop character, and reflect the theme without overshadowing the primary narrative. And yet, the overall premise should crumble if these storylines are removed.

So don't add a subplot simply because that's what all the craft books told you to do. These additional storylines must be incorporated in such a way that it becomes vital to the overall narrative. If you can't identify how or where to add subplot or the addition adds nothing to the main plot, cut it!

[1] A **foil** is a character used to highlight the traits, motivations, and values of another character (usually the protagonist) through comparison. The foil may be the total opposite of his opposing character or nearly identical except for one crucial difference, but the juxtaposition should create a thematic or emotional dynamic between the pair like shy versus outgoing or responsible versus reckless. Common literary examples include Sherlock Holmes and Dr. Watson or

Harry Potter and Draco Malfoy, but don't confuse the opposing nature of the foil with the definition of antagonist.

A foil is mean to highlight the different path another character could have taken (either good or bad) while an antagonist is a main character or entity who acts in direct conflict with the protagonist's goal. An antagonist drives the plot forward by creating obstacles while a foil is primarily designed to reveal facets of another character that wouldn't be possible without the inclusion of his mirror-like counterpart. In essence, foils aren't about opposing the protagonist's actions, they are meant to oppose the protagonist's characterization.

An excellent example of both foils and subplots is *Harry Potter and the Half-Blood Prince*, wherein Draco Malfoy is tasked with finding a way to sneak Death Eaters into Hogwarts and to kill Dumbledore. A dark path that's meant to demonstrate the evils Harry could have fallen privy to if he hadn't been strong enough to avoid his more ominous urges. This contrast becomes even clearer when we consider the book's main storyline where Harry is undergoing the noble task of finding the horcruxes that are necessary to defeat the Lord Voldemort.

Standalone or Series?

Before starting your manuscript, decide whether your story will act as a one-time tale with a self-contained storyline or if you'd like to continue the protagonist's adventures in a series. This is important to pinpoint early because each choice will have a different effect on your approach to things like characterization and plot. This decision will also color how publishers market the book — many of whom traditionally prefer series for their continued revenue potential.

To begin, think about what kind of story you want to tell, what type of hero you have, and what sort of problems you want to solve. For example, traditional mysteries like amateur sleuth stories and private detective fiction lend themselves more easily to series because of the open-ended number of potential adventures and cases. On the other hand, thrillers are often standalones since they tend to have more definitive endings. However, there are no hard rules in this regard. In fact, dozens of authors like Tana French and Rachel Howzell Hall have had success in both spheres, so don't let peer pressure or a publisher's wish list be your deciding factor. Consider your needs first.

And yet, I cannot express how important it is to make this decision as early as possible so that you can either plot a finite conclusion or plant seeds for a sequel with a protagonist whose problems and profession can move forward from book to book. Not to mention, this question will absolutely be the first thing agents ask during your quest for representation.

So here are some points to consider. I have marked them as pros and cons even though many of them can fall on either side of the argument.

Standalones

- ❖ Pro – freedom to tell the story in any format

❖ Pro – freedom to draft characters without concern for future narratives

❖ Pro – typically have a ticking clock and high-concept hook, which make them more compelling

❖ Pro – protagonist can have a drastic change at the end of the story (e.g. fatal injuries, jail time, relocation, new profession)

❖ Pro – freedom to start a completely different work upon completion

❖ Con – success determined by immediate sales

❖ Con – generally must have the "perfect" premise to draw large audience

Series

❖ Pro – can rely on premise *and* repeated characterization to draw an audience

❖ Pro – larger margin of error for bad plots since audiences are coming for the characters just as much the conflict

❖ Pro – can develop a character or setting in detail and show their progression over time

❖ Con – tied to a specific character or setting for the long-term and the task of keep them fresh

❖ Con – continuity; characters must stay consistent from book to book and thus typically undergo smaller changes at the end of each story (e.g. falling in love, loss of family member, minor injuries)

❖ Con – readers who haven't read the whole series may be less inclined to buy new entries

❖ Con – publishers judge the work on the sale of the first two books despite series typically being a slow sell, not catching fire until the third or fourth book

Standalones

A standalone is a novel with an autonomous plot. Some prominent examples include *Pretty Girls* (2015) by Karin Slaughter, *The Woman in Cabin 10* (2016) by Ruth Ware, and *Something in the Water* (2018) by Catherine Steadman. In such books, the characters receive a thorough conclusion and are destined to exist within a single text. So in some ways, the standalone offers greater flexibility than a series in the area of characterization because none of the players have the burden of recurring in future narratives. The author can present each person in a manner that logically enhances the plot rather than having to develop them as a potential fixture. This flexibility also lends itself to a more unpredictable ending than the series where it is implied that the heroine, or a portion of her team, will emerge healthy enough to slay another day. By contrast, the standalone's decisive ending allows the *will she, or won't she succeed* story tension to have a much larger emotional impact since the author could choose to have the heroine lose her freedom or even her life in pursuit of her goal.

Standalones also rely more heavily on their premise as the success factor for the novel while series have the luxury of using returning characters as part of their draw. To put it bluntly, the standalone's plot must be doubly effective because the characters won't be coming back to redeem themselves in a second book.

Series

A series follows the activity of recurring characters through a number of books, usually four or more although many consider duologies and trilogies in this category.

Some prominent examples include the Gray Man Series by Mark Greaney, the Rosato & Associates Series by Lisa Scottoline, Harry Bosch Series by Michael Connelly, and the Stephanie Plum Series by Janet Evanovich. Within this style, some authors, like Connelly, choose to follow the exploits of a primary character while others like Scottoline use the setting (a law firm) or the characters as the connective thread, which allows her to switch focus to a new lead from book to book.

Regardless of the approach, readers often look to a series for comfort, citing their love for the characters or the setting as their main reasons for returning again and again. As the series progresses, the audience knows they will learn something new about those involved, the world those people exist within, and/or the overarching problem.

The ending of each novel must restore some order to the chaos and provide answers to the immediate conflict, but the personal or professional headaches of the characters will continue to shape the books to come. This is an exercise in continuity *and creativity* for the author because you will also need to develop your recurring players in such a way that anyone joining the series midstream can quickly adapt. So if you choose this route, start a series bible as soon as possible to keep track of the elements crucial to the world being built. This will aid in continuity and allow for consistency in characterizations, physical traits, locations, lineage, body count, et cetera.

For more information on how to plan a series, read *How to Write a Series* by Sara Rosett and *How to Write a Successful Series* by Helen B. Scheuerer or visit Sarra Cannon's Heartbreathings YouTube channel for her free five-part "How to Plan & Write a Series" tutorial.

Revision

According to the *Online Etymology Dictionary*, the origin of the word "revision" comes from the Latin *revisonem*, which means "seeing again." When we revise, we are reexamining our work in an effort to see it differently. Consider the revision process your opportunity to revisit the manuscript's big picture ideas and discover new ways to make them clearer and easier to understand. This act is often lumped in with proofreading for typographical errors as well as editing, which is really a separate process that deals specifically with correcting grammar and logic. But no matter how you choose to define the term, most writers consider revision a hassle or a step to ignore altogether.

A young writer I met in graduate school, Tamara Gould, once gave me some sound advice when I started complaining about needing to polish my novel: "Revision is difficult not because it means writing but because it means rewriting. It means finding a compromise between what you wrote, what you planned, what you want, and what you need." I think that is a fantastic spin on the basic idea that *revision is re-envisioning*. While both pieces of advice are sound, I especially love her take because it gives us a specific point of focus for when things seem overwhelming.

Now, I've found from my own experience that this fear of revision typically involves some combination of two basic problems. Either the writer hasn't found a suitable revision process (i.e. they don't know what to review, change, move, add, or delete), or the writer has realized a harsh reality: Revision challenges whether your manuscript is publishable either by forcing you to decide whether it's worth spending significant time to make it better or convincing you to abandon it for something more marketable. That challenge is often such a daunting gamble that it leaves people frozen with indecision.

On the other end of the spectrum, the small group of people who find pleasure in revision often grapple with a different problem: When is the right time to revise? Should I begin while my manuscript is in progress, making corrections as I go? Should I wait until the first draft is finished? Or should I set the manuscript aside to give myself some emotional distance while the ideas marinate?

Unfortunately, there is no correct answer. Each writer must decide what works best for their process, which again may prove daunting but is an essential part of authorship.

Now, if you find that you're a writer who starts each drafting session by revising the work of the previous entry, that's perfectly fine! Just don't let your inner critic trick you into dawdling over the same passage for weeks at a time. Instead, merely use that method of review as way to reintroduce yourself into the world of the story, then be sure to move forward as planned. Of course, this early revision method won't eliminate the need for a full first draft reread and rewrite, but it will certainly put you in a stronger position at the end of round one.

In contrast, *Bird by Bird* (1994) author Anne Lamott advocates for turning off your self-editor and getting a complete "shitty first draft" onto the page before starting the initial revision. Her theory is that if you allow yourself to play freely without edits or restrictions, you'll shed some anxiety and tap into a creative well that you wouldn't have been able to access without such freedoms. Just remember, if you tackle her approach of writing forward without pause, it still may be wise to keep a simple list of the things that need tweaking. This will help you formulate a revision plan without much effort and allow you to begin troubleshooting your completed first pass as soon as you're ready.

"Writing is about hypnotizing yourself into believing in yourself, getting some work done, then un-hypnotizing yourself and going over the material coldly." ~Anne Lamott

Regardless of your approach, as you finish the first draft and prepare to consider the full manuscript for first round revisions, there may be an emotional attachment to the ideas. This might lead to a blind spot that could impede your ability to improve the work. If you feel that's the case, put the manuscript away for a week or two. Distance and time often breed objectivity. The space offered by a simple break may allow you to successfully change gears and view the work with fresh eyes.

Revision Questions

Even though waiting two weeks to revise a first or second draft may be the best way to bring new insight to the piece, it isn't always practical. So we should work to have tools at our disposal that will help us become our best critics and encourage us to make the tough decisions — e.g. cutting a fun but unneeded character, strengthening the motivation of the protagonist, or rewriting dialogue that sounds stilted. The rest of this chapter will address ways to improve your ability to see your fiction anew and provide you with questions to streamline the revision process.

Before you begin revising, think about the intended purpose of your prose. What images do you want to create? What information do you want to include? What emotions do you want to evoke? It is easier to rewrite, or *re-envision*, if you remind yourself of the desired result.

Then prepare yourself to revise from the perspective of the reader. Put yourself in their shoes as you consider the elements of your novel. Because at the end of the day, suspense stories are commercial fiction and that means you must provide a certain level of satisfaction to the audience. To help see the writing anew, print out the pages and read them from the hard copy to give yourself a fresh perspective. Another technique is to convert the document into a PDF or EPUB and read it on your tablet so that you can't nitpick over commas and other minor editing errors. You could even read the text aloud and record the session to ensure the language flows the way you intended. Do whatever it takes to force yourself to read as a reader and only write down the big picture ideas — characterization, motivation, plot, setting, mood, et cetera — that don't quite work.

Lastly, consider these questions as you work through the first draft of your completed manuscript. Don't be overwhelmed by the number of questions per category. Simply focus on your weak spots. Remember to correct the big picture ideas first. Avoid spending precious hours agonizing over the hero's wardrobe choices if the story still lacks a strong opening hook or reeks of bad dialogue.

Structure and Pacing

❖ Does the book have a good opening that starts quickly and grabs the reader? Examine the first scene as well as the overall premise.

❖ Is the action purposeful? Does it move the story forward? Is it believable?

❖ Does each scene have a purpose that advances the plot and adds a complication to the overall story question?

❖ Does the plot make sense? Do the story elements follow each other in a cause-and-effect sequence?

❖ Is the pacing correct for the genre? Is it well-modulated with highs and lows? Does the narrative hold your interest throughout? If the story marred by irrelevant details, numerous flashbacks, and bulky backstory, do some rewrites.

❖ Does each scene or chapter stay in a single viewpoint?

❖ Have I adequately foreshadowed all plot twists (e.g. an unreliable narrator)? Are the plot twists believable and supported by the action leading into them? Have I amplified the suspense where applicable?

❖ Is the writing immersive? Revise if the narrative calls attention to itself — inaccuracies, verbosity, repetitiveness, et cetera — or pulls the reader out of the story world.

❖ Do all subplots resolve by the end and enhance the resolution?

❖ Do I have a strong closing scene and image?

Characterization

❖ Is the protagonist sympathetic or empathetic enough for the audience to root for? Is the characterization consistent? Does the protagonist have a clear goal with a complete arc?

❖ Is the protagonist making a proactive effort to obtain a goal and overcome conflict? Does this person's unique abilities, expertise, experience, profession, or personality contribute to the solution? If not, rework the investigative action for clarity.

❖ Do we meet the villain in the first half of the story, and do they have a viable motivation for their actions? Is that person a worthy adversary? Are the story stakes established via the introduction of this character long-standing and consequential?

❖ Are the secondary characters well-developed and believable? Do they have their own agendas or are they merely ciphers designed to fulfill the whims of the hero?

❖ Do the characters stay in character? Is it clear how each character helps the conflict or purpose of each scene?

Dialogue

❖ Have I effectively balanced internal and external dialogue, action, and narration?

❖ Is the dialogue realistic? Do the conversations advance the plot? Avoid excessive monologues or information dumps where the characters tell each other things they already know.

❖ Do each of the characters have their own speech patterns and rhythms? Does their dialogue enhance their characterization? Is their language appropriate to their age, education, profession, et cetera? Is it clear who is speaking at all times?

❖ Is the story consistent in its tone? Does this tone balance with the theme?

Setting and Time

❖ Have I built an engaging world for the reader? Do I use strong descriptions that engage all five senses? Is it clear for every scene *where* the characters are, *when* it is, and *who* is present?

❖ Is the setting appropriate to the genre? Does the setting strike the right mood, enhance the telling of the tale, and inform characterization?

❖ Have I kept track of how much time has passed throughout the story and been consistent about that element from scene to scene? Create an outline that marks the passage of time between each event. This will help you stay consistent.

❖ Does the story follow a clear order? (Note: This doesn't mean the story needs to unfold chronologically. What is important here is that any shifts in time serve a purpose and become clear as the tale progresses. The events as presented must have a clear cause and effect.)

❖ Is the story cohesive? Does it meet the audience's expectations while at the same time bringing something new to the genre?

If you can't answer "yes" to each question, continue working until each missed element meets these minimum standards. If it helps, grab a critique partner to work with you or take a few days to consider each category. This will allow your subconscious mind to work on any challenges you're facing and give you a fresh perspective on issues you may have overlooked.

Or if this revision approach is too overwhelming, consider each scene in your novel and write down its narrative purpose as well as what you want the reader to understand about each interaction. This will allow you to see if your scenes connect in a cause-and-effect manner and determine whether there are any unnecessary sequences. Remember, each sentence should propel the story forward, and each scene should impact the scenes that follow by complicating future events. If you have a hard time pinpointing the purpose of each scene, consider readjusting the goals and motivations for your characters so that each passage has a conflict resulting in a dilemma that leads to a new problem.

Tracking Problems

As you're completing the rough draft, keep track of any potential issues or areas for revision by listing them in a separate document or notebook. Personally, I also make notations within the manuscript using brackets to remind myself of what needs to be fixed. Since they typically go unused in fiction, I find that brackets make for an easy search (some authors use the TK "to come" distinction for the same reason). For example, if I decide my main character keeps a switchblade under her pillow whenever she takes a man home from the bar, I'll write **[follow up on switchblade]** or **TK - use switchblade** at the bottom of the scene as a reminder that I need to tie this street-savvy behavior into some critical aspect of the plot. You can also highlight the spot using the comment feature if you're writing in Microsoft Word. If you're using Scrivener, you have even more flexibility because you can use the annotation, comment, document notes, or project notes features to organize and store ideas.

With that in mind, here is one more revision tip: We all know the old adage, "Show, don't tell." Yet, many fiction writers still default to narrating important actions as if everything happened in the distant past rather than showing the audience things in real time. "To show" is to present a full sensory picture — complete with colors, sounds, smells, tastes, reaction, and emotion. Use strong verbs and adjectives to take the reader on a journey. Let them discover what the scene is about and who the characters are by allowing them to interpret the action and dialogue.

"To show" is the lifeblood of fiction — it enlivens your story, enhances characterization, develops a connectivity with the audience, and provides a catalyst for suspense. Of course, you'll occasionally use telling to introduce brief pieces of exposition or to aid a transition. However, if you lamely "tell," i.e. summarize, your most important scenes, the reader will feel cheated of the opportunity live vicariously through the characters and complain that the story felt stagnate.

❖ Telling: Mike was deaf, so he asked her to repeat.

❖ Showing: Mike watched her lips intently. After a few seconds, he shook his head and signed the words, "Too fast, slow down."

The second example paints a much clearer picture for the audience and allows the reader to interpret the moment. Do the same with your fiction.

Now, consider a real-world example of the "show, don't tell" concept in action by referring to an excerpt from the third chapter of *The Big Sleep* by Raymond Chandler (1939).

> She slammed her glass down so hard that it slopped over on an ivory cushion. She swung her legs to the floor and stood up with her eyes sparking fire and her nostrils wide. Her mouth was open and her bright teeth glared at me. Her knuckles were white.

The author, Raymond Chandler, could have easily encapsulated the moment by saying, *Mrs. Regan was angry*, but he cleverly chose to create an image that you wouldn't forget.

Critique Partner Feedback

More often than not, what's really needed in the early stages of writing is a critique partner. This is another writer who reads your work and provides feedback, helping you to recognize story inconsistencies like the change in a character's eye color or motivation from chapter to chapter.

Whether you're a newbie writer, a seasoned author, or an all-around prolific genius like J.D. Robb, having a critique partner is paramount. Why? Most people aren't able to view their work objectively. Having a partner, gives you an opportunity to see your work from the outside and understand how it affects an audience — after all, successful fiction is primarily about eliciting an emotional response from the reader.

A trustworthy critique partner can help you improve by offering an outside perspective. This includes providing support during times of self-doubt and holding you accountable with regard to deadlines. But the true value of a critique partner is that he or she will help you develop the tough skin that comes with receiving criticism gracefully — a skill that's essential when submitting work for publication.

Since a critique partner is traditionally a fellow writer, the input may be less nuanced than an editor's feedback but more craft-oriented than a beta read (i.e. test read) from a friend or family member. That's why choosing a critique partner is tricky. We want someone who will take the work as seriously as a paid professional would but who will also deliver that honest feedback with the compassion and encouragement of a mentor.

To be clear, don't use friends and family members as critique partners. Their love will either lead them to be too kind or overly brutal in a misguided attempt to spare you public humiliation. You want to work with someone who understands your goals and knows your genre.

I have three critique partners who I met online. Each act as a sounding board, telling me what works and what doesn't. They dig into my manuscript, pull out the structural flaws, and propose corrective measures. Sometimes they suggest craft books to aid my understanding of characterization, setting, or grammar. Other times they provide links to short stories or novels to inspire creativity. Regardless, I know that something is particularly troublesome if all three writers focus on one element like a poorly paced scene or a character whose personal history needs further development. Their feedback polishes my work and fosters my confidence.

You can find a good critique partner through the matching programs offered upon joining such national organization as Mystery Writers of America, Sisters in Crime, Romance Writers of America, International Thriller Writers, and Savvy Authors or look to your local writer's associations and other community-based organizations such as the National Novel Writing Month website.

Better yet, search for a partner while taking a writing class. Select an affordable online course or visit your public library. Many branches have writer meetups and free in-house courses. Use the classroom setting to find someone with a similar level of experience — ideally, slightly above your own so you have room to reach beyond your current tier. If you're unsure where to start, the coursework will create a foundation for the relationship by establishing a mutual understanding of what constitutes good writing.

Whether you find your partner in person or online, consider a few additional guidelines for selection:

Search for someone in the same field. This may seem trivial. After all, writing is writing, right? But remember, critique partnerships are about reciprocation, which makes this relationship more extensive than the one-sided interaction of a beta read. Initiate a feedback loop with someone who not only enjoys your style but who also understands your subject matter. This will prevent you from having to explain genre expectations to someone who is unfamiliar with them. For example, cozy writers are expected to give their readers a happy ending with justice restored but psychological thrillers end much more ambiguously. So your thriller partner may argue that it is more poetic or realistic to have the heroine sacrifice herself at the end. Disagreements of this nature are an unnecessary headache. Keep the peace by selecting someone within your niche who understands the tropes of your trade.

Look for a partner who is committed to craft. If you find yourself paired with someone who constantly wants validation, they probably aren't going to look at your work with a critical eye. A critique partner shouldn't simply stroke your ego or act as a yes-man. A good partner shares your vision but also gives constructive revision advice. The goal is to find someone who can help you overcome your weaknesses while bolstering your strengths. Choose a partner whose talents you respect and whose values you admire. This professionalism should resonate in all their interactions with you. If not, pause the relationship. Receiving feedback from someone who isn't interested in doing the hard work doesn't serve either party.

Choose a colleague with shared objectives. Avoid anyone who diminishes your passion for writing. The goal of the partnership should be to lift each other up using your combined efforts. Ask your partner about their habits and expectations. Perhaps you're both working toward a specific task like self-publishing or drafting your first agent query. Whatever the goal, make sure you and your partner have discussed those ideas before committing to a long-term relationship. Outlining your objectives ahead of time will allow you to push each other, and you'll accomplish more.

Select someone responsible. Establish rules for delivering feedback. Agree to be honest with your critiques but also let your partner know what topics are off limits. If your story contains a scientific element like ballistics that you'd rather leave for an expert's review, make sure to let your partner know that upfront to avoid wasting each other's time. Furthermore, agree on a turnaround standards and commit to that deadline. A common work ethic is key. Will you exchange pages weekly? Monthly? Chapter to chapter or project to project? The relationship is yours to design. But if you or your partner can't deliver within the agreed upon period, the relationship is not worth cultivating. Nothing is worse than someone who doesn't follow through.

As you move forward with these strategies, keep in mind that finding a critique partner requires effort. Like dating, you may go through several relationships before finding the perfect one. As you start your journey, think about your ideal partner and create a list of do's, don'ts, and compromises. Realize that no one is perfect, so the list may bend and flex as you move closer to finding a partnership that works. The key is that the relationship must start with trust, honesty, mutual respect, and professionalism in order for you both to grow.

With that said, I know you may still be thinking: *How do I know if I am getting good feedback?* If you're lucky, your partner will provide a reason for her comments, which should make it easy to assess feedback. But if the critique you receive isn't that thorough, take a moment to consider why they chose to comment about certain portions of your manuscript. Have you created something that is unclear, have they misread your intentions? Have you failed to include something or added too much of something else? If there is clear problem with a feasible solution, the comment is definitely worth considering. But if you examine the critique and find that it is more personal preference than problem, more bias than befuddlement, then you may want to take a step back and make your own assessment.

Another approach is to imagine your target audience. Picture their reactions to the flagged portions of the narrative. If the results align with your critique partner, make the change. If not, find an alternate solution. Basically, like most aspects of life, you'll need to find a balance between your instincts and your experience, which will grow along with your writing.

Bottomline, even with a critique partner, learn to trust your own judgment and be honest about the story you want to tell. Only you have final control over what goes into the manuscript, and only you will truly know when your story is ready for that next step.

Editing Software

Print a hard copy of your manuscript to catch the small errors that are often overlooked on the computer screen such as incorrect spellings, missing words, poor grammar, diction, and awkward sentence structure. Most agents and editors will exercise some leeway in this regard, especially if you have a strong hook and great characters, but you should still work for perfection. Remember, your novel will face stiff competition and being the consummate professional will help differentiate you from the crowd.

Web programs like *AutoCrit*[1], *ProWritingAid*[2], or *Grammarly*[3] can help in this regard, but they sometimes overlook homonyms, inverted word order, proper nouns, missing question marks, pronoun agreement, et cetera. Anyone interested in becoming a professional writer should learn the basic rules of grammar and syntax so they can check behind the checker. I highly recommend investing in a few guides to help improve your skills. Here are my top picks:

❖ *McGraw-Hill Education Handbook of English Grammar & Usage* by Mark Lester and Larry Beason

❖ *Essentials of English* by Vincent F. Hopper, Cedric Gale, et al.

---

1. https://www.autocrit.com/
2. https://prowritingaid.com/
3. https://www.grammarly.com/

❖ *Line by Line: How to Edit Your Own Writing* by Claire Kehrwald Cook

❖ *One Word, Two Words, Hyphenated?* By Mary Louise Gilman

❖ *The Best Punctuation Book, Period* by June Casagrande

❖ *Self-Editing for Fiction Writers* by Renni Browne and Dave King

❖ *The Writer's Little Helper* by James V. Smith, Jr.

❖ *Revision and Self-Editing for Publication* by James Scott Bell

Of course, if these feel too advanced or if you find their advice confusing, search for texts that work best for your goals or seek help from a professional. Organizations like the Editorial Freelancers Association[4], Book Editing Associates[5], and Reedsy[6] all have free resources on their websites as well as reputable editors for hire at reasonable prices.

Before you decide to work with someone, interview the person to see if they complement your personality because the revision and editing process should be a collaboration, not a conflict. Consider asking these questions and any others that may help narrow your search:

❖ What other authors have you edited?

❖ Have you edited books in my genre?

---

4. https://www.the-efa.org/
5. https://www.book-editing.com/
6. https://reedsy.com/

❖ What types of books do you normally review?

❖ May I see some of the editorial responses you've provided in the past or speak with the authors you've advised or get a sample edit on a short piece?

Can a Writer Revise Too Much?

Possibly. If you find yourself whittling away at the humor or if your friends say your manuscript has lost its spark, then you could be revising out the elements that make your piece unique. Don't be so focused on perfection that you lose sight of the goal: publication. In such cases, you may be overediting due to the fear of criticism. And while that feeling is valid, getting feedback from industry professionals and sharing our work with the public are two of the main ways you'll grow as an artist. Worst case scenario you'll be told that your manuscript isn't good enough for publication and be given some guidelines for correction, making the revision process easier. Best case scenario, you'll be rewarded with good reviews, which will help you work more confidently and efficiently next round. Either situation is a win if you choose to look at them both as learning opportunities.

Now, I am sure you're asking: *Well, how many drafts strike the right balance?* That number is different for everyone, so I would encourage you to avoid thinking about drafts if that concept brings you anxiety. Instead, think in stages. First, complete what Anne Lamott calls "the shitty first draft." Second, reread the entire work several times to review for the big picture concepts in the areas of structure, voice, content, and clarity. This second step is known as revision and the tenets are covered by the list of questions provided earlier in this chapter. Once you're satisfied with things like your story's characterization, pacing, plotting, dialogue, and action, move to the third stage: feedback. This is when you will utilize your critique group, hire a developmental editor, or consult the feedback of a beta reader. The results from this stage may require that you engage in another full round of heavy rewriting…or not — the results here will depend on experience. The final stage is the editing process where you will do a final polish of the manuscript by fixing the smaller issues like concision, repetition, word usage, punctuation, grammar, sentence structure, capitalization, spelling, et cetera.

- Phase 1: Rough Draft
- Phase 2: Revision
- Phase 3: Feedback (Critiques)
- Phase 4: Editing and Proofreading

Just don't let all of this information overwhelm the goal, which is to strengthen your work so the reader has an immersive experience. You want audiences to be so enraptured that they forget they are reading, so take revision as seriously as possible and rewrite, rewrite, rewrite. It may take four drafts for the manuscript to make sense and another three before it sounds effortless, but your persistence will pay dividends.

Conclusion

Your writer's voice is a combination of your personal beliefs, feelings, and observations of the world. The hard part is to stop yourself from judging your ideas long enough to create something. If you're struggling to get words on the page, take a step back and consider why you are doing this. Is this a matter of ego? *I have to write a book because that's the cool thing to do.* Or do you really have something to say?

If so, I recommend that whether you want to write a heart-pumping crime thriller, a dazzling courtroom drama, or morally gray medical mystery, you examine three or four novels within your genre that accomplish what you hope to do. Make sure they are works published within the last four years so that you observe the most recent developments within the genre. Study them thoroughly then map out the sequence of events for each scene and act. Once you have that information, compare those scene maps to your current outline to determine if you're hitting all the major beats to satisfy genre expectations with regard to pacing, action, characterization, plot reveals, et cetera. Does your work have the potential to conjure the same level of excitement as published works within the genre? If not, tweak your outline. Perhaps the reason you're stuck is because something is missing from your plot.

The point is if you really want to make writing a serious part of your life, you must stay the course. Put in the work, and trust that the answers are inside you. You've taken the first step by investing in this book, now take the second one by investing some time and faith in yourself.

Author's Note

Thank you for reading this book. Please spread the word.
Write an online customer review.
Gift a copy of this book to a friend.
Join my mailing list to hear about upcoming Writer Productivity Series titles, which will cover writing faster, comedy in fiction, and writing dialogue.
Follow me on social media and recommend this book.

Website:
https://ajthenovelist.com/

Twitter:
https://twitter.com/ajthenovelist

Instagram:
https://www.instagram.com/ajthenovelist/

Pinterest:
https://www.pinterest.com/ajthenovelist/

Facebook:
https://www.facebook.com/AJ-the-Novelist-693083501559738

Bookbub:
https://www.bookbub.com/profile/andrea-j-johnson

Goodreads:
https://www.goodreads.com/author/show/19764533.Andrea_J_Johnson

Mailing List:
https://ajthenovelist.com/sign-up/

Glossary

Act – a unit of analysis for dividing a narrative into sequences; although not marked as with a play, the emotional beats of a commercial fiction novel can be divided into three to five acts

Action – the behavior, gestures, or body language that illustrate a character's feelings and attitudes—this behavior should propel plot, provoke reactions, and build conflict

Adventure Fiction – action-filled stories whose main conflict pits the characters against the environment

Afterword – like the foreword at the beginning of a book, the afterword is typically written by a prominent artist other than the author to explain some aspect of the text (usually social/historical data or facts); although the afterword appears at the end of the book, it should not be confused with the epilogue

Alibi – proof of having been elsewhere during the commission of a crime or any circumstance that seemingly prevents someone from having committed a murder

Analogy – an extended simile

Antagonist – a character or element in direct opposition or conflict with the protagonist

Anticipation – expecting and/or evaluating a potential event without being exactly sure what will occur; looking forward to an event or moment; when the reader is able to use the information given to them by the story and their own life experiences to make a prediction about what may or may not happen next

Antihero – a central character who is deeply flawed and has a twisted moral compass—e.g. doing the wrong thing for the right reason—but whose tragic flaw becomes her source of potential redemption for herself or others, e.g. Walter White from AMC's *Breaking Bad*

Archetype – based on a recurring concept in culture such as a symbol or character type and speaks to a universal aspect of the human experience

Background – information about a character

Backstory – action that took place before the current events of the plot; the details of a character's past that occurred before the story's start

Beat – a statement used between lines of dialogue to increase the emotion or tension of a scene, usually includes gestures or thoughts that anchor the speaker to the setting

Beat sheet – a document that identifies the key emotional moments in a narrative and lays out what needs to happen in each act of the story

Beta reader – someone who reads a writer's manuscript prior to publication to confirm the work has met the audience's expectations for the genre

Brand – the identifying elements of a company, product, or individual; the relationship between the product and the customer where specific expectations are met

Capers – a subgenre of mystery told from the criminals' point of view that involve a light-hearted crime rather than a murder; see also *heist*

Catharsis – purging of emotion; the post-climax release of tension that refreshes the spirit

Character arc – the character's internal journey during the story and how she transforms (positively or negatively) by the end

Character quirk – a strange or interesting character trait

Character trait – characteristics, behaviors, and attitudes that create a character's personality

Characterization – the act of providing a portrayal or description of a character

Characters – the people who occupy a story

Chekhov's Gun – the assertion by playwright Anton Chekhov that any noteworthy details within a story must eventually contribute to the overall narrative

Circumstantial evidence – indirect evidence; evidence inferred from one or more sources

Cliché – a word, expression, or phrase that is predictable or overused

Cliffhanger – a suspenseful situation left unresolved until the next beat, chapter, or novel

Climax – the height of a story's pace, action, and tension prior to the ending; the final conflict where it is decided if the protagonist will win and achieve his goal

Clue – a piece of evidence or information used in crime detection

Coda – the portion of the story that serves to round out, conclude, or summarize the lessons learned in the main tale but may also attempt to serve its own interests by answering or posing a new question about the characters' personal lives—unlike an epilogue, a coda is not marked to indicate its separation from the main story

Complication – an action or event that introduces a new conflict; the obstacles or opportunities that undermine a character's ability to achieve his goal

Conceit – an extended metaphor that compares two unlike things in a congruent and often clever manner

Conflict – problem or predicament; the opposing force or obstacle that keeps a character from getting what they want—often broken down in literature as man v. man, man v. nature, man v. himself and acts as the main struggle for the story

Concrete language – specific; referring to the tangible and perceivable characteristics of an object or situation

Copyeditor – an editor who checks for issues of mechanics

Corroborating evidence – information that strengthens or confirms already existing evidence

Covert murder – an attempt is made by the murderer to cover-up the death

Cozies – a mystery subgenre known for eschewing explicit violence, sex, and gore in favor of off-stage murders in idyllic settings with coverups, suspense, misdirection, and (most importantly) a feel-good ending where justice is restored; also known as *cosy* or *cozy mystery*

Critique partner – a fellow writer who provides feedback on story structure and content prior to publication

Deceitful murder – the murderer attempts to make the death look like something else, e.g. an accident, self-defense, act of God, suicide, et cetera

Deductive reasoning – the process of demonstrating that if certain key statements are true, then other statements based on them are also true; following one or more factual statements through to their logical conclusion

Deep point of view – a style of writing that strives to place the reader in the protagonist's mind by removing elements that place a barrier between her and the audience

Denouement – French for "untying"; the post-climax resolution of the plot; an essential solution to the plotted conflict

Description – a narrative explanation of the who, what, where, when, and why conveyed as imagery that is either sensory, emotional, poetic, or data-driven in its output

Developmental editor – content editor; also known as a substantive editor

Deus ex machina – Latin for "a god from a machine," which in the days of ancient Greek and Roman drama referred to an actor or deity statue being lifted over the stage by a crane; a plot device in the form of a person, object, or event that appears suddenly and instantaneously fixes an impossible conflict or problem—can be used comically but contemporary literary critics consider this a contrivance, e.g. the entrance of Fawkes at the end of *Harry Potter and the Chamber of Secrets*

Deuteragonist – the second most important character in a story; in classic Greek drama this is the person whose importance falls after the protagonist

Dialogue – speech or words spoken aloud by characters, signaled via quotation marks; (consider dialogue a clear way to keep the story active in the absence of physical movement as dialogue is one of the keys to conflict)

Dialogue tags – the verb after a line of dialogue that signals who is speaking or how the words are being spoken, e.g. said, exclaimed, shouted, asked, et cetera

Diction – word choice

Direct characterization – when the narrator or other characters explicitly describe what a character is like

Direct evidence – positive evidence; any fact attested to by eyewitnesses or information stated in documents that affirms the genuineness and veracity of the data

Disturbance – an event that foreshadows the upcoming turning point

Dramatic irony – when a gap appears between what the audience knows and what a character believes or expects

Duology – two related works whose collective narratives form an overarching story arc or theme

e.g. – for example

Empathy – the ability to understand or be sensitive to the experiences and feelings of another person

Epigraph – a short quote that speaks to theme; usually placed at the beginning of a story or amidst the front matter at the start of a novel

Epilogue – an optional follow-up section that briefly covers personal events that occur some significant period of time after the story's main question has been resolved and concluded, typically marked to indicate its separation from the main story

Epiphany – a sudden realization or insight into a subject's greater meaning

Escalating stakes – the consequences for success or failure increase as the story progresses

Exculpatory evidence – information tending to excuse, justify, or absolve the alleged fault or guilt of the defendant

Exposition – the initial phase of the plotting arc meant to establish setting, characters, situation, and potential conflict

External conflict – the struggle between the protagonist and an outside force such as nature, society, or an adversary

Falling action – the point of the story after the climax in which the resolved conflict leads to the conclusion and a catharsis for the audience

Figurative language – a word or phrase that conjures an image in the mind of the reader by creating a change in the usual meaning or order of words and/or by comparing or identifying one thing with another, e.g. similes and metaphors; also known as *figures of speech*

First person – an internal narrator who refers to herself using the pronouns "I" or "me"

Flashback – a break in the present narrative to present something that happened before the start of the story

Flashforward – a break in the narrative structure whereby a scene from the fictional future is inserted into the fictional present or is otherwise dramatized out of chronological order

Flat characters – predictable characters with no dimension or personality, e.g. Kenny from *South Park*

Foil – a character who serves as a contrast to another (usually the protagonist) and is meant to draw attention to the strengths and weakness of both parties; a character meant to put the protagonist's action and choices into context

Foreboding – a prediction of misfortune; the feeling of an ominous mood rising

Foreshadowing – a hint to future events

Foretelling – reflecting or briefly hinting at themes that will be further highlighted over the course of the narrative

Foreword – a short introduction to a book, typically written by someone other than the author

Frame Story – the literary technique of placing a story within a story; a story where the introductory narrative sets the stage for an additional (or multiple) narrative

Genre – the category in which a story falls; in commercial fiction, this includes mystery, romance, science fiction, fantasy, et cetera

Gimmick – in fiction, this is often an approach or device used to create what is supposed to be an innovative or clever fix but is actually implausible or insincere

Goal – what each character wants or desires

Heist – a subgenre of mystery similar to a caper where the story is told from the criminals' perspective; however, these stories tend to include violent crimes motivated by revenge

High concept – a story with a unique or innovative premise that easily hooks the audience and deals with the genre's tropes in unexpected ways

Hook – the concept or opening lines of a novel, designed to grab the reader's attention and induce further reading

Howdunit – the narrative's solution focuses on how the murder occurred

Hyperbole – exaggeration or overstatement

i.e. – that is; in other words

Imagery – the sensory component of description that's often created through figurative language such as similes and metaphors

in medias res – Latin for "in the middle of things"; all fiction should start in progress

Inciting incident – an event that upsets the protagonist's ordinary world and sets her on the journey that will occupy her throughout the narrative; also referred to as the *destabilizing event*

Indirect characterization – when a character's traits are revealed implicitly through her speech, behavior, thoughts, appearance, et cetera

Indirect dialogue – a summary of dialogue usually used to transition between scenes or simplify a long one; authors use this technique when the audience needs to know a conversation took place, but doesn't need to witness the words verbatim

Inductive reasoning – making an inference from a general observation or small sample

Info dump – when a writer reveals a large amount of information or backstory all at once instead of spreading it out

Intangible clues – a piece of legitimate evidence that cannot be physically defined such as the habitual behavior of a suspect or an eyewitness statement

Internal conflict – the protagonist's struggle against himself such as flawed drives, habits, or impulses

Internal dialogue – a character's self-talk or inner monologue; thought

Irony – when a statement or situation is characterized by the significant difference between what's expected versus what actually happens or what's understood versus what's meant; in literature, there are three types of irony: verbal, situational, and dramatic

Legal thriller – a subgenre of mystery where the legal system serves as the backdrop and framework for the narrative, e.g. *Presumed Innocent* by Scott Turow

Locked room mystery – a subgenre of traditional mysteries where the crime unfolds under impossible circumstances such as a murder that occurs in a locked room or a victim found murdered in an untouched patch of snow, e.g. *The Hollow Man* by John Dickson Carr

Logline – a one-sentence summary or description of a narrative, usually a screenplay, designed to hook the listener; a short description of a text's premise; also known as *elevator pitch*

Maid-and-butler dialogue – a conversation where a character relays information to another even though both characters already know; an obvious attempt to inform the audience of something; the author's failure to show rather than tell

Manuscript – the term used to refer to a work in progress or an unpublished novel

Mary Sue – a character, usually female, portrayed unrealistically free of faults or weakness

Means – the ability and resources to commit the crime such as access to the weapon or knowledge about the method of murder

Metaphor – a figure of speech where two unlike things are compared, e.g. "Love is a battlefield."

MacGuffin – an object, event, or character in a narrative that helps trigger or propel the plot but doesn't necessarily have as significant an impact on the resolution; often the item's perceived value comes from what it represents to each character as opposed to what it does or what it's worth

Macro-editing – working to revise big picture issues; to look at the manuscript with regard to content, clarity, voice, and structure

Mantle – a responsibility or collection of actions the protagonist cannot reject, ignore, or set aside; the event or interaction that compels a character to undertake an endeavor they'd usually ignore

Micro-editing – working to correct small editing issues of mechanics like concision, repetition, word usage, punctuation, syntax, grammar, capitalization, formatting, and consistency

Milieu – the physical or social setting of the narrative; the overall atmosphere or feel of a story, including the environment, culture, history, geography as well as the mood and tone of the text

Misdirection – the act of diverting an audience's attention towards away from one thing so that it fails to notice another

Mixed metaphor – when two or more usually incompatible comparisons are tangled together in a manner that's unclear and often unintentionally humorous, e.g. "It's our turn at bat, so let's see this project into the end zone."

Modus operandi – Latin for "mode of operating"; in criminal law, this term refers to a pattern of behavior so distinctive that separate crimes or wrongful conduct are recognized as the work of one person

Monologue – a long uninterrupted speech given by one person—can be internal as thought or spoken aloud as dialogue

Mood – the emotion a scene evokes in the reader

Motif – a recurring symbol, sound, action, idea, or phrase within a literary work meant to strengthen the narrative by adding images and ideas to the theme

Motivation – the things driving a character's desire or goals; drive

Motive – an actionable idea or reason to commit the crime

Narrative – the written events of the story as told by the viewpoint character or narrator

Narrative question – the major thematic dilemma or central conflict that's tied directly to the stakes of your narrative and must be answered by story's end; although not a literal question this problem sets the reader's expectations for what the book will deliver; see also story question

Narrator – the person telling the story

Noir – a genre of crime/detective film or fiction characterized by cynicism, fatalism, moral ambiguity, and edgy settings; e.g. *The Black Dahlia* (1987) by James Ellroy

Novel – a written work of 50,000 words or more

Novella – a written work of 45,000 words or less

Omniscient point of view – a third-person point of view where the narrator is all-seeing and all-knowing

Onomatopoeia – a word that approximates the sound it describes, e.g. "buzz"

Opportunity – time to commit the crime unseen; an unencumbered chance to follow through on intention

Overt murder – no attempt is made to make the crime look like anything other than a crime

Pacing – the rate of a story's forward progression

Pantsing – the act of writing a novel "by the seat of your pants" without advanced planning

Perfect alibi stories – mysteries where the events of the crime are in reality shifted in time from what is initially perceived so that it appears the proposed killer does not have the means and opportunity to commit the crime; most often used in howdunits but an overall great way to create a plot twist, e.g. *Salvation of a Saint* by Keigo Higashino

Perjury – telling a falsehood under oath

Personification – a figure of speech that endows something nonhuman with humanlike qualities or abilities, e.g. "Death brushed against me."

Personal wound – an internal struggle or blind spot a character has difficulty overcoming or seeing past

Physical setting – place where the action unfolds; also known as *spatial setting*

Pinch point – a small turning point

Plot – the narrative events that unfold as the protagonist overcomes obstacles to achieve her goal; the five main phases of plot are exposition, rising action, climax, falling action, and resolution (or denouement)

Plot device – any technique in a narrative used to move the action forward; also known as *plot mechanism*

Plot hole – an issue, inconsistency, or contradiction in the plot that makes it illogical or unbelievable

Plot point – a significant event that moves the story forward; see also *turning point*

Plot reveal – the answer to a question, which the writer has prompted the audience to ask earlier in the narrative

Plot reversal – (add as the see also for turning point) an event, person, or piece of information that takes the narrative in the opposite direction; *see also turning point*

Plot twist – an unexpected development that shatters what we thought was true; a story turn designed to drastically disrupt things the audience believes they already know and view the story in a whole new light

Plotting – the act of planning your novel structure in advance; the arrangement of the action

Point of view (POV) – the perspective from which events are viewed and the story is told; the focus and voice of the narrator; also known as *viewpoint*

Point-of-view character – the person whose perspective the reader uses to view the story; also known as *viewpoint character*

Police procedural – a subgenre of mystery that depicts the cops using the tools of their trade to solve crime

Preface – introductory remarks written by the author, typically stating something about the book's subject or purpose, positioned after the publishing information and front matter, like the dedication, but before the prologue or first chapter

Premise – the story's main idea or concept; a short but hooky statement that outlines the plot

Presumptive evidence – information that is considered to be fact until proven otherwise; see also *circumstantial evidence*

Prologue – Latin "spoken before"; the section of a literary work prior to the first chapter meant to provide important background to the main story although the purpose of the information may not prove immediately obvious

Proofreader – someone who reads through the document to make sure the copyeditors' marks and suggestions have been honored

Prose – the ordinary form of spoken or written language without rhyme or meter as distinguished from poetry or verse

Protagonist – the main character

Purple prose – writing that tries too hard to be descriptive and is verbose in doing so; also known as *flowery language*

Red herring – a false lead that throws the reader off track or briefly carries the protagonist away from her goal; a classic example of a powerfully plotted mystery that uses these false trails is *The Five Red Herrings* by Dorothy L. Sayers

Resolution – the narrative's conclusion

Revision – the process of looking at your ideas and finding ways to make them clearer and easier to understand

Rising action – the events of the story leading up to the climax; the idea that conflicts should increase as the story progresses

Rashomon Effect – an instance when a single event is described in different or contradictory ways by the people involved; named after director Akira Kurosawa's 1950 film *Rashomon*

Scene – an event that takes place in a single setting in a set amount of time—a novel is made up of several scenes divided into acts

Second person – a narrator who refers to herself using the pronoun "you"

Secondary character – a person who is part of a subplot or central storyline but does not play as large a role as the main characters

Series – a group of novels that follow the activity of recurring characters through a number of books, usually four or more although many consider duologies and trilogies part of this category

Series bible – an outline or organized collection of information about your series such as location, character breakdowns, and the summaries for past and future plots

Setting – the time and place where each scene occurs; the unifying element of a story, which ties time, location, culture, mood, tone, characterization, and theme into one milieu

Simile – a figure of speech that makes a direct comparison using the words "like" or "as," e.g. "She's as cute as a button."

Situation – the basic events depicted in a literary work (i.e. what happens); different from conflict in that this refers to the overall circumstances and may or may not involve a struggle or problem

Situational irony – when a character has an expectation that undergoes an unexpected reversal or is fulfilled in an unexpected manner

Stakes – what's emotionally and/or physically at risk for your character; the element that drives rising action and makes the story question worth answering

Standalone – a novel with an autonomous plot

Stereotype – an undeveloped character whose traits stem from a widely perceived misconception associated with them

Story question – the major thematic dilemma or central conflict that's tied directly to the stakes of your narrative; know your story question before you begin to outline (it should be part of your premise and the foundation for your writing); see also narrative question

Stream of consciousness – free association; a narrative technique commonly attributed to the Modernist Era (1900-1940) where a narrator's internal monologue is written to mimic real-time thought patterns and emotions, e.g. *Mrs. Dalloway* by Virginia Woolf

Style – an author's distinctive manner of expression through his diction and imagery

Style sheet – a file that defines the layout and other items of consistency for a large document

Subgenre – a smaller category within a genre

Subplot – the secondary plot in a work of fiction

Substantive editor – content editing; see also *developmental editor*

Subtext – the underlying, implicit, or metaphorical meaning of a dialogue or text; an idea hinted at but not plainly expressed

Subvert – when your words, action, or approach criticize, undermine or overturn the usual way of doing or thinking about something

Surprise – a one-time event that is unexpected

Suspense – elements that induce the states of feeling excited, anxious, or uncertain about what might happen—often created when a question is raised and the answer is withheld to place the audience on edge; the purpose is to make the reader more concerned about the characters and form an empathetic connection

Suspension of disbelief – the willingness of the reader to set aside their judgement and accept the story being told; a term most often used with cozy mysteries since their storylines hinge on an amateur sleuth rather than law enforcement solving the crime

Symbol – an image, concept, person, or thing that stands for something else

Sympathy – one's personal feelings or sorrow for someone else's misfortune

Synopsis – a summary of the novel's events, including its ending

Syntax – the way words and phrases are put together to form sentences; word order

Tagline – a clever slogan or statement used to market a product, not to be confused with *logline*

Tangible clues – a piece of evidence or information that points to where a suspect has been, i.e. things you can taste, smell, hear, touch, see, or analyze such as fibers and fingerprints

Telegraphing – providing the clear meaning or outcome of a dramatic action—in literature this is seen as lessening the final effect by hinting so heavily that the truth or surprise is spoiled

Temporal setting – story time or the current reality for the characters; same as *plot time*

Tension – the reader's anticipation of conflict rising; the immediate feeling of discomfort that arises when a certain action or event unfolds

Theme – what your story is trying to say or prove about its topic

Third person – an external narrator who refers to the action using the pronouns "he," "she," or "they"

Thriller – a subgenre of mystery that focuses on a high degree of suspense, adventure, and intrigue to fuel the narrative

Tone – the attitude the work takes toward the material; in fiction, this often reflects the protagonist's attitude toward the story situation

Tragedy – a genre of storytelling where the protagonist is undone (often a fall from greatness) by his own flaws such as avarice, hubris, or jealousy, e.g. *Citizen Kane*

Tragic flaw – the trait that brings the downfall of the protagonist in a tragedy

Tragic hero – a protagonist whose traits earn him sympathy from the audience, but whose flaws ultimately lead to his downfall, e.g. Willy Loman in *Death of a Salesman*

Trilogy – three related works whose collective narratives form an overarching story arc or theme

Trope – the storytelling conventions common to different genres

Turning point – an unexpected event, person, or piece of information that raises the stakes and sets the protagonist on a new path; the three moments of action and/or decision that leads from Act I into Act II, Act II into Act III, and Act III into Act IV in a commercial fiction novel

Unreliable narrator – a storyteller who lies, misleads, or withholds information from the reader, either intentionally or unintentionally, casting doubt on the narrative

Verbal irony – when a word or expression takes on a different meaning (usually opposite) than its surface meaning

Voice – the narrator or author's emotions, attitude, tone, and point of view as expressed through diction

Whodunit – the narrative's solution focuses on who committed the murder

Whydunit – the narrative's solution focuses on the motive for the murder

World building – the act of infusing the setting with specific details about the culture, government, geography, politics, religion, etc.

www.ingramcontent.com/pod-product-compliance
Lightning Source LLC
Chambersburg PA
CBHW020136130526
44590CB00039B/186